SEEING SIDEWAYS

AMERICAN MUSIC SERIES

Jessica Hopper and Charles L. Hughes, series editors

Eric Harvey, *Who Got the Camera? A History of Rap and Reality*

Stephen Deusner, *Where the Devil Don't Stay:*
Traveling the South with the Drive-By Truckers

Hannah Ewens, *Fangirls: Scenes from Modern Music Culture*

Sasha Geffen, *Glitter Up the Dark:*
How Pop Music Broke the Binary

Hanif Abdurraqib, *Go Ahead in the Rain:*
Notes to A Tribe Called Quest

Chris Stamey, *A Spy in the House of Loud:*
New York Songs and Stories

Holly Gleason, editor, *Woman Walk the Line:*
How the Women in Country Music Changed Our Lives

Adam Sobsey, *Chrissie Hynde: A Musical Biography*

Lloyd Sachs, *T Bone Burnett: A Life in Pursuit*

Danny Alexander, *Real Love, No Drama:*
The Music of Mary J. Blige

Alina Simone, *Madonnaland and Other Detours into Fame and Fandom*

Kristin Hersh, *Don't Suck, Don't Die: Giving Up Vic Chesnutt*

Chris Morris, *Los Lobos: Dream in Blue*

Eddie Huffman, *John Prine: In Spite of Himself*

John T. Davis, *The Flatlanders: Now It's Now Again*

David Cantwell, *Merle Haggard: The Running Kind*

David Menconi, *Ryan Adams: Losering, a Story of Whiskeytown*

Don McLeese, *Dwight Yoakam: A Thousand Miles from Nowhere*

Peter Blackstock and David Menconi, founding editors

SEEING SIDEWAYS

A MEMOIR OF MUSIC AND MOTHERHOOD

KRISTIN HERSH

University of Texas Press ◆ *Austin*

Requests for permission to reproduce material from this work should be sent to:
    Permissions
    University of Texas Press
    P.O. Box 7819
    Austin, TX 78713-7819
    utpress.utexas.edu/rp-form

♾ The paper used in this book meets the minimum requirements of ANSI/NISO
Z39.48-1992 (R1997) (Permanence of Paper).

Library of Congress Cataloging-in-Publication Data

Names: Hersh, Kristin, author.
Title: Seeing sideways : a memoir of music and motherhood / Kristin Hersh.
Other titles: American music series.
Description: First edition. | Austin : University of Texas Press, 2021. | Series:
American music series
Identifiers: LCCN 2020056889
        ISBN 978-1-4773-1234-6 (cloth)
        ISBN 978-1-4773-2310-6 (library ebook)
        ISBN 978-1-4773-2311-3 (non-library ebook)
Subjects: LCSH: Hersh, Kristin. | Women singers—United States—Biography.
| Women alternative rock musicians—United States—Biography. | Singers—
United States—Biography. | Alternative rock musicians—United States—
Biography. | Mothers—United States—Biography. | LCGFT: Autobiographies.
Classification: LCC ML420.H387 A3 2021 | DDC 782.42166/092 [B]—dc23
LC record available at https://lccn.loc.gov/2020056889

doi:10.7560/312346

This book spans thirty years of music and motherhood. From 1990 to 2020, or thereabouts. I use no names other than my sons', since these four chapters are meant to reflect their individual voices. Children are a wildly important opportunity to wake up to the fact that you are not the story. And they accomplish this with such a gentle hand.

When I was sixteen, I was hit by a car, and ever since, music has been coming into my head, in color, whether I want it to or not. My sonic orientation—synesthesia and hearing music no one else hears—has been variously attributed to this car accident, to misdiagnoses of mental illness, to the coping mechanisms of PTSD and concurrent dissociation, to a southern hippie childhood, to . . . well, to lots of things, really. I've always maintained that I'm simply a musician and that this mutation plays an irksome role in a consumerist culture steeped in facsimile. I could be wrong about this, but I kinda doubt it.

My sons, like all children, are a vivid example of life living itself. So is real music, real anything. Without the boys, I might not have understood that music is not a disorder or a product but a series of Big Bangs. Life begets life begets stories. *People* are not disorders or products either, no matter what they tell us. The tragicomedy on this plane is real pretty in the boys' hands, in other words; its sweetness happifying and heartbreaking. So music and motherhood go together for me. Two engaging ways to disappear behind beautiful, blooming things.

Kristin Hersh

All scars are beautiful. Because you lived.

—Bodhi

DOONY

♋ surf cowboy

I slip under the water
I fall into the sea

come
everyone

When the ball of fire rolled across my kitchen, I was sitting at
a green ceramic table with a man who'd once saved my life in
a freezing, roiling Malibu ocean. Point Dume, where the Statue
of Liberty turns up at the end of *Planet of the Apes*. We called
it Point Doom, but even the rescue was pretty goofy. The Pacific
gets cold. Clean but hard to think; makes you sluggish, stu-
pidish. The man said my mute little body felt like a sack of
potatoes as it was swept away—had no internal mechanism, no
wherewithal—and the beach monkeys just sitting there watching. Those little Malibu ground squirrels. It was TV to them. I

was a strong swimmer, but sleepy and unwilling to fight. Again. More of a wait-and-see swimmer, anyway. Guitar and baby had grown my muscles up to pretty hard, then pretty hard life froze them into still fibers wrapped around bones. Cuz they wouldn't fight for me; they were just looking for a fight, any fight. Bones're steady, wait-and-see swimmers, but muscles twitch and react, and you gotta hold 'em back like surly drunks so you don't get the shit beaten outta you. Again. Bones remember.

The man's giant hand thrust itself through the surface, into the salt realm where I'd been tumbling in and out with the tide, cut up on rocks, gradually getting the feel of not breathing. It was surprisingly easy. Now *that's* a useful muscle. Think of all the fun we could have if we exercised our right to not breathe. Note to self: don't forget how suddenly an epiphany grabs your face and yells at it, then kisses you on the cheek and wanders off, not even sticking around to watch you flail, see if you learn to fucking deal. Stupid epiphanies. Down again, into churning green salt. Second note to self: *ow, but your lungs freak.*

And the green salt asks, what're you gonna freeze and what're you gonna let burn up? What do you wanna zombify and what do you want to disappear to*night*? Right now, to-fucking-night, set it on fire? I mean, on the off chance that any of this is up to you. Which it probly isn't, but it's how we seem to get by: "I think I'm writing this story . . ." Third note: *Also, your heart goes nutz.*

When air and land happened again, I couldn't stop laughing. The man found nothing funny, which made it way funnier. Dripping and laughing, the beach monkeys and I were on the same page. TV to the man.

♋ cold water coming

cold water coming for the warm water junkies
poor sucker freaked and couldn't swim with the monkeys

Also, your heart goes nutz.

We had only been adults for a few years, me and this man, who seemed an awful lot like a grown-up to me. As if he had actually *grown up*, while my friends and I still looked and acted like children. He was tall. Loud on occasion, when it was called for. As label manager at our record company, he had joined my band on the road and then followed me home to this little island when the tour ended. Or rather, we found ourselves together, looking for a landing place. And landed at this green ceramic table in a sort of coma, in a sort of . . . ye olde colonial kitchen, on this island off the coast of New England. Sometimes a true moaning, blue New England: blue-collar cobblestones, a moaning blue harbor, creaking ropes plus moaning wind, down the cobbled blue street. The man had quit his record company job to manage my band—for ten percent of not very much—and join forces with a subculture as obsessed with the love of music as we were with hating the music *business*. I told him I'd leave too; go indie, go anything, go anywhere . . . that I was morally obligated to no longer participate in an industry that denigrated music and women. So he and I held hands and agreed to face a faceless corporate beast together, knowing full well that we were doomed.

Welcome to Point Doom, dude. I'm guessing you're giving up a hell of a paycheck.

Hell's paycheck isn't worth it.

Ok. You know what ten percent of not very much is?

He smiled. He did this often.

So we'd spent the last couple of months at this table, pretty much. Over which hung greasy air made of dust motes and unnamed particulate, but also the bumpy grief of a lost child: this was our coma. When the baby was taken, I froze on a memory that both shut down my faculties and expanded my perception of the event into a blitzkrieg tapestry; a painted backdrop spilling over with hurricane and desert, too much and nothing. I didn't know that this was PTSD; I only knew the hurricane maelstrom and desert emptiness. That this one impossible memory never ended because it was too much to stop. Time stops *other* events. This event didn't end. It was an always. The pain was so great, I found myself able to leave my own body, and not only when I played music. I had always loved the superpower invisibility, but disappearing was no longer invisible.

Kris. Wake up.

I'm awake.

Not entirely.

Pilgrims. They must have hung this grease in our kitchen's air. We hoped maybe pirates. We even had rum some kid in another band left in my apartment. Just said, "Spirits," and then held up a bottle of Captain Morgan, cape flying. I stared at the Captain, full of cartoon joy and spirits. Then slid *Ball of Fire* with Gary Cooper into the VCR and excused myself, handing the kid my bright-red telephone cuz I knew he liked to make crank calls. Stepped out into dry snow to buy a liter of Coke, trying something: sticky rum and Cokes tonight. That's all we ever did, us broken kids: try another something and then drop that ball too. Cuz all we could really do? Was play music. And wonder when everybody else took the class that walked them through this grown-up shit.

♋ freeloader

I'm a broken kid
I'm lonely enough to make the air around you sweet

When I got back with the Coke, the rum kid was balancing my phone on his knees, chattering at a Home Shopping Network operator in front of an audience of townie kids; pseudo-adults in a postchildhood limbo we figured was nature vs. civilization. Listening, we all tried sticky rum and Cokes. Well, *they* did. I'd been a mother for three years and mothers have to stay sober, *want* to stay sober, no matter how much it hurts. My baby had been taken, but I was still a mother, convinced that any minute now, he'd be placed in my arms the way he was when he was born. Any minute now, so can't blur edges in case essence blurs. Safety first, etc. Any minute now, the cruelty would show itself as such, even to the cruel, and mother and child would be reunited. Only happy endings in a child's storybook, and Baby Doony had only ever heard children's stories. Any minute now, because we can't go on any longer.

Alcohol was not going to touch my broken heart or my disappearing act anyway, which was why the townie kids had gathered here: the young are drawn to pain, knowing that their very presence is healing. So these flannel-clad kids and this New York man who pulled me outta the Pacific, the ghosts of two fire-bellied newts and Gary Cooper, a dude named Cinderella in the apartment upstairs, plus rum and Cokes on the floor. Cuz nothing that isn't sad and funny is worth doing, I guess. And that night we decided that everything we'd seen on sitcoms growing up was both sad and funny. *The Love Boat*, we figured, was the rum-and-Coke-iest. Isaac the Bartender'd sticky up some lovelorn orange and glossy actors who were about to learn a lesson. The lesson that lovelorn devolves into love-shattered and then, oh my god, you're in the ejector seat, shot up into the air, but then you adventure-land in Hawaii where orange and glossy Love awaits with flowers around its neck . . . coulda been *Fantasy Island*. Gary Cooper wasn't working; we wanted our childhoods back. A boy stepped out onto the front porch to steal Cinderella's *TV Guide* out of his mailbox.

Borrow, not steal.

He flipped through it.

"Love Boat. An icy widow learns a lesson in charity."

Icy.

Yeah, icy. What did Gopher do?

He was your yeoman purser.

He was not.

Of course he was.

I bet she wasn't icy, just whiny. A whiny widow.

Hope she learned her lesson.

Your yeoman purser. I can't stop saying it.

You don't have to.

My TV just played movies, not TV, so the only lesson *we* learned that night was that sticky doesn't sit well. Ended up quietly bonding over the decentest way to kill lobsters—which is actually a sorta demented way to kill *anything* (thrust a pointy stick into its brain). And that there are men named "Newt," two newt ghosts watching from some dusty corner. The Captain Morgan kid slumped against the wall as his crank call went on and on—art on the wall, essentially, since I had no art on the walls—something about Jesus on a String. *Home Shopping operators aren't allowed to hang up on you*, he whispered, covering the mouthpiece. Then he demanded to know how they'd sold out of all the Jesuses on strings when he'd just seen Jesus hanging from a string on his own TV moments ago, and also what she'd done with all the Jesuses on strings if they hadn't yet sold out of them. While the baffled woman waited patiently to explain that this product never existed.

Whaddya mean you haven't sold any? Then I'll buy all of them. But I really only want one Jesus on one string.

Hopefully, this woman was able to shark sleep with half her brain and write grocery lists or make TV-watching plans while she explained, again, that Jesus only came with no strings attached. By midnight, warm, watery rum and Cokes dotted the floor and the kid was gone. Everyone but the man had walked home to their townie pad or a drunk dad's basement. The man was unwilling to drive back to New York, was willing to stay the night. He seemed incongruous on this children's cartoon island, sleeping under the gaze of Captain Morgan.

Why are your friends all children?

I'm a child.

Yeah. Why are you all children?
Because we didn't grow up.

As a child with a child, I was a cartoon with gravity. As an adult with no child, he was fearless. In the hope of starting over? He and I lived in circles while we waited for the courts to determine our future. The spirit of Captain Morgan, posing next to the yellowing refrigerator, straddled cartoons and life-as-slow-death. The Captain's rum, capped and forgotten, his new home a greasy countertop, his new neighbors a bottle of Fireball and a dull, drooling fridge. The Captain's smile did not fade. He was a confident, flexible dude. *He* didn't grow up either. Cartoons are important; zombie-freezing him was the right thing to do. Other things would burn up around him. Mostly memories.

♋ candyland

life is unkind
'til it burns up our memories

Two months ago, the memory that didn't die:
Your mother needs you, it's an emergency.
My mother? I can't leave, I just put the baby down for a nap.
I'll watch him. Go, it's an emergency.
My mother's blank face. No emergency.

There is a cop standing on
the front porch.

Pieces of paper: child abandonment, restraining order, domicile, bank account. Child what?

Child abandonment.

I didn't abandon him; I left five minutes ago. Where is he?

The cop told me that if I came within thirty feet of my own baby, I'd go to jail, then turned to leave. I yelled after him.

Tell me where he is!

A legal kidnapping was taking place. The cop turned his back calmly and walked to the police car parked at the curb. When I got home, the house was empty.

I was twenty-two. The title of my first song. I wrote it when I was nine. For some reason.

♋ 22

```
a backward movie
we missed the beginning


and the end
```

This is when I started having trouble with time.

The man seemed able to accept this. I looked across the green ceramic table at him.

Let's go to New Mexico.

They won't let you go back on the road until custody's settled, Kris.

But Doony was so happy there. That's gotta count for something.

It matters. But not to them.
So, yeah . . . *now* is not where I was.

✶ ✶ ✶ ✶

Baby Doony on my hip, I stepped off the van into the fiery, cold New Mexican sun. The wind whipped at his hair and he laughed, dug his face into my neck, then caught my eye, wicked, gleeful. Chubby fingers pulled back shining curls and he showed me his surprise-eyes. Black, leafless trees shivering happily on broken sand and snow lines. A crazy foreverscape.

Doony climbed higher up me and pointed at where he wanted to go: into the forever.

♋ aching for you

we're born again vagrants

Wake up.

With increased intracranial pressure, we first lose the concept of time. Only after that do we lose location or people; hearts are placed, but not placed on a linear timeline. When he was taken, the baby was hidden. I drove all night looking for him, all over this island, banging on doors, his car seat empty behind me. Now any movement I made toward him to keep him safe could put me in jail, keep us apart indefinitely. The emptiness of arms missing a child who needs them in order to be okay.

The baby's not okay.

And all the music we played, all the noise we made. Music in my head, in the air; music was an always too. My bass player, parked outside my apartment, waiting to take me to practice. I rest my chin on my guitar case in his truck and watch dry snow whip across the windshield as he drives; watch the gray road and gray sky become a black road and black sky. He shifts gears and looks at me out of the corner of his eye. An asking and knowing squint he rarely loses.

In a basement, under a bare bulb, our drummer is already playing; so we join him and tear through hours of songs, exhausting ourselves. I stop yelling and bloodying my fingers long enough to watch them work and think, *thank you*. I always do this when we practice. Cuz music turned out to be passion, of all things: an exercise in circular breathing and becoming a you without a name. Nothing like the stuff they sell called "music."

My bass player is dripping wet, my drummer's chest heaves. This noise is categorically different from what our record company wants us to do. Like an energetic eruption; happy swearing or something. No pride or shame, unless it's the *power* of shame. It has an electrical component, heartbeats align with it, an alive thing that has no more interest in us than an apple tree does, and it comes to everyone in open moments. My bandmates and I gather the most interesting apples we can find . . . and those are pretty not pretty. Wormy, bruised, and misshapen, you know. But boy, are we obsessed with those apples. We carry 'em down to the basement and pitch 'em around the room. Smashing guts to fall in love to. This keeps us clean; transmutation is detox, of course.

And the bags of McDonald's the music business hawks,

claiming they grew that shit on trees. Poor listeners. I hug my drummer.

See you tomorrow.

It's after midnight.

See you today.

Then back in my bass player's truck, resting my chin on my guitar case all the way home. He sideways squints at me, then at the road; that weird question-and-answer face he makes. And stars appear.

♋ glass

in this hyper-chlorinated pool of humanity
you're very clean
in this insatiable, unstable subspecies
you're very sweet

And townies fill my apartment again, politely holding beers, trying to figure it all the fuck out, which they were never gonna do. When I moved to this island as a southern child, these Yankees were unkind, so I worshipped them. And now I was grateful for their kindness. Nothing to say; cruelty can't be understood except by the cruel. Who throw blizzards of paper covered in typing. Served papers. One sentence can take the baby, can put you in jail. The lawyers told me I might be able to keep my son if I didn't play music.

I'll quit.

It's too late for that.

So the townie kids and I fall silent, and that's full. Now we knew: the adults we were supposed to become? Were out of their minds.

* * * *

Maybe pirates. I mean, we had rum now. Guitars and Baby Doony's cool, old metal toys filled the hearth, which was missing one fireplace; it was a tiny town of road atrocities instead. Road atrocities like Potted Meat Food Product and candy ants in candy sand, trucker speed, Sugar Boogers, a brochure from the Potato Museum. Buncha broken "unbreakable" guitar picks. Cartoons scribbled on parking tickets. Cartoons are important. We got an inordinate number of cartoonists at our shows. Lonely, fiery people with cool secrets. They'd draw us while we played, then sign the drawings and promise to die soon, making the scribbles more valuable. All I remember about them was their smallness and their smiles: glassy eyes behind glasses.

Glassy rattling, an aquarium missing two fire-bellied newts. Glass and water. Glass doesn't have to be fragile or even transparent. Sea glass is opaque and unbreakable. Sea glass held up the cartoonists' cartoons, the unbreakable broken picks, and Polaroids of Doony on beaches, Polaroids of sand and water; sea glass is sand and water. Brushing a finger across a packet of Sugar Boogers, a townie tells me my New York boyfriend is . . . and searches for the right word.

Tall.

I know. But it's not his fault.

♋ cartoons

I'll shut up soon
then we'll go home
covered in band-aids and casts

This kitchen'd been updated in the seventies with grim-gold linoleum and a leaning, wheezing, graying fridge. Poor old, cold dude. Grim-gold sunshine, half gray and soothing, hung grease-heavy in the kitchen air, which was different from air in the other rooms . . . like draped light. Colonial grease; tallow or something.

Lawsuits, the law in suits. The business of music loves money, does not love music. The legal ramifications of contractual vs. moral obligation. As teenagers, we'd been tricked, time and again, by so many people, just waiting to pounce and sue for future money. They all pounced at once now. And lawsuits around the baby: passion and misguided passions, love turned to hate. And more money. I'd heard of this, but . . . my kindness was real, like everyone's. I'd reached out to those who'd reached out to me. And now it was shrouded by noise, fear, anger, and by my own maternal strength and frailty. It's hard to find humanity in those who hide theirs, as badly as we may want to. The man from New York was shivery and sometimes grayish in all this, even though he was golden by nature. He grew his hair to keep warm, grew a beard to keep warm, and: grew. Fearless, he did not hunch, he swelled with power and hope. I hid in his shadow, shrinking.

They could be at the door, on the phone, in the mailbox. We escaped on the road. I want running away back. That was life. That was home.

I know, Kris. This is just a hover home.

How did love wreck everything?

♋ tar kissers

all my sympathy for you
sitting straight on the back of mother hate

Like coming to. In the interstitial moments between broken time's effects, court is ongoing. They're holding the baby's feet and pulling. Taking the baby was supposed to kill me, but mothers can't die, so that plan didn't work. I'm alive and disappearing instead. No one knows what to do about that. Least of all me.

They're trying to use a diagnosis of mental illness against you.

Misdiagnosis. There's nothing unstable about me.

You'll have to prove that.

Other people held the music's feet and pulled. Trying to escape a major label that never wanted someone like me in the first place was futile. They wanted the *pretense* of passion, the *pretense* of love, the *pretense* of beauty. Music and humans are unpretentious, unsalable. I didn't belong there, but they wouldn't let me go. The bees under the auspices of this hive were human beings and there was kindness between us, even music between us. But the hive ran the show and we just buzzed over telephones about it.

*How much would it cost me to buy myself out of my con-
tract?*

You can't afford it, Kris. Trust me.

*Yeah. But I lose you guys money. I'll never be a Barbie-ho,
playing product and calling it art.*

*I know that; we signed you because of your integrity. You're
on our roster because of all the people trying to do what you
won't.*

So sign them and let me go.

They sign with us because of you.

That's terrible.

What did you think it would be like here?

Which was a good point. When an anomaly thinks she's an
exception to the rule, she usually needs to study the rule book
again. *People* think, corporations don't. Nothing there is necessary and nothing necessary is there. And no window left open
to escape into clean rain because without a heart, without skin,
there's no feeling; no need for clean or rain. People made sense,
the rules didn't.

Lawyers, so many different lawyers, and the lawyers fight
each *other*, that's how it works, like a video game: *hold on,
I got a guy.* Each individual lawyer is also a human, but one
tasked with attacking and taking. All directed at me, at my
name, which isn't me, grimming my mailbox, my phone, and
then fluorescent-lit offices, courtrooms. I only did one thing to
deserve all of this: I fell in love. And yeah, it wrecked everything.

Our snow is tiny, dry crystals swirling around us. Theirs is
blizzards of paper. I just froze.

How can the baby be gone?

There is a cop standing on
the front porch. There is
always a cop standing on
the front porch.

A hover home. Which, well . . . totally counts, because you can
climb out the window. Into dousing thunderstorms or the dry
flakes of a coming snowstorm. But what if a memory catches
fire and drags itself off time, burns all over your forever? What
window helps you escape that?

*They can have the fucking music. I quit everything but the
baby.*

They all want money.

I don't have any.

They don't care.

Found this in an old song notebook:

These influences are taking the form of oxytocin then cortisol, of
hiding in showers as if they're rain, of hiding in a van as it races
through the desert, of hiding in memories of the baby, of gripping
losing and accidental stealing. The wandering off kind of stealing:
I let go, shouldn't you let go too? Of hiding in sex as if it's a sagey desert,
I'm naked, shouldn't you be naked too? Lawsuits and black-wet highways,
hiding in memories of New Mexico, snow-skittered dry highways
and McDonald's coffee, hiding in fleeting kindness as if it's reedy
wetlands, McDonald's milk, hiding in showers again as if they're
rain again, hiding in memories of a gas station in New Mexico,
ghost-like isolation and gnawing ghost hunger and . . . ghosts of

the baby and me when we were happy. Friends and lovers became enemies on angry paper and noisy phone calls; our only home, dry static motels like rain shadow and housekeepers' thick shells. These women must miss their babies too. Please don't clean my room, I made my bed, go home to your children. Anger is just the deepest disappointment we're capable of. I'm losing the baby but he's alive so I can't die. Hot tears and cold numb are the same awful, of all things, and I know the baby must be crying too, somewhere.

♋ milk at mcdonald's

every car crash on st. andrew

Doony's not ok.

I looked for him, but everywhere I looked shut my eyes. And it all played out in this hearth missing one fireplace; a shrine to what just happened.

Gray and yellow were the only colors left. Like sinking down to the sea floor, watching the rainbow disappear wavelength by wavelength. Gray and yellow fought over us: scary sun beamed through soothing clouds, which then threatened and sank down until gentle, yellow light filtered through them and warmed into exposure and then burning overexposure, when gray storms raced to our rescue. But storms don't care if your mute little potato-sack body gets slammed down. It all happened so fast.

And then you wait. Wait for them to decide your future, so your life circles and repeats. Hours become days become weeks become months, and sometimes a month was a minute that burst in both directions. Time was now fucked.

* * * *

Doony's black eyes with white New Mexico sun in them, reflecting a deeper blue. The wind whipped his curls into them while he drew in the sand with a stick. When he turned to look at me, a crow landed in the black tree above him and he gasped.

* * * *

Bottles and bottles stacked on the counter, holding the fridge up. As it groaned. Heavy breathing into humming and then it just . . . quit. Poor old humming, mummified frigerator.

How many little baking soda boxes lived out their lives inside here?

An army of them. An army of little baking soda boxes.

I bet just this one.

Yeah, probly.

We closed its smudgy gray-yellow door and kept it closed until we tiptoed out of that apartment. We didn't need a fridge, weren't eating a ton, were broke and tense, humming and mummified, living in circles. And this morning, we were actually still.

Hungover. That's different.

Still zen.

Ya think?

Buddha loves a hangover. Hangover's part of the high.

The bad part.

A dénouement.

A punishment.

♋ clay feet

this is no time to fuck up
scooting around the linoleum on all fours
what for again?

Found the baby a popsicle in this dusty, dark gas station. New Mexican light is a snow-white, polar-bright blue, and the freezer all lime green and neon pink. I hold the cold and hand him the stick. Doony presses the wrapper to his cheek and startles at the ice or the crinkling or my eyes on him, I dunno. He twitches and grins. Wind and sun are the same thing here.

✳ ✳ ✳ ✳

And the Krazy Kat desertscape of New Mexico more in front of our eyes than the norms' world. Krazy Kat comics are always open on the green ceramic table; so much beauty printed on paper. Not ugly money or legal documents, paper as weapons. A courtroom is a study in pain. I mean, norms aren't as normal as they think they are.

And the child is illegitimate?

Illegitimate?

Please answer the question. Is the child illegitimate? Yes or no?

I'm not married.

So the child is illegitimate.

No.

Remember you're under oath.
No child is illegitimate.
Objection. Prosecution is confusing the witness.

> There is a cop standing on
> the front porch. There is
> always a cop standing on
> the front porch.

In some dusty corner were the fire-bellied newts who'd committed suicide escape, they hated living with us so much. Maybe
the dark devils chasing us, or maybe they didn't like fish food
. . . maybe newts have their own dark devils, I dunno. The newts
bummed me out. Whatever their deal was, it wasn't really my
fault. Unless it was captivity, which it coulda been. But *their*
breathless freedom took the form of expiration. They didn't
like our world, became ex-newts in it. Their inertia was actual
stillness, actually breathless: they stopped breathing. Which I
would have killed to do—I'd learned that skill in Malibu while
the beach monkeys watched—but there was love and a child.
Apartment life doesn't suit those looking to slip into marshy
reeds and I could relate. But only *ish*: there was manic love and
a depressed child. Seismic activity like manic depression, you
gotta honor. Life is manic, it is depressed, it is intense, it is full,
it is everything, including numb and shut down when numb and
shut down happen, which isn't often enough for most of us. So
we numb ourselves and shut each other down. You know, sprea-
din' the love. This does not mean we are manic or depressed; it
means that life is what it is.

Marshy reeds are for those who aren't called to duty. No mud was gonna take me yet; no mud would have any of us because we had each other.

The nurse said I'm not depressed, that my life is just depressing.

You're sad about sadness.

Who isn't?

No shit.

I have to prove that I'm not mentally ill when they're all nuts.

This is not a new story.

Some people think they're themselves and you're you. That the more pain they inflict, the less they'll feel. I asked the man what happened to confuse them.

They know not what the fuck they do.

They know exactly what the fuck they do.

Well, that's actual pain, then.

But the baby. I was gifted his body and psychology. I'm custodian of that tiny system and it doesn't deserve this.

I know. I mean, I don't know.

❋ ❋ ❋ ❋

"Visitation," they called it. Three and a half days a week, Doony would be with me again. I picked him up at a building surrounded by a chain-link fence and we stayed very still, holding each other, for a long, long time. Such a still, silent child. He was cold and rosy-cheeked on the walk home, then happy to see his toys, books, and clothes in my apartment. We dropped into the rocking chair together, exhausted; he was in our coma too. From that old song notebook:

The baby said this today, about a dream he had. "We were in a row-boat full of holes, just you and me. I am small, so I fell through a hole into the water and you jumped in to save me. Then I fell all the way down to the bottom where it's dark and you couldn't find me. You were crying." This is the most he's said all day.

He'd only started speaking a few months ago and his first words were, *hey, look at the helicopter*, pointing out the tour bus window. I froze at the time, quietly freaking, while he got pissed and pointed at a helicopter flying past. *I said, look at the helicopter!* So I did. There was a helicopter and we looked at it. He rarely spoke now. Understood everything, I could see it in his eyes, but had little to say.

Christmas is coming, baby. What would you like? Elves have gotta build it all, right? They need time to work out how. You know, blueprints and stuff. We'll hang your stocking now, though. And when you know what you want, draw me a picture.

He wasted no time, grabbed a fistful of crayons and his almost used-up pad of drawing paper, threw himself on the floor, and got to work. I watched, had sort of forgotten that a three-year-old's drawings are indistinct at best. Twisted my head around like a dog, trying to understand.

Good idea. And . . . you want a purple one? With . . . yellow?

Nodding, he embellished with more yellow scribbles, did not look up. I tried to guess what he was asking for, but it was hard. His overalls bunched up around his waist and he tugged at the straps, then got back to work, grabbing a red crayon and adding what looked like hair.

Is that hair?

He shook his head, made piercing, dark eye contact, then

emphatically drew some more red over the red to explain. Sometimes he was here, sometimes he was gone, and sometimes he was behind a chain-link fence. When they saw him talking to me through the fence, they'd call him away.

From the same old notebook:

Relinquish control. It was imaginary, anyway.

♋ bo diddley bridge

freaking
sweetly killed

Turns out the red hair-ish was a helmet. A red helmet on a nut-cracker soldier. One that cracked nuts, specifically. We had one whose head came off when you put a nut in his mouth and Doony's idea was: not that.

A sage princess pumpkin, hard as rock and green with ice, on the front porch; an ice lantern that would never be a jack-o'-lantern on fire, waiting for the fire-bellied newts, peering through sun-mist, looking to come home. Maybe the fire gone outta their newt bellies, so they need a hearth again. A hearth also missing a fire, which plays out the last story in sea glass, holding up a fuzzy Polaroid of Doony on a beach: sand and water, and sand and water: sea glass. The repetition'd be a torture if we weren't hypnotized by it. Welcome home, newts.

✳ ✳ ✳ ✳

The silhouette of my bass player in his truck out the window, waiting to take me to practice. My drummer is a brightness, my bass player a singularity.

Thank god for you.

We gather apples and pitch them around the basement again. So far, I don't seem to have done much right in my life, but I will say this: prayer is better than televangelism.

♋ william's cut

I lost every hope I ever had
but I like it too much

That night, the man and I drive to New York to find a nutcracker soldier that cracks nuts. I ride shotgun, staring into nothing. The view is still wiggly, but at least it races.

Old Saybrook, can't read the sign without hearing it in the train conductor's voice. It whizzes past, gray drizzle and mustard-gas yellow, both with an odd glow on the dark highway. Sometimes you wonder what America is, moving through it the way we do. Sometimes, not often; as the question is more about what people with and without power *think* it is.

✻ ✻ ✻ ✻

Dead boxcars, sideways, on dead train tracks in cold sun. A dark snake body, basking but cold. A dark crow, a dark tree. I lift the snake and it makes brief eye contact before warming itself, twisting around my arm.

Doony is one of them, his hair and the sun shining together. He's not of this species.

* * * *

Spin the shocks, I guess? There are poisons here on this plane, and most of them are injected by venomous snakes who'd rather go about their business. We call it danger because we're a species-centric species, but if you do not stumble mindlessly, snakes and viruses and shadows will remain glossy intrigue. "Poison" only means it hurts *you*, and who are you? If you're meant to engage and pain each other, you and the danger will be pain teammates, making the most of shock, of contagion, of enemy, of death grip, of partnership, of damage. You'll face the venom, but it could take years.

All of this fucks with time. The snakes have not needed to evolve for millennia, the viruses never stop. Your liver and its analogs'll teach you to spit poison, to live broken or healed. Or we shrug and die like shadows, cool with that too. Cruelty is a tough contagion; occasionally, it's an out-of-control population shift. But I suppose inherent in every unbalancing, there is focus and concurrent balance.

Opposed forces don't immediately disengage. *Did I call this violence? Dis-ease?* What is interplay? What is dis-integration? What is an enemy? Every entity is both a system within a system and an organism. Every song a body; soul is its substance, this incarnation only its style. Same with us. This fingerprint will write its own story of engagement.

So yeah, spinning shocks, we had no option but to live the minutes. And totally learn to spit; it's important.

Kris.

Oh yeah. In a car, headed toward New York. Drizzly road signage.

Stamford. Always in the conductor's voice. Thanks for that, dude, I love your voice. I love your job and its squeaky gleaming and weird hours. Just that this America through the window doesn't always feel like a healthy one.

✳ ✳ ✳ ✳

It snowed not as weather, but as a parasite. Never accumulated. Last year and every year before that: icy, gray mounds and failing snowmen molested by crows, but this year? It just . . . didn't stop dry snowing. We'd leave the crooked island and the dry snowflakes'd follow us. Like it was our own personal climate, to get fake snowed on. Snowflakes always in our hair, our totem precipitation. Drive to New York cuz you need a nutcracker soldier that actually cracks nuts, lean out the window, and the snowflakes gather and spin around you, float down and disappear.

The highway whizzed past, a soft, gray, ill, and comforting escape, sick with Jersey grime, blurry. Blurry was how I felt and blurry I could handle. Anything that smoothed rough edges was welcome. The man spoke gently.

I know people who could get the three of us fake passports. You just need to be sure it's what you want.

New Zealand?

Sure. It's far away . . . and safe. They speak English.

He watched the road over his red scarf.

You could never play music again. Not in public, anyway.

*We probably couldn't come back to America or see our friends
or families ever again.*

You're my friend. The baby is my family.

He drove, staring ahead, while we considered a muddy future.

*But if they put you in jail, you couldn't see us anymore,
either.*

I couldn't speak. He reached for my hand.

I'm only trying to help.

The highway was so blurry.

I'm worried about the end of the world.
                                        —*Krazy Kat*

You ok?

Sure.

Well . . . you're gonna have to get out of the car.

Oh. Am I not out of the car?

. . . no.

What am I doing?

I thought sleeping, but now I'm not so sure.

I just . . . wanna go somewhere else, so that's where I went.

*Yeah. You're gonna have to go here now. Where's your
twenty? I'll buy you some gum.*

Always bring a twenty-dollar bill to the city. Then buy something for fifty cents and share out the rest when people who
need way more than that ask for it. If you got it, do the same
with a hundred-dollar bill. Especially when it's cold.

Wherezza nutcrackers at?

Toy stores are closed, Kris. We'll go first thing in the morning. You need a drink.

You're an enabler.

You aren't an alcoholic yet. I'm working up to enabler.

Duck into an icy bar on the icy Hudson for icy margaritas in plastic tumblers and a plate of fried alligator, the snowflakes follow you in and settle under your barstools like dogs. A dénouement, a punishment, a high hangover only the Buddha could love. Also a foreshadowing: it was supposed to be New Orleans in here and it kinda was. Just enough.

Herradura Silver, please. Two extra shots?

Stared at the bartender's back, missing frames. Snail vision. It felt like I'd been on tour for years.

It feels like you've been on tour for years because you've been on tour for years.

Oh.

What's wrong with musicians' brains?

I dunno. Something. I wanna learn a glossy, orange love lesson on a love cruise. I wanna adventure-land in Hawaii. I want a lei. And maybe a Fantasy.

Our love lesson is: people hate us.

I went around and around and around with this, trying to make sense of it, hitting repeat, losing the plot. Why the hell does anybody ever *care* enough to attack?

This'll keep you warm.

The bartender was playing bartender, but he meant it, so that was cool. He added an extra shot to our margaritas with an ersatz New Orleans prayer, then held up his two middle fingers to us. Waxy dead fingers; corpse yellow-gray, scored with lemon-slicing slices.

Frostbite.

No shit.

Wear gloves.

Ok.

A loud waitress yelled something too loud to hear and it made the bartender spin around and do something I couldn't see. I tried to eat some alligator, couldn't swallow. Always slow on the outside, I was slowing down on the inside, becoming the cold. It felt wonderful. I looked at the man.

I wanna stay here forever.

This is maybe heaven.

You know? Yes. Not the heaven but a heaven. An heaven. Cuz of the comfort and the ice.

He mouthed the words, "comfort" and "ice," to see if that was true. I tried to explain.

The driest you can be is in the woods, in the rain, when you find a lean-to some hippie built and left for you and whoever needed it, like a rabbit or something, and you think, holy shit, people are cool. I know cuz that happened once.

The man was squinting at me. He had no hippie blood and was wary of those without rules.

I figured, or you wouldn't have said that. Cool people are cool. Not all people.

What if all people are cool and they just forget how to act?

Then we keep forgiving them until their bullshit peters out.

Now I squinted at *him*.

Is that what bullshit does?

♋ petal

I've never been afraid to die
I've never been afraid to live
I've never been afraid before

I watched the man from New York City be in New York City. Kinda hopped up.

I just get off on this place. It's the energy, the buzz.

That's not energy, it's shopping. And you hate shopping. I don't get how you ever worked at a major label.

He grinned.

They make the rules.

Of what game?

The game that decides who gets to eat. Seems less stupid when you're facing its repercussions.

No, it doesn't. That's when you see how stupid it really is.

He laughed. Like all musicians who are not entertainers, I . . . am . . . a . . . dog. He decided that he was a dog inside and a winner outside, but it wasn't quite true, and for that, I was grateful. Something guileless in his never having been hurt. Something guileless in my assumption that he'd never been hurt. The bartender finished wiping down a glass and struck a pose in front of us, his waxy fingers resting against whaling-captain sideburns. I looked up at him.

How'd you get frostbite?

Catskills.

We waited. He stared.

Oh. That's a good story.

Yeah, well. I'm just a bad camper.

In that hippie's lean-to in the rainy woods, I'd tried to imagine what it was like there in the snow. The biggest hippie heart can't keep out cold if you're a bad camper. I felt sorry for the bartender and his yellow fingers. I'd heard that the tingling when frozen digits come back to life is intolerable—coming back to life outta numb—wanted him to know we're all bad campers sometimes.

I climbed a waterfall once? Camping? And when I got to the top, there were all these crosses for the dead people who'd tried to climb the waterfall and failed.

Cool.

Except they shoulda put the crosses at the bottom. I mean, I was hangin' by my fingertips, watching the water rush around all the crosses and thinkin', they didn't die going up.

Ah.

So. You know. I'm also a bad camper.

I wondered if it would tingle intolerably when *I* came back to life. The bartender grabbed two shot glasses and filled them for us. Normally, I would've given these away. Musicians get a lot of free drinks; you gotta be smart about that. And me, no control over my own face; still blank-eyed, affectless. What else can you do but fall blank? Hurts to lose numb.

૭ mississippi kite

you get burned
you get cold

* * * *

His tiny, round sneakers smudging the sand into dust that flies up in swirls and catches sunlight, Doony erases his sand drawing and begins again, studying the crow edging closer on the shaky black branch. The baby spit calls into the whistling wind and the crow answers. Sounds like music.

* * * *

Rank, murky, it was dark on the sidewalk, but there were lights everywhere: neon signs, headlights, streetlamps, storefronts, marquees, traffic lights.

Night isn't night here.

The man studied the glare around us.

New York doesn't sleep.

I nodded.

I've heard that.

We once lived this day's opposite: a garbage strike in August. Heat lifting dirty paper, cans rolling into swirling crud in white hot air. Nobody does garbage like New York. Walking down the shimmering sidewalk, we wrote a new garbage script:

Fishbones.
Grapefruit rinds.
Coffee grounds.
Banana peels.
Jagged tin can lids.

Cartoons are perfect. Cartoons will save us. We're garbage here and having seen how beautiful that can be? Loved those who'd thrown us away.

The man smiled down at me. I felt like he only stopped smiling to well up. And not just about sadness. He welled up with joy or beauty. The opposite of affectless.

Could you eat?

I shrugged and he pointed into a steamy window.

Heartbreak soup.

♋ power and light

hearts thrust into heartbreak soup
desperate times

Staring into my *chirinabe*, the steam enveloping my face. I looked out the window, which wasn't actually a window but a picture of snow-covered white birch trees glued to the back of a window frame and hung on the wall. It looked like Vermont. Or Switzerland.

I'm not sure I can do this.

I know.

Didn't expect to lose a baby.

Nobody does. But Doony's still here. I mean, he's alive.

I watched the swirling steam on the surface of the soup.

Sometimes I wish he wasn't. Then I could just go to heaven and take care of him. I'd have no problem doing that. But what kind of mother wishes that?

The man watched his own swirling steam.

People live through nightmares. Sometimes.

Or I could be a ghost, then no one could keep us apart. Or an angel for his whole life and . . . blow danger away from him.

He stared at the white birch trees and blue sky out the fake window.

Maybe we should view this as an experiment. You can't do one-day-at-a-time because you don't want your darkest day to determine your future, so it'd be a big-picture kind of experiment.

I considered this.

What are we looking for?

He turned away from the window.

A happy ending.

✳ ✳ ✳ ✳

At three a.m. the next morning, we lay in the dark, listening to the radiators clanking and sighing. Trucks lumbered down the street, their brakes screeching. It was steamy hot in his apartment, but I pulled the sheet up around me anyway, studied his darkness as he spoke.

I'll keep you here, if you want. I'll make it my mission.

A truck slowed and stopped outside, compressed air whistling from its brakes; the radiators hummed.

♋ chipping teeth

don't forget the happy ending

✳ ✳ ✳ ✳

Desert wind harmonica'd through conifers and a bottle clanked with it. Doony chased the bottle as it spun and rolled, alive. Sun can't blister, can't sear, through a wind like that. His curls grabbed it and shone cold. When he looked at me, half-lidded, I scooped him up and carried him back to the motel. By the time I'd found the key and fumbled us into the room, hip-checking the door shut, he was asleep.

✳ ✳ ✳ ✳

℥ candyland

I was born with a sad song in my mouth
he gave me a reason to sing it

I held a large wooden soldier up in the air. It bared its teeth down at me in a snarl; feathers adorned its helmet. This tiny West Village toy shop was a carefully orchestrated elfin sugar-plum planet, which allowed them to jack up the prices tenfold cuz desperate parents are up against it this time of year. I was a desperate parent.

The clerk was a soft, smiling young nerd with glasses around her neck, who was practicing being a soft, smiling *old* nerd with glasses around her neck. The kind of lady who looks the same for her whole life cuz she decided to turn into her grandmother a long time ago, which was nice of her: she was very smiling. I turned the soldier to face her.

Is this a nutcracker?

Yes. It's a nutcracker soldier. From The Nutcracker.

And it cracks nuts?

Again, it was very important to Doony that the nutcracker on his Christmas list crack nuts. Last Christmas morning was a super sad fight with the slippery head of a nutcracker soldier that wouldn't adhere to its own neck. All of our nuts were still intact. NUTCRACKER THAT CRACKS NUTS is what he had me write on his list. Bitterly. The woman channeled her grandmother, laughing softly.

I think it cracks nuts. It's a nutcracker.

Do you know that it cracks nuts? The reason I ask is that my little boy really wants a nutcracker that actually cracks nuts.

She looked at me, blank, then put her glasses on to study the mechanism of the soldier's jaw. I was impressed; I would've guessed that her glasses were fake. The jaw opened and shut with a swing of the arm. I laughed.

Hey, like that Barbie whose tits grow when she hits puberty. You swing her arm and she goes up a couple bra sizes? Growing Up Skipper?

The woman looked sick.

What?

Never heard of her? But you work in a toy shop.

She looked sicker. The man appeared at my side, holding a giant doll upside down by one foot.

So, what's the upshot? Does it crack nuts?

The charming old bell on the charming old door jingled and a camel-coated couple walked in, pulling a complicated stroller through the doorway. The clerk let her glasses drop and peered hopefully through us, but the couple didn't seem to need any help. Her smile had become the kind of smile that's making itself tired. She turned it on the man.

I haven't seen it crack nuts. But it's a nutcracker. It's from The Nutcracker.

That's a ballet, right? Yeah, so . . . ballet. It's important to her little boy that it actually crack nuts is all. Do you have any nuts here?

She shook her head and excused herself—*just you two*—and left to wrap gifts at the register. The man shrugged.

I don't trust ballet. Does he want a doll?

He didn't mention wanting a doll. Not unless it can crack nuts with its head.

In one swift motion, he gripped the doll fiercely and smashed its head on the shelf. The store clerk looked up from her wrapping in alarm.

That'd crack a nut, I bet. How 'bout we steal some nuts and come back?

Or . . . buy some.

I was beginning to see how he might have fit in at the record company. He looked down at me.

You play with dolls when you were a little girl?

No, we had a spool.

He used the doll to scratch his head.

A spool. Of thread?

Well, a big one. Not of thread, of cable. My brother and I could do anything on that spool. Ran around the yard like circus bears.

Circus bears.

Like circus bears, yeah.

We both eyed the shelves, looking for spools. The camel-coated couple and their camel-coated baby were at the register now, being grandmothered at, chuckling quietly about a "perfect Christmas."

The man smirked.

Wanna go?

Yeah. I need a schmancy coat before she cares about Doony having a perfect Christmas.

We're buying the freakin' soldier.

He laid his doll back down on the shelf and its dead eyes went to sleep.

♋ milk street

trying to shield your glass newborn from the
dodgeballs

The sidewalk in front of the man's apartment was the coldest place on earth. I gripped the wooden soldier in a razor-blade wind that raced across the East River, down my neck, and into my spine, as he checked all his pockets for keys. He had many, many pockets and the keys didn't seem to be in any of them. Grinning wildly, he started over.

An aquarium full of fish-keeping paraphernalia rested on top of his boot on the sidewalk, which, on Christmas morning, would contain a buncha circling fish and two sulking newts. He had promised me that he could create a beautiful, watery dreamworld for Doony in the living room: a movie that never stopped, and the baby could name twenty pets at once. The man yelled something I didn't get into the biting wind, which was maybe not words, and held up his keys. I bent my frozen face into a smile. Not a good smile, I bet. Probly the soldier's wooden grimace.

♋ silver sun

bend your molten face to smile

Carried our bags of stocking loot plus the nutcracker soldier and fish tank up three flights of stairs, then the man had to fish for keys again. I didn't lock anything—bikes, cars, doors— didn't even *own* keys to my apartment, but in New York, peo- ple lock everything thousands of times. This time, it wasn't so cold, so I watched him under the buzzing fluorescents. Listened, I guess; there's more information in sound. Fumbling over his red scarf, the grime of a billion city moments rubbed into the walls and floors, the man hummed and jangled. When the door to his apartment swung open, Christmas toys spilled through it, clunking together; we could hear the radiators' clanking and sad singing, breathing steam into the living room. All these sounds went together. The prettiest was the sound of half a dozen snow globes rolling together, which sort of *whirred* . . . curved glass buzzing against curved glass.

On the wall was a picture of my band, sitting on a staircase, grinning crazily, and on the desk, a collection of gross candy I had sent him from the road: candy ants in candy sand, Sugar Boogers, pork-chop gum.

We carefully placed Doony's Christmas presents on the

couch and admired them. I had this desperate hope that I could turn Doony's enormous sad eyes into happy little elf squints with these gifts, if only for a morning. If I'd had any idea what praying was, I would've prayed for this.

We don't have much money left.

Well . . . we can finally crack nuts.

Just scared it's all been leading up to this . . . everything. All the shit we been through wasn't the shit. The storm's just been brewing.

Now comes the storm.

—*Krazy Kat*

✳ ✳ ✳ ✳

I had been setting myself on fire a lot. Leaning over candles, a diaphanous sleeve evaporated around my arm. Our ancient gas stove lifted a blond braid in crinkling blue flames. I watched, quietly fascinated. Fire . . . finds you? A grease dust fire in the trash can; that leftover pilgrim tallow, I guess. Engulfed in smoke, I stood over it, watching, as paper curled and floated, breaking down and breaking up. My Salvation Army skirt caught the edge of a drugstore receipt and, smoking, seared in communion with the rest of the trash.

Look out the window. All the little-girl Irish mothers lining the block and the old Irish mothers and the little, old Irish mothers, unwhiny widows, well: these ageless angels leave their burning hearths to smoke on the front steps. Yeah, fire finds you. Reaches out a fingertip and sets you on itself; like-minded entities, you and flames, sizzling to disappear. A deep, angry summer in winter. God, do we love the babies, soapy dishes, men, and townie friends in our houses, but we'll step into the snow looking for more fire, it's so important to us. Smoke had filled the kitchen by the time the man walked through it to pour a glass of water on the burn party. More smoke. Wicked cool. Physics plays out always.

The man got pretty used to leaning over and putting out flames, watching me watch his hands. Same hands that shot through the surface of salty green in Point Dume while the ground squirrels watched. At least fire wasn't bitter or selfish, like an angry person. A hungry bear climbing down from the hills, it was just digging through my garbage life. *The bear can have it.* The man was a bear wrangler but I was on the bear's side. When flames lit it all up, it was warm for a second. Then the man extinguished them gently with his cold arms and it was like two opposed kindnesses.

But cold was winning. Winter shines, winter wins. Physics plays out, always.

Should you be catching fire?

Hmmmm.

I mean . . . this often?

I don't do it on purpose.

No. You don't do anything at all.

I think I don't wanna fight anymore.

It doesn't make you look not crazy. Let's start with fighting fire and see what happens to the fire in you.

You can't help but look out colonial windows on a cobblestone street. The picture appears to be moving. Wiggly glass is like an altered state of participatory view. Another little Irish smoker opened her ye olde door and joined her neighbor on the porch in a T-shirt and her husband's winter coat. They were elegant, those women.

And the whole time? Music plays. A soundtrack no one else hears is unusual apparently, but I was real used to it.

♋ glass cats

outside is blue
in this house is golden

Fish Christmas came and went, the pouting newts just glum, not yet disappeared; no pointy sticks through their brainz. The ball of fire was still just a spark in a god's brainz, I guess. The second law of thermodynamics was questioned that winter; the role of momentum and entropy's arrow. Caught in a slow spin. And all we could come up with really was: *more pie*. Doony stood on a chair, thrusting his hands into a bowl over and over again. He was talking, he was gleeful; what a sunshine. Little backward knuckles trying to grip flour, giggling when it ran through his fingers.

Dust!

Clapping his hands in the air. Clouds of flour hung around him, coating his golden curls. I peeled a mound of apples and he squealed through the dust clouds.

I'm not clapping, I'm getting the flour off. Powder!
When can it be a piecrust?

When I finish playing with this snow.

He clapped his hands again.

I'm not clapping, I'm getting the flour off. Snow!

Murmuring at the pile happily, he molded the flour into a hill and poked a hole in the top.

This is a igloo.

He clapped his hands in the air again, making more clouds, admiring the air around him and whispering.

Fog. I'm not clapping.

I whispered back.

Are you clapping?

No.

Reaching down to the table, he pulled a long strip of apple peel away from the others and held it up to taste it. I took it gently.

Peels are chokey.

And pushed a tiny piece of peeled apple into his mouth. He clapped flour clouds.

Why do you keep clapping, baby?

I'm not clapping. I'm getting the flour off.

So it is flour. Good. Cuz I'm supposed to make a piecrust.

It's not flour . . .

Pinching a little in his chubby fingers and tossing it into the air. The flour settled on his lashes and he blew upward to clear his vision.

This is birdseed for a tiny bird.

He tasted some, pretending to be a tiny bird. Flour in his mouth stilled his enthusiasm, but only for a second, then cloud-clapping started up again. Doony was opening his tiny mouth to call the flour something other than flour again, when my bedroom door crashed against the wall and he froze, mid-clap.

The man leapt into our grim-gold kitchen, legs spread in a power stance. He was wearing long underwear and sneakers, with a towel cape tied around his neck. My swimming goggles and bathing cap were squeezed tight around his head, and he had pressed a flour handprint onto his chest. The baby shrieked happily.

Who's that?!

I stared.

I'm not sure . . .

The goggles bounced crazily on the man's face.

WHO AM I? I'M COOKING MAN, OF COURSE! IS SOMEONE HERE COOKING?

Doony, still frozen mid-clap, looked at me in shock and delight. Cooking Man watched through foggy goggles.

WHY ARE YOU CLAPPING, SON?

I'm not clapping. I'm getting the flour off.

He clapped his hands to demonstrate.

FLOUR, HUH? I HEAR THAT'S GOOD FOR MAKING PIECRUSTS.

The baby spoke quietly.

It's not flour. It's sand.

TOO BAD. SAND DOESN'T MAKE GOOD PIECRUSTS.

I stopped peeling apples and watched. There was an awkward silence as Doony pressed his hands into the flour again without taking his eyes off Cooking Man. As he clapped more flour clouds into the air, Cooking Man relaxed his superhero pose.

YOU'RE CLAPPING AGAIN.

Doony giggled and sputtered.

I'm not clapping, I'm getting the flour off! I mean the sand!

He convulsed with laughter, hands deep in the bowl of flour. Cooking Man looked cross-eyed in his goggles, the rubber strips at his temples bouncing.

WOULD YOU LIKE SOME COOKING ADVICE, SON?

The giggling escalated. Doony gripped flour with both hands and threw it up into the air.

(A) DON'T COOK WITH SAND AND (2) DON'T THROW FOOD.

I finished peeling the apple I was holding and added it to the pile of naked apples. Doony stared at Cooking Man, pupils dilated with wonder. I opened my mouth to speak and Cooking Man's hand shot up.

NO NEED TO THANK ME, MISS. JUST GLAD TO BE OF SERVICE!

Doony and I stared.

WELL, GOT TO BE ON MY WAY. LOTS OF PEOPLE COOKING TODAY. SOME OF THEM DON'T KNOW NOT TO COOK WITH SAND.

I nodded.

Well, that's not us anymore. Really appreciate you stopping by.

Doony watched in amazed silence as Cooking Man walked back into the bedroom, waving.

GOODBYE, CITIZENS! HAPPY CUISINING!

He slammed the door behind him. Doony stared at the closed door, astonished.

Who was that?!

I think he said his name was Cooking Man.

Minutes later, the man walked out of the bedroom dressed as himself and hugged Doony from behind. Twisting around to look at him, Doony splayed his floury hands.

Did you see that guy?

The man looked at him, blank.
What guy?

♋ heel, toe

I'll carry you

That night, I lit some candles and pulled our rocking chair over
to the corner, positioning it in front of Doony's Christmas fish
tank. Outside the window, patches of dusty snow glowed blue-
black. The man had gone back to the city and Doony and I
were left to try and fall asleep alone. It wasn't easy. Black holes
like sleep didn't seem safe enough to fall into anymore, and we
didn't want to spend what little time we had together unconscious. So I put him on my lap in his dinosaur pajamas and we
rocked, watching tiger barbs, neon tetras, and glass cats shimmer. As hypnotic as a fire, but more colorful, just like the man'd
said it would be. One was always dead in the morning—unlike
pets with which I was familiar, like dogs—but at night the gliding fish were awfully soothing. Even the newts were nice to look
at before we knew how depressed they were. I pointed to a little
pink fish.
Who's that?
Schlaphandrie.
Oh.
We rocked and watched.
Slapandry?
No . . . Schlaphandrie.

He dozed for a minute, then woke up talking fuzzily.
Maybe Cooking Man will come tomorrow.
Maybe.

♋ el dorado

there's a blue blizzard in our heads and I'm too sore to
sleep

The fireball had not yet burned itself through our kitchen wall,
past the frying pans and sea glass, those three dead things: a
refrigerator and two petrified newts, the fire gone outta their
bellies. And don't give me shit about that; I would've scooped
the newts and flush-buried 'em, but I couldn't *find* them. Bafflingly. Probly wasn't trying too hard, scared that they had
thrust pointed sticks into their own brains to escape my life and
I didn't wanna see those little mummies, their bloody heads too
big for their bodies. Thankfully, some kinda newt rapture flew
them up and away. Or maybe they'd slipped out a window in a
thunderstorm. I couldn't bear being separated from the sound
of a cracking sky, either; always flung open windows, wanting
to climb out when the sky threatened.

But still, screw you, newts. I mean, the fish seemed happy
enough. *They* weren't committing sushi at me. I was kinda
pissed at the newts. *What's your point?* Miserable isn't fair. *I*
was flailing and failing and *I* stuck around. Around and around
and around the aquarium. You can't take a baby's mother away.
You can't take a mother's baby away. We more than flail and

fail, we catch fire and race out the window looking for the baby
in thunderstorms. The sky cracks and the baby falls too.

♋ candyland

I lost a boy
and now I look for him through every window

✳ ✳ ✳ ✳

New Mexican ice sun. This cold burning where the sky cracked
a long time ago. Cracked open in a bright searing. Black, leafless trees were never not here.

A red ant runs over the baby's overalls. I brush it off and
whisk him up. We are each other's somewhere. Outta nowhere.

✳ ✳ ✳ ✳

In the courtroom, I laughed. Bitterly, but still. I wanted to cry,
so I laughed. On the witness stand, pelted with questions about
money, my recording contract, touring and how much money
that makes. Nothing about the baby. *Just give me the baby.
No, give the baby his mother.* The room full of adults: blank
eyes, myopic cruelty. Always some good in there, in every single
body, in what's left of the child they once were. This is why we
mothers will seem to evade time, freezing our kids at certain
ages, reminding a man that he likes ladybugs, because we're
right. He *does* like freakin' ladybugs. That's him.

I swear that's who they *really* are, these cruel grown-ups: their own goodness. But the impulses that fly through them . . . well, they set you on a bad fire.

Objection. Prosecution is confusing the witness.

Prosecution is confusing. So I laughed.

Wake up.

A greasy sunshine morning, apple pie, a toddler clapping flour into the air. Watching him through sunlit particulate. If we could be children just a little longer, my son and I. Move into a toy barn with the plastic cows and maybe a little plastic cat, chasing plastic mice. Children aren't safe, but toys are. How badly did you wanna live in that barn when you were little? What a bitchin' commune *that'd* be. And we wanted back in, me and the boy, heartsick. The man put his arms around both of us; cold arms, trying. Watching the flour clouds over our shared stomachache, watching them dazzle the baby. The baby clapping slow snow into that pirate pilgrim kitchen, the cold seeping into every crack. The slowness.

The money was gone. A minute ago, I'd had a savings. Years of work. The lawyers took it all. I'd written the last rent check I could write. Rolling out a piecrust, I glanced resentfully at the hearth full of toys, scary road shit, and sea glass. Should have been a fire in there, keeping Doony warm.

Why isn't the fireplace a place for fire? Fire is in all the wrong places in this kitchen.

Pie will save us. Pie is perfect.

Well . . . not this pie, but yeah.

We don't have to eat it. We can make it an offering to the pie god.

The coolest god.

By far.

The *Paris, Texas* soundtrack on repeat because it sounded like New Mexico to us and we had to go back. We knew it was all pretend, but it was a beautiful dream.

New Mexico will save us. New Mexico is perfect. Even better than pie.

I-70 West . . . don't look back.

♋ faith

was it me or the cold made you give up hope?

Ball of Fire, with Gary Cooper and Barbara Stanwyck . . . also on repeat cuz it looked like Time to us. Which we didn't think we had. Also spun our pseudocommie sensibilities as American like a lot of movies from the thirties. Mostly, Gary Cooper was a big nerd come to visit us from Black-and-White Land and we loved that.

The geeks shall inherit the earth.

The geeks should've already inherited the earth.

They're just running late. They know it's important. Their glasses are slipping down and they tripped. But they're on their way.

As red as the *Daily Worker* and just as sore.
                                        —*Ball of Fire*

I wanted the road back so bad. Touring is swimming. Imagine you could make an ocean out of anything, and in this case it's cheap motels. You fashion a net for your friends and throw them all into the ocean, jump in after them. Into an environment to which you are ill-suited and oddly suited. No gills? Stop breathing . . . *use* that goddamn muscle to parse wants from needs. And you know what? You have, like, one goddamn need, maybe two, tops. You're a body, so yeah, maybe air and water. *Maybe*. But that's not what we're here to figure out.

You sleep with bleach on your scratchy sheets and green chlorine traces wrapped up in your hair, wrapped up in each other's hiding, down the staticky hall. Breakfast is in vending machines unless you're a baby. I foraged for health food and he never went hungry. Slept in my chlorinated arms, bathed in the filthy-with-bleach, bleached-clean, bleach-dirty motel bathtubs. In towns where everyone knew everyone, we knew no one. It was like being ghosts.

The sun in the parking lot is filtered and moving, the van bright hot or metallic cold, depending on the season, which you don't fight. Not the hot, not the cold, not any season or topography.

My oddly quiet baby. For three and a half years:

He'll speak when he's ready.

Driving and diners, storybooks and crayons, raisin boxes. Sleeping in a car seat, in a dressing room, in my arms, on my lap in heat, in cold, in the van's radio cloud filtering like sunlight, sleeping in the day, staring at night, staring in the day, swimming in pools, toddling around pools, around and around, catching him before he tripped, before he fell, before he hit the ground.

He'll talk when he has something to say.

INTERVIEW:

Q: You look like Gidget.

A: Is that a question?

Q: How come you look like Gidget?

A: What's Gidget?

Q: Sandra Dee, you know. And then you start yelling. It's incongruous.

A: Yeah . . . I'm sorry.

Q: That's ok. You got a real shotgun thing too.

A: Like white trash? I know.

Q: Just not sure what you're going for.

A: Me neither. Was I supposed to go for something?

And every night, unzip the Sandra Dee bodysuit to reveal the monster within and hope it's one we all share. A syringe of memory later, we slip out the back.

♋ no shade in shadow

and moving back in time
we're moving back in time

In Krazy Kat's New Mexico, racing cancels itself out. An open hugeness bigger than the sunshine that filled it. Cold sun killing down from a sky that isn't a blue we've ever seen before.

The baby climbs up my hip to rest his chin on my shoulder. Pumping gas with my drummer at a gas station on a highway off a highway, like a dream about a gas station or a story about a gas station. Like you turn around and it's gone, which is, of course, what always happens to us. Turn around and *we're* gone.

The gas station sells some weird and some water cuz there's no water here and plenty of weird. Cigarettes—cigars but *ette*— though the proprietor smokes a pipe. She is frozen in beauty. My drummer stares at her through the smudgy window.

How old is she?

A thousand. Or maybe our age, hard to tell.

I bet after we pump gas out here in the sun a few times, we'll look like her.

God, I hope so.

I'm leaving my heart here. Gonna come back for it later.

Me too. We're coming back, pinky swear.

What does one give and keep?

—*Krazy Kat*

And the gas station sells candy ants in candy sand and Potted Meat Food Product and trucker speed and cool little metal toys and grime, and it has this sign in the window:

HELP

The "WANTED" behind some dusty plastic bottles of antifreeze.
Also this sign:

LIVE DONUTS BAIT

Baby on my hip.
I'm in love.

♋ sand

race through the country
the perfect carnivore
pull over and stop to breathe
there's grape jelly on your sleeve

If we worked here? Our band wouldn't have to suck to succeed.
We could live human lives of love and quality and weather. This
gas station becomes a sort of totem for us: there is no win, and
the only fail is going after one. Real life . . . holy hell. Right at
your fingertips.

And now, staring at diner food. Half the time, you can't do it.
I can't do it.

A pyramid of grape jelly ramekins. Tiny boxes of Apple
Jacks and Froot Loops.

Those jacks have never seen an apple.
Those loops have never seen a fruit.

Even the baby stares, unseeing.
He can't do it either.
Let's take a walk.

Music: how can there be a word for it? Makes no sense. A unified theory of everything in two syllables. After the show, get in the van and shark sleep home to the hotel. Clouds of chlorine. Which is a poison, I guess? But god, it's all we breathe.

♋ chipping teeth

you smell like chlorine

Wake up. We have to go to the fair.
The man blinked in the dim light of my ye olde bedroom.
Fair? Do we have to?
What did I just say? There's really nothing else to do here. Duh.
But that's why it matters.
Noooo . . . that's why it doesn't matter.

Big hog, I told him. We hit stuff with outsized hammers: children playing with toys. Grew outsized vegetables and inedible sour things like crab apples and rose hips. Cool chickens in a little wooden hut, heirloom or something. He stretched and grabbed the car keys, but not because of chickens.

Was it the hog? It's real big.

Smirking down at me, he helped me into my New York City coat.

No, I just do everything you say. Will they have coffee?

Mmmm, they're not so much coffee people as, like, cider and . . . cider.

Gotcha.

Don't underestimate the heirloom chickens.

Cold and sun and cold, sunny car, smelled like snow.

I already have.

Well, stop.

We parked in a field and then I dragged him over to the chicken coop. Peering in, you see the sentience, their eyes like a dog's. And *chicks*—chicken babies that aren't fried eggs in a diner—fuzzy miracles following each other in a cloudy line. So much like our fuzzy miracle babies. He was instantly overcome.

Chickens are fucking cool.

Chickens are so fucking cool. At least these ones are.

I don't know any others.

Me neither. I bet, like, ninety percent of chickens are cool, though.

Yeah, maybe. And ten percent are chicken dicks. How come there aren't any rooster dudes?

Guy with the stick said they peck eyes.

They do? What guy? Whose eyes?

I dunno, that's all he said.

Maybe it's more than ten percent.

Probly.

This fair happened every year on the island. But we weren't . . . the jelliest of makers or the chickenest of owners. Our out-sized vegetables were biggish, I dunno. And you can't joust or mud wrestle, really, without practice, and who has their own mud pit to practice in? So we weren't great at any of this. Buncha townies hiding their tattoos under flannel and wool for a day. Seeing it through the man's eyes kinda highlighted the trying. I mean, none of us are farmers; we were just delaying growing up for one more weekend, I guess. The guy holding the bull's halter worked at CVS.

I don't think it's his bull. I mean, I know it's not his bull. His landlord doesn't allow dogs.

The man was quiet, mystified and happy. I chatted up at him.

It's just . . . we do this every year. Grew up watching grown-ups do this. Haven't gotten it quite right.

Well, your grown-ups grew up. You guys didn't.

No. Sweaters are nice, though.

It's all very charming. Love the hog.

Big, huh? Let's bring home some kinda bale.

Ice sparkles and preserves in suspended animation. Zombie hopes. Best a dream can do is be served on the rocks, then mummified, a pointy stick through its brain. And we do love that hog. It's just so *large*.

The weather is broken: thick sun, fog-infused but dry as these weird dry snowflakes that fall and never land. We wander in the impossible dry fog, a sunset the color of berries glowing on the dog-eyed chickens, the sun-mist straw. No one was selling bales of anything at the fair, so we brought home a sage princess pumpkin that never rotted, never caved, never faltered in its front porch newt vigil.

We are animals: if winter is always coming, then spring is always coming too. Is hungry but hopeful, making buds and babies, lime green leaves and neon pink buds, the colors of popsicles in a New Mexican gas station. Nothing to eat yet, so you don't feel lack. Nobody steals when there's nothing to steal, not like in courtrooms. Hunger looking for hope in the branches and underground. Hope could be anywhere, so you see it everywhere. Eyes wide open, skin singing.

Spring is coming.

Winter is coming.

He took my hand.

Sure. But so is spring. Don't lose hope.

The zombie princess pumpkin, icy sage. Winter is a cold gratitude, because life is on a fire that may go out soon. One of the few pretties that isn't stupid—is actually beautiful—winter sparkles with empty. Out of money, we expected to be out of hope, just couldn't get there. It was all so elegant.

What're we gonna do?

I dunno . . . 'spretty, though.

♋ winter

winter wears high heels
and the light is dazzling

❋ ❋ ❋ ❋

Black, leafless trees. Living shadows. The van empty and tilted alongside some pretty trash, I walk up into dry hills, lifting rocks and branches, looking for snakes. If only snakes bit, I coulda learned about venom and damage, but they won't. They glide up my arm to check out the view, then meditate.

Love everybody, baby.

Doony looks up darkly. He knew this but he's learning something else.

* * * *

Kris.

> There is a cop standing on the front porch. There is always a cop standing on the front porch.

A dead flower, blooming. What happened is always ready to jump out and happen at you again. The smallest trigger reminds it to come back and then you duck with flying colors.

♋ mercury

we quit making out to attend this meeting
with old ladies on tremendous amounts of coke

Bees buzzed in the hive around us, phones rang, voices murmured, intercoms interrupted, coffee was walked down hallways. We studied the gold records hanging on the walls. Each bee was art, but the swarm was artifice.

Norms aren't as normal as they think they are.

Nobody thinks this is normal.

What you do is, you make out before you go into the meeting and then they can't hurt you with their weird record company jujitsu, using your own stomachache against you. You gotta remember that you're an animal; an essence some people have lost, striving to be bigger than other people. Animal is where music is. So that's wicked scary, that these people are in charge of the country's soundtrack, but it's still so goofy. The emperor's new clothes is just such a ludicrous concept.

And it's always the same: we're made to wait. Wait to sit in chairs lower than their big chairs. Or sit around a Zen table on meditation cushions next to a Buddha water feature. I try to come to this table open-armed but they do lousy math in the entertainment industry: women are *things* whose cultural win is to flatter rich white men who've bought their own hype into parting with their resources. And guess who scripted this pimping? Rich white men, hoarding resources again; boring and damaging and in almost every sphere, just elaborately cartoonish in this one. A cartoon either laughs at ego or becomes it and then *we* laugh. I dunno. They can't win, because there's no win in it. Music was everywhere but here.

Chicken dicks.

Can we go yet?

I wanna take out my knees. Remove them cuz boredom.

Does that help?

The saddest and most hopeful thing here was all the real people who made up the bulk of the swarm. The secretaries were cool. The janitors and even some executives who were real music listeners . . . people who lived in their bodies, people who weren't money-safe. They just *worked* in this hive that smelled like magic markers, buzzing with money bees. American success is a weird party. The kind of party where people rip off their faces to reveal a monstrous emptiness. And somehow? It was still really, really boring. I wanted out so bad. When you realize, holy shit, I signed up for Hitler youth and check out the other signature on this contract, it's Zombie Satan, no kidding, I met him and his cronies and I signed my name with his pen, but I wasn't Hitler, I was just youth and there's been a terrible mistake—

Kris.

What? Was I not controlling my face?

This is why they hate us.

Yeah, I don't blame 'em. I used to be so nice.

Blink and the meeting is over, remember?

'K.

Unable to buy or talk myself out of my contract, we decided to try our best here. To maybe bring some hippie-commie to a peak capitalism table. Blink and the meeting is over. In the meeting? We said what we always said. Essentially this:

Marketing could be honest: sharing substance instead of trying to fool dummies into buying style. There aren't actually any dummies, anyway, and you alienate the musically literate when you throw fashion at them; they know what an insult it is. You also alienate listeners looking for depth when you define them by the superficial, calling them ages, races, and genders. Market this record as a search for those who want to hear it; a symbiotic relationship, cuz we'll keep those listeners forever. If it has to be about the bottom line? You will sell more in the long run if you earn listeners' loyalty by offering quality. Which, in music? Doesn't cost any more than suck does.

As usual, we might as well have spewed cornflakes across the table.

I mean, I mighta been getting pontificatey, to be fair. And the poor bees, trapped in a waxy coating of greed. Even *need* would've stilled them in amber, coated as it was in a thousand aimless wants. Poor fucking bees, just buzzing to keep up with the buzzing they think they hear.

Just run.

Doesn't snow in there and we needed clean. Our dry snowflakes waited faithfully on the sidewalk outside of the record company like dogs by a schoolyard chain-link fence. And actually, most of the bees melted away in the elevator on the way down. I looked up at the man.

God, you're boring when you tell the whatchamacallit.

Truth.

Yeah, truth.

Sorry. Look at your messed-up fingers . . . like a dancer's feet. It's disgusting, what you do. Your guitar's blood-spattered.

Sorry.

No, I mean record companies have nothing to do with music. Nobody can stop you from donating blood.

They can't stop me from bleeding, but they're my fucked-up Red Cross. I could play music without releasing it. Or release it without working it. That's honest, an honest life. I doubt St. Peter's first question is gonna be, "Did you attract attention?"

He might notice if you don't survive, though.

The whole concept of survival is such a conundrum.

INTERVIEW:

Q: Nobody likes your band and some people love you. Why?

A: Nobody likes us?

Q: . . . and some people love you. I'm a writer, so that's what I aspire to.

A: Uh . . . we're not for everyone. I'm kind of on a mission and that gets obnoxious. No, I *think* I'm on a mission. Even worse.

Q: Which is it? Are you on a mission or do you just think you are?

A: Well . . . I'm me, so I dunno.

Q: What's the mission?

A: I don't think there's much music in the recording industry. Mostly just product. A spontaneous impulse like music . . . just seems like everyone should play their *own*. This business monetizes then corporatizes something real by making it fake.

Q: Right. That can't be a popular idea.

A: You wouldn't think so, except that it's so obvious. Musicians turn up with enthusiasm for sharing and then are spit out if they don't play along with image . . . and the dumbed-down template that's mostly left us with actors *pretending* to be musicians. Even fewer songwriters here cuz they die.

Q: Actors?

A: Actor/model/dancer/singers. They . . . dress up for photo shoots and play characters.

Q: So when they fake it, what's missing? Magic?

A: Yeah. I mean, everything is missing, but even the term *magic* points to our obsession with measuring. Magic just means we haven't figured something out yet and, really, measuring doesn't figure anything out, just hands us some more hubris we don't know what to do with.

Q: I get that. And what about women?

A: *Which* women?

Q: I see your point.
(I laughed.)

A: I didn't know I was making a point.

Q: "Women" isn't a category.

A: Oh. Yeah, sure. That *is* a good point. Women aren't necessarily alike; being female is not an inherently feminist act. "Men" isn't a helpful category either. Cool people're humans. Some women are fucking amazing: strong, funny, selfless. They're not in the music business. I just didn't know this was a fashion industry.

Q: How could you not? There's no art in arts and entertainment.

A: Yeah, I dunno. Thinking there was room for musicians and songwriters here too? But they only want real musicians when they're faking it. I mean, a song could land on absolutely anybody, but only in a moment of grace. And that moment won't share itself with egoic concerns like money or fame, which is what the business offers musicians and people pretending to be musicians.

Q: So no rock stars.

A: Rock stars should *never* have happened.

Q: Amen.

A: Music is the color! It's sound-sex. It's a great, intense world. But even though songwriters are expressive, some of us are shy, so attention is a turnoff.

Q: But aren't you a performer? How do you get on stage?

A: The shape of a venue just facilitates listening. My only value proposition is focus. But stages also attract people who want the spotlight, which is an artificial cue to look. Meaning that we've perverted attention to serve marketing. Sorry. Sometimes I get pontificatey.

Q: That's cool. So who is listening, then?

A: People who *need* this. That's not everyone. These listeners never forgot the visceral response they were born with or maybe sound shakes their spine. They're raw. Pain or love sometimes wake people up. Passion, I guess. But you know what? Don't buy records. Play your *own* music.

Q: Uh-huh. I'll try. How do you define success?

A: Impact, not units sold.

Q: Can you measure impact?

A: Probly not.

♋ baseball field

talking at the radio
just one of the places to shoot off your mouth

The interview over, the journalist reached into her bag and pulled out a Polaroid and a blue Sharpie, handed them both to me.

Could you sign this please? It's us five years ago.

Looking at the picture, I saw two teenagers standing on the sidewalk outside a club.

Hey, it is us. We've met before?

Briefly.

I'm sorry, I didn't realize.

You gave me the chords to a song of yours I couldn't figure out.

Jesus. Why would you want that?

It was driving me nuts.

Oh. Well, it's nice to see you again.

The girls in the photograph matched perfectly. T-shirts, grandpa trousers, and worried half-smiles. In the picture, she looked grim. In the room, she also looked grim.

We were seventeen.

Right before everything.

Right before everything.

Taking a red Sharpie out of her bag, she drew a shared speech bubble between us:

HELLO, EVERYTHING

WE'RE ALMOST READY

Bones and the bones of trees, whitened and blackened by wind and sun. The baby rode, squinting in wind and sun.

The next morning, we had a diner breakfast with aspirin and bought five-dollar coats at the Salvation Army because we were cold. The man's new coat was too long and his sleeves were too short.

Normal people would already have coats. Like, in preparation for winter, which comes every year and always has.

Yeah. You didn't grow up either. You think you can fool me by being tall?

He laughed, way up high. His new coat sleeves made him

look like a toddler who'd outgrown last winter's coat, but there was a cigar in his coat pocket that he was gonna smoke that night, so I couldn't really tell if he was a kid or not. That shape he made, the dark Captain Ahab shape, with the red hover-circle moving down the street, a little Captain Morgan, even . . . I knew to look for it.

Some future promise also glowed deep inside him and crammed into the detail of everything he said. Not an escape as much as it was a spin: dusty snowflakes could feel like *this*, could look like desertscape, silence without violence. Check out the moon that shines on us when sun and clouds stop fighting. It was already like that in New Mexico.

It'll be ok. It'll be ok in the desert.

It'll be ok because it's all going to melt anyway.

Damn straight. It's all going to melt.

Driving to the island that night I looked up and saw white sparks in the sky: lousy fireworks, bursting off each other like a sky mistake.

♋ civil disobedience

you can buy me breakfast
then find me a coat
here's a big fat aspirin
maybe you'll choke

that's not funny

In the morning, I picked up a newspaper and saw a picture of those lousy fireworks—broken sparks—on the front page. A plane had exploded over the highway, over us, over the McDonald's by the gas station. People scared and burning and falling. Somebody's baby afraid, while I watched. Maybe a giving up, maybe some relief from the hard. But the left behind loved ones? Death by fireworks hurts them forever, I imagine.

Death by fireworks means no empty promises.

It does?

Sure. What a way to go . . . look at 'em go! On fire in the sky? Hell yeah. It's a tragiclimax.

✶ ✶ ✶ ✶

Not long afterward, the burnt-orange newts eloped to their deaths. I guess. Maybe to their patch of marshy reeds. Maybe they found a home and that home took them. I hope so.

> There is a cop standing on the front porch. There is always a cop standing on the front porch.

Wake up.

Court tomorrow. I have to find a dress that makes me look like an adult, that makes me look like one of them. In order to keep the baby, I have to look like the kind of person that would take a baby. These adults that we are supposed to become? Are out of their minds.

♋ hazing

I'm up now
you're crazy

The townies on the floor that night were mostly straightedge and not drinking, mostly wanted a place to go that wasn't cold or a drunk stepdad's basement. I was a cardboard cutout of myself with a bloody cow heart duct-taped to it and they understood; propped me in the corner where I could do no harm. We gentled them with road stories and they gentled us back with the Minnesota Personality Inventory. Like SATs for sanity.

True or false. I move toward trucks filled with explosives.
You like those trucks best.
True. 'K, true or false, I make my own clothes and shoes.
False. You only make shoes.
Right. True or false, I have never had any hair on my head.
When they left, so very slowly, we leaned against each other in the dark, listening to the plastic sheeting on the windows fluffing in and sucking out.
I'm sure some people do like trucks filled with explosives.
Maybe those guys never had hair.
And make their own shoes.
The newts' suicides were not wholly unexpected.

✳ ✳ ✳ ✳

When you're sleepwalking, you think you're gonna sleepwalk forever.

Waiting for them to make a decision, waiting to find out if we needed fake passports or a real home, and wouldn't that be amazing? A home. Our marshy reeds. You have to walk in step with each other, in the rhythm of the sleepwalk, because when you wake up? It happens fast.

♋ sleepwalking

this is too short a pier
it's too sharp here

There is no numb.

How did we not know this?

I know how we didn't know this. But why didn't anyone else tell us?

Yeah. Everybody knows this shit.

We should make a list of all the shit everybody knows.

And then what? Just know it?

Yeah.

Well . . . have someone else make the list.

Cinderella sang in his apartment upstairs, over the fluffing of plastic sheeting and cold wind. It sounded real pretty, both noises together. Nightglow began at dusk, which didn't begin, you would just notice that it had come. Like trying to watch bamboo grow: you have to look away to see it. Night glowed now, didn't fall, like this strange new snow. The man lifted a bottle of tequila and held it up as a question.

No thanks. I gotta stay clear.

Just soften.

We were feeling enthusiastic about potatoes. Something a townie boy'd said about peasants like us and the earth all made of dirt: "That's why they call it earth." We were put here to commune with the unpretentious potato; therein lay enlightenment. We are bumpy, brown, of the earth and to her we shall return. Ashes to ashes to dust in the wind. He was pretty baked.

I'd buy that, though. I'm totally a potato.

Me too. The character actor of vegetables. Is a potato a vegetable?

I dunno. It's not a leading man.

Or lady.

It was sorta beautiful and Cinderella serenaded us potato people from above. But . . . then he started dancing and I guess he was wearing winter boots. Or maybe clogs.

Tap shoes?

Our hangovers kicked in before we went to bed, listening to the plastic sheeting whappin' back and forth in a winter wind. Had an actual alarm clock that ticked like a bomb. Charming until now. It also glowed in the dark. Two unfortunate qualities in something that lives on your bedside table. It was banished to the closet under a mound of pillows that night.

Maybe . . . never wind it up again.

Potatoes.

Right.

♋ hungry

snowflakes and dust look the same on the ice
herradura silver

And this morning, our breakfast potatoes sat sadly on their secondhand china on the secondhand green ceramic table; tasted,
then ignored. I felt guilty. They were so lumpy and plain but
they'd risen to the occasion, dressed up on party plates, you
know . . . trying. And we'd turned our hungover noses up at
them. They looked just like we did, looked like our nausea felt.

We're still potato people, we just don't want to eat them.

Awake, but not entirely. Saturday morning animation: a
fuzzy cartoon, soothing and sickening. My nightgown was cold
but soft over rawbone, under sweaters. We spoke as sound,
didn't listen, spoke as a humming soundtrack. Murmured as an
excuse to smile at each other. Hangovers so suited this dream. I
squinted through the kitchen fog, trying to make sense of what
the man who'd saved my life at Point Doom was saying. He was
talking about a menu? So I interrupted.

*Wait. You mean you literally dreamt about Chinese food?
Or did you just go to bed hungry?*

He didn't look nearly as hungover as I felt. Unshaven, maybe.
And his hair was messed up, his green eyes red. Christmassy.

*I did go to bed hungry, but when I close my eyes, I dream
plans.*

Plans?

He woke up enough to become briefly earnest.

*The blue-plate lunch special at Ming Moon is a good deal—
four-fifty and it comes with an egg roll.*

An egg roll's a good plan, I guess. So you had a dream that told you what to eat for lunch?

If we order the special, it'll be a prophetic dream.

He was yawning and grinning, which meant that soon it'd be time to go. *I dream other worlds in other languages or without language entirely. My dreams dream other dreams. I can't find words for the pictures I see when I close my eyes. A Chinese menu, my god.*

You're my dream hero.

I love him because he's the kind of guy who gets drunk on a glass of buttermilk.

—*Ball of Fire*

* * * *

Sun blazed through the window of the tour bus as Doony rested his head on my chest and we drew together. He sat on my stack of heavy immunology and virology textbooks, big enough to create a booster seat. A pad of paper spread across our laps, pens held lazily, the lines erupting into giggles when something struck him as funny.

A flock of black birds flew over and with us, and he sprang up to watch carefully. A desert highway is a straight, vivid thing. When the last bird flew away, following the road the bus followed, he slumped back down and dotted the paper again and again.

Birds. All the birds. So many birds. And now they're all gone.

✻ ✻ ✻ ✻

I'm driving in the pitch black, driving in circles all over the island, knocking on doors, looking for the baby. I drive all night. The car seat behind me is empty. I'm always driving in circles; the car seat is always empty. The island is a circle and I am always driving.

✻ ✻ ✻ ✻

As the ball of fire sung through the air, headed toward the chain-link fence that lined our yard, aiming for bare tree branches squeaking against the worn brown shingles and salted holly bushes lining the exterior wall of my apartment, the man rubbed his Christmassy eyes.

What did you dream about?

I hesitated.

I dreamt . . . that we were at the top of the Mount Hope Bridge, leaving the island.

He stared. I cleared my throat, tried to turn mush into thought into words.

I dreamt that . . . the ocean? Was thick, like Jell-O. It was a physicality we could put our bodies into and took up the same space as the water, but in its current, it was also time, like a hurricane. Meaning that its substance shifts though it is a continuous entity. If you measured its particulate, there would be no constant.

I looked up. He was still staring.

And . . .

Brief eye contact, to check in.

If we could only learn to swim in this particular Jell-O—
Oobleck?
Sure. This particular oobleck, then we could jump off the
Mount Hope Bridge with impunity. Sorta hang glide off the
edge. I mean, in the dream, we were supposed to do that
because otherwise, somebody could push you off and if you
weren't ready, you'd drown in your own misinterpretation of
the space-time continuum.
Quicksand.
Yeah, you'd fight your own efforts. Hopeless.
More silence. Nothing to fill it with.
No egg rolls.
No egg rolls.
Probly about hope, huh?
Yeah.

Reached for a toddler who wasn't there. One hand always waving vaguely in the air, hoping to land on soft curls. Wanted to call out for him and hear his baby-animal-cry answer. My hand landed on a knee and the man grabbed it.

This is when the ball of fire burned through my kitchen wall, about the size of our two heads pressed together; spinning, hot fire-breath. We watched it whirl over the clanking bottles and bottles, past the dead fridge, our two heads pressed together. It was over in a moment. But a really long moment. The spinning and burning and sparks . . . like the plane crash fireworks, it just didn't make a lot of sense. Fire crashed into the opposite wall and made the frying pans bang against each other; shake on their hooks. And then it was gone, leaving burn marks on both walls.

We waited for an explanation, looking at each other, blank. The man stood up slowly, stilled a pan.

It's hot.

I didn't move. Was used to things not making sense. He took a piece of candy out of a hanging egg basket. We didn't have eggs, so we put cinnamon Jolly Ranchers and Fireballs in the basket. Coincidentally. He smiled at me.

I blame you.

* * * *

I need a dress for court. One that lies. Shoes. I need lying-lady shoes I can't walk in.

* * * *

Suddenly, it's all over and there are no more circles, there is no more sleepwalking. The circles were a spiral anyway. Each time we came back around, we were somewhere else. And now we were somewhere else.

Every day my mind grows keener, my good arm stronger, my silly enemies more futile.

—*Krazy Kat*

Wake up, but don't wake the baby. We're in New Mexico. Look out the window: horses.

RYDER

♋ Costa Rica

tonight your dream is safe with me
tomorrow we wake up in LA

Sea lions moaned, scooted, and rolled across the sand. Point Dume was just as we'd remembered it. The sound of moaning, scooting, and rolling is a bellow. The sea lions sounded like a bellows keeping their fires lit, sucking in air and blowing it out, moan-scoot-rolling across the beach. Though dried blood from the sharp rocks still snaked down my shins, I much preferred water to land. And these creatures looked more graceful down there in the green tumult. They seemed to have a water/land conundrum going on too, but I dunno. Mammals, but better equipped than us. They breathe air, so . . . essentially the same, completely different. Flexible dudes.

Seems important to anthropomorphize sometimes. Just to check in:

You guys cool? Had enough to eat? Feelings fucked with?
I love human mammals, but.

We are less graceful in green tumult. And sometimes we breathe the wrong stuff. No way to live. The man and I watched sea lions until they wheezed and fell still, when he began telling me about his family.

I had a thumb uncle. Uncle who was a human thumb.

Thumb?

Bald head, no neck. Extra neck, twice the size of his head. Never buttoned a shirt collar cuz he can't. Shaped like a gumdrop.

Next time say gumdrop before thumb.

Sure. Someone married him too. Bop.

He stared at the bellowing sea lions without seeing them. I stared at him.

Bop is the person who married the thumb?

Yeah.

That's a dog's name.

Uh-huh. Face like a jelly bean.

The gumdrop married a jelly bean?

He nodded. A pair of watery sea lion eyes looked up into mine. They looked awfully sad.

Why are they sad?

They're not. They're pinnipeds. Pinnipeds have sad eyes.

Maybe pinnipeds are sad.

Maybe. These are all bulls. Their women are in Alaska having babies.

No shit.

The watery eyes stared and I stared back.

Did they procreate?

Who?

Bop and the thumb. Are there little thumbs?

Oh. Yeah.

Do they have necks?

Super necks. Wider than their heads.

Wow.

The sea lion would not look away. I *could* not look away. The man sighed.

And I got another uncle who's a thumb breaker. Child molester. Monster.

Oh. Much worse.

I come from a long line of much worse.

Squinting up at him, baffled.

I'm sorry.

And he laughed.

My point being that you don't have to marry me.

I gazed out at that roiling sea.

You saved my life. I think I do.

♋ flipside

how dare you save my life?

The morning of our wedding, I woke on the island with Doony in my arms, then listened to Hank Williams, waiting for the dry cleaners to open so I could pick up my mother's wedding dress, carried up north from Chattanooga, Tennessee, by one confused, biscuit-baking grandmother.

You're marrying a man from New York? Well. I'll pray for you.

She baked biscuits all morning. Doony tasted one. I looked out windows. Crumbs on his lips.

Dust.

Dust?

Nodding, he wiped his mouth with the back of his hand and ran to the Christmas tree, stopped short in order to be dazzled.

You ok, baby?

Doony raised one eyebrow.

At nine o'clock, we drove to the dry cleaners to pick up the largest item of clothing I would ever wear, then to a castle overlooking the ocean under dark, heavy December clouds. The castle was also dark and heavy; it loomed over a dark, heavy ocean. Probly all real dark and heavy, but we didn't see it that way. *Real* weather means you have balls and so does your pearly princess gown. Grim did not occur to us. Dark heavy was something to look through and something to see through. We could have been wrong about this.

Doony's tiny tuxedo matched the man's; his shiny, black dress shoes slipping and skidding entertainingly on the carpet, which was enough to keep him from being wholly terrified by the way I looked. He was just *mostly* terrified by the way I looked. When he pulled a little white rose out of my hair and pressed it into his lapel, I realized that he was doing his best to speak the language of a formal event that did not speak to him. He made claws out of his fingers and grimaced to show me this; a fearful tiger cub. Someone swept him away then, with a Styrofoam cup full of something warm.

What a big boy! So heavy! How old are you?

Doony held up four fingers and gazed over the shoulder as it carried him away.

I sat, dressed as pearly crazy, staring out a window, wanting to jump into the icy ocean, knowing full well what it takes to breathe. Not even sure the speeding, dripping hurricane air out there was breathable; too fast, makes one gasp with its lung thrusting. When my father appeared in the doorway to walk me down the aisle, I told him I wanted to hike my skirts, grab the whole wedding party and march them down to the sea, jump off the cliff and swim. Do something normal on this weird day.

Well . . . that wouldn't be normal.

No. But neither is this.

How about: swim in everything.

Ok. Gotta learn how, you mean?

Yeah. Takes a while.

Oobleck or ocean or hope, he was probly right about this. The baby and the man walked down the aisle together, in their matching tuxedos, and the three of us were married. Essentially the same, completely different. I hadn't seen the man since yesterday, in observance of a custom meant to reinstate my virginity; the long hair and beard I had known all year had been stripped off by a barber early that morning, revealing a plain man, a Ken doll, a clean-shaven leading man. I wanted to bare my claws in fear, *mostly* terrified by the way he looked, but I smiled at his American joke instead and held a hand out to each of them. The two blood tests I took the day before had told me that I was: (1) allowed to get married and (2) pregnant. Which I already knew, brand new virginity notwithstanding. I was so very morning sick.

The justice of the peace, who seemed a little drunk, referred to us as "Dwayne and Wanda," the placeholder names inserted into the wedding ceremony he read from. So it's possible that we were never legally married and that Dwayne and Wanda lived happily ever after.

We could change our names.

I wasn't clear on our surname.

Hmmm . . . yeah. I didn't catch it either.

Also possible that Dwayne and Wanda committed some crime we'd get blamed for and that's why they fucked off.

Oh geez, I didn't even think of that. They're hitched now, though. Legally hitched.

And us all livin' in sin.

Gross.

Soon, my pearly gown had a purple stripe of wine down the front—not mine, an enthusiastic guest's—and looked much prettier. The man's raw face shone with tired, with gracious smiling. Married, I kissed Doony a honeymoon goodbye through our two deep stomachaches and held him in his tiny tuxedo, now rumpled and covered in crumbs.

Can I come?

Children think adults run the world. They never understand when you say you can't do something. *Who's stopping you?*, they think, *who's big enough to?* And rightly so. Everything *is* our fault. I held him longer and held him too long and held him some more. Still wasn't good at letting go of that baby. And he was not a squirmy child, so he took the love and panic until hands gently pulled him away with a story. A story of something other than mother. And some Tic Tacs, I think.

Then we drove. Away from the dark, wet, honest heavy and into the bright, wet, lying city; looking for lost on a highway, our favorite place. A pretty, oily shimmer on the road, in the air.

But . . . no moon. Shouldn't we have a moon?

The human lights were human happy; an artificial hearth everywhere you looked. The sky black. Opposed safeties: essentially the same, completely different. Not many clues as to how to act on this weird day-without-time. The castle on the sea had no moon. The city had never had one.

The moon'll come back when we hit the highway.

Oh, I'm not worried.

And Texas has a big ol' moon.

♋ a loon

you look at me cross-eyed and I don't know what to do crazy loon

I stared out the wet car window for hours, thinking and not thinking. The moon didn't show up, though. Not the one I was looking for. That moon wouldn't come knocking at the window for a long, long time. It takes years sometimes, for a particular moon to show itself.

Changed out of our wedding costumes in the night van,

blending into a group. Not a band this time but a film crew; essentially the same, completely different. I'll stop saying that now, sorry. Our honeymoon was movement—our favorite stillness—and a finger lift of effort that was not going to ask me to remove my Sandra Dee skin and become a monster, then crawl back inside my bodysuit, like the music kind of living in a van did. This was a sleepy, strange thing: ostriches, snow, Texas. Some New York friends who doubled as a film crew had talked their way into our honeymoon van, dragging their equipment behind them. We were all so very dazzled by the idea of ostriches in Texas, hoping for more ludicrous beauty, as if we hadn't seen enough. Just couldn't get enough of that stuff. And so we thought: movies. A movie will make it fake-a-listic and true.

A guy waiting on the dark sidewalk, his thumb out, lit yellow. Winter rain swept into the van with him; into the damp, woolly, and escapey van that'd be our home for a while. Another body, some bulky equipment. Drive around and gather more bodies, more metal cases. And then the van became a familiar system— pulmonary, limbic, circulatory—shook off bright, yang urban for fields of everlasting dark, wet yin.

How come this is our only home?

Cuz we don't belong anywhere.

Huh. But this is maybe a more-than-sum-of-parts dealie.

Oh, well . . . yeah.

And not gonna tell you what to do, but: a mushy, bright cold of fields, gas stations, and dumpster meadows. You can live on this, round-the-clock, a beautiful thing. It means you *are* a hover home, a tortoise, and nobody's watching, which is the only perfect. Some transmutation, maybe. But mostly a land of needs, no wants, then no needs . . . this is one of the places where you can stretch out an arm and touch music's bubble with a fingertip.

No where.

But we weren't driving for music, we were just driving, trying to get to snowy ostriches. Took a fuck of a long, lovely American radio time. Truck stops are a particularly bewitching beacon of crazy beautiness on a night highway. Truckers are lonely-ass folk, lonely as comedians, and they meet up over lousy food like comedians, under fluorescent lights. Musicians are not like this; we go limp on the road, go dark, live a cult life. We watched these truckers carry their damp towels outta the shower, shop for speed, beef jerky, and Red Bull, then peer around Burger King for other guys doing the same, waiting to let go all the words that piled up on their tongues while they drove and thought, thought and drove.

The cinematographer and I pretended to read novelty vanity plates as truckers swarmed the Burger King.

I hope, I hope, I hope, that their memories of fast food are sweet family ones. That they aren't trying to live on this shit without any help from their physiology.

What?

Tell me about the blood-brain barrier vs. Burger King.

Oh, ok. I'm sure that bacon double cheeseburger reminds him of Friday nights when his dad was nice because he just got paid and his mother was happy cuz she didn't have to cook and his brother didn't hit him for a whole dinner.

Thank you.

You're welcome.

Ya know, one of the most beautiful places I ever saw was

a McDonald's in New Mexico in the morning. In Spanish,
McDonald's is ok.

See?

And the lady truckers, heavy and gorgeous, done with crap
and burdened only with fried softness, which they wore in
country songs. Sometimes America sells itself as very American.

♋ san francisco

I was born in america
born with the fists of a saint
way, way out of range

The man and I wished we'd been married for twenty or so years
instead of twenty or so hours. Held hands over the gear shift
while the crew slept to murmur-quiet Hank Williams.

Died in a car.

Yeah, but so did lotsa people.

Died in a really nice car. Didn't make it to thirty.

Let's make it to thirty.

One night, getting-there night, an unsure limbo—*that road*
sure was pretty, motion sure is safe—midnight, a crazy house,
a nowhere cardboard. The engine cut and Hank stopped singing. This Texas McMansion grew up out of the Hill Country,
and it was the opposite of the Hill Country. Its silhouette in the
door, unmoving. Sniper still. I sat in the van between the lighting tech and the cinematographer, wary. The man stared from

the driver's seat, then opened his door and let in the sound of rushing, slammed it shut again to become another silhouette pasted into the crazy house's doorway. The van breathed quiet now that we knew about the rushing noise outside.

Do you think America is a failed experiment?

Well . . . not yet.

Maybe it's more of a joke.

Yeah. But it's not funny yet either.

And the whole time? Music plays. Doesn't seem to care that I'm listening.

♋ a rushing

first a spark
then a firewall

When dawn happened, so did morning sickness. Vomiting by a gatepost in the cold was a chilled pink, and ostrich silhouettes appearing on the prairie. They ran and stopped short. Froze. Very *Looney Tunes*. I felt for them: I felt *sad* for them. My heart went out to these strange beasts lost in Texas. Which is maybe patronizing, maybe anthropomorphizing, maybe projection.

You guys cool? Had enough to eat? Feelings fucked with?

They may not have felt as lost as they looked or as lost as I felt. I love Texas and they probly do too. It's stunning and alive, shot through with a wind that has blown through squalor and been swept clean by tawny husk, then blown through greeeeeen. Texas is fucking cool. Anyway, the female ostriches were brown brushstrokes, enormous finches; the males were black shadows and white light. Knees lifting over straw bent by early winter wind, but real tentatively. They definitely looked lost, so that part wasn't just me. It was the way they stared into the distance, then ran toward it, stopping when they got close.

The people in this town had adopted a look sometime in the fifties and, I guess, stuck with it. Mostly just: Elvis. Elvis and Mrs. Elvis and all their little Elvis juniors—cuz Elvis was married to each other—and Elvis the butcher, Elvis the rancher, Elvis the veterinarian, the shopkeeper, the secretary. Elvis worked at the bank, delivered mail, doled out donuts and change, dropped the kids off at their bus stop. He was also a few dogs. One of whom, a teacup chihuahua, ran its life away, biting ankles and crying for help. Its woman watched without emotion. We watched *with* emotion.

Is he ok?

Does he look ok to you?

So Elvis, America's king, and these birds, but only "birds" in the way a shark is a "fish." Like a new take on something you keep contained in your house, you keep harmless in your mind. Can both cut you in half. Which we clearly deserve. The ostriches stood, blinking drag-queen lashes in the snow. Or they ran, too upright. People—our species—were dreadfully upstaged by them. We couldn't keep our eyes on the humans, wanting so badly to hear what the giant birds had to say. Giant, goofy dignity doesn't speak so much as transmit, though.

As our cameras gazed at him, the lights illuminating his bumpy features and clothing, boom mic poised over his head, a rancher told us that ostriches were big chickens.

Big chickens? Really?

Oh, yeah. Big dumb chickens.

Do they peck eyes?

That chicken could definitely reach your eye. And I'm sorry, I try to be respectful, but this dude who was dumb enough to think ostriches were big chickens told us they were dumb *because* they were big chickens. He was giant and goofy too, but he had no dignity.

Dumb, dumb, dumb. These big chickens are so dumb.

They're dumb?

Oh yeah.

Shaking his head about the dumbness of ostriches, he rolled his eyes at the unimaginable idiocy of not being human. English isn't even their *second* language . . . these dummies don't talk at *all*. Thinking he was better than other creatures: the American joke. I found this terrifying and heartbreaking. *Do you think you're better than other* people *too? Worse than other people? What did you forget?*

The ostriches were misplaced soldiers, confused and ready for battle. Seemed real edgy. We filmed their lost stares, almost silent, not truly silent. A thumping, a bellow not unlike sea lions and their moan-scoot-roll. Air in a chest cavity whooshing to match the rushing prairie wind. The people were not silent, though they didn't whoosh. They spoke a lot of words without saying much; answered questions, then didn't stop talking, just kept going after the answer was over. This was both boring and fascinating. Cuz people are strange that way. They claimed to be crazy and actually *were* pretty crazy, but didn't know it. So they'd repeat it: "I'm just nuts!" Waiting for it to sink in, I guess.

Elvis the butcher, the ostrich butcher, so oddly still.

Mannequin still, sniper still in another doorway, not sure the guy breathed. For all their restless chatter, some of these Elvises were intensely motionless. *Is his heart beating*? Huge. Oily. Shy. I liked him. He told me that the ostrich bodies are like ours, so he felt like he was butchering himself and that his knives must be sharp in order to do this well. His belt buckle was bigger than my face and he was real into biltong. Ostrich penis biltong, except he pronounced the word *penis*, "pen" "is." Maybe he'd only seen it written. He made me extra sad and hopeful cuz he was so touching.

Sometimes I just sit in my truck, watching them. Put the radio on and watch their feathers blowing in the wind. I can watch for hours. They move real, real pretty.

And he was the one who killed 'em and chopped 'em up.

I tried watching them, Elvis the butcher–style. Sat in the van huddled against nausea, watching feathers blow in that husked, green wind. The dude was onto something. Death was fully present for him and he so admired life. His equation was weighted in both directions; mastering stillness to absorb movement. He couldn't help it. Guilelessly childlike, to live in the sphere of your senses. Knives present, no weaponry.

✱ ✱ ✱ ✱

Dyed red wisps of lady hair twitching over her fur coat in a biting wind, sticking to her hot-red lipstick. Bozo redness. She called her lumpy husband "Booger" or "Sugar"—but mostly "Booger"—and kept her arm on his shoulder. Which woulda been sorta sweet except her arm was extended at all times, as if she were trying to keep him an arm's length *away* from her. His hair was a bluish silver and so was his jacket, which he called "rock and roll." Asked if it was too hokey for a documentary.

Hokey is documentary gold.

Okay, then. So keep it on?

They were both very much about *a million dollars.* Fixated on that number and noun. The word "dollars" came up a lot, always with the modifier "a million." They were going to get it. Not an *if* thing but a *when.* And they were gonna do that at the expense of these ostriches and their bodies. The cinematographer told me I wasn't controlling my face; that I was sad-squinting at them. So I tried to be lighter about their uncomfortablenesses. They're alive, you know. Organisms. Just kinda scary.

Dancing into the kitchen in a negligee to scramble us eggs for breakfast, the redheaded woman took a hammer and chisel and started whaling on an ostrich egg. Pink feathers on her sleeves caught droplets of goo when the hard shell cracked. Emptying two enormous eggshells into a frying pan, she hummed and kind of whimpered, then burst into song, her whisk flying.

Crazy, I'm crazy for feeling so lonely . . .

Red-haired lady Elvis had a hard shell. She had a hard smile. Her smile was not for us, not for here or now, but for the million dollars in her future. She was our species. And she was right: she was crazy and lonely. Butcher Elvis was an animal child; soft while wielding sharp knives. Wounded and strong, hacking at bodies with love and respect. He was our species too. Butcher Elvis did not smile.

And the ostriches staring into the rushing prairie air, racing toward a mirage, then freezing. Staring, still. Following another mirage. The teacup chihuahua still running and running, still screaming, biting any ankle that got in its way. Still not looking ok.

A mother cat and her litter of kittens underneath a shed, caught between garbage and the cold.

A macaw in an airless breezeway: "I can't do it . . . I can't do it . . . I can't do it."

He says that because my daughter came inside crying one day. She tried to teach herself how to ride a bike and fell again and again. She's twenty-seven now.

Twenty years of *I can't do it*. Maybe patronizing, maybe anthropomorphizing, maybe projection, but: fuckin' brutal. *You guys cool? Had enough to eat? Feelings fucked with?* Convening in driveways and parking lots, outside barns and in diners, we'd ask each other what was going on.

Human hubris. Our animal nature is screwed up, so our animals are screwed up. We think we're more important than them.

But we are animals.

We left that in Eden with happy nakedness.

So we made them crazy and now they're telling us that we're crazy?

They're right. We are.

And always the rushing sound. Blasting the prairie.

✻ ✻ ✻

There was an ostrich sperm sample collected in a 7-Eleven plastic tumbler: Big Gulp. A rape pretty much, pillowcase over its head. The lighting tech swayed in her revulsion, which gave the scene a porn thing it didn't need. The ostrich yelled into his pillowcase, bellowed like a sea lion. We couldn't back away from this because behind us, a coyote was dying, bleeding into a grate, having been accidentally shot out on the prairie early that morning. The humans responsible for all of this were our species.

Newly pregnant, I was having trouble staying conscious through the nausea. If only I could puke this up, but it was in my *eyes*. The cinematographer closed his.

I'm sorry. I just can't watch. Hope it's in focus.

Dude. You're good. I think I'm gonna die.

How do we unsee this?

Please, Lord, let us unsee this.

Pregnancy wasn't just making me sick, it was making me care deeply about everyone and everything.

Poor coyote. Why?

Why anything?

Yeah, but, specifically, why this?

When the Big Gulp cup was released, we ran out into the odd, rushing air. The lighting tech had a tub of Noxzema in her purse, which she took out and passed around.

It smells clean.

We'll never be clean again.

Let's try and remember the grossest things we've ever seen. Or heard of. I think it will be cleansing. Or maybe we can at least blot this out.

So we sat in the van and told each other every disgusting urban myth we knew; every happened-to-my-cousin, every greed-turned-regret, every practical joke that backfired, every adventure-land you didn't land, every captured-on-Polaroid badness and medical mistake story we knew. Breathless and spent, we lapsed into personals ads ("personal sads") we read from the local paper.

Fishing fanatic seeks same for fishing.
Dang, shoot me. He just wants to go fishing?
She.
She just wants to go fishing?
She wants to go fishing in love.

I had imagined that these people who lived in the rushing outside, with animals, might teach me about nature. But they didn't live outside, they *went* outside and tried not to feel it. They *lived* with televisions and heat. Both blasting. That coyote, bleeding into a grate, was the only creature I saw with grace and agency—living—and it was dying. One of us killed it by mistake. I coulda kept looking for a Texas rancher that breathed like a prairie, had some kind of grace, but I was too nauseated with morning sickness. So ill that a farmwife took pity on me and bustled me into her warm, stuffy living room, TV blaring. I could *see* the rushing noise through her steamy windows, but I couldn't hear it. She was warm and stuffy too; trapped in her warm, stuffy clothes, stuffed into her warm, dumpy body. She radiated kindness and game shows. Like the butcher, she pulled her truck up alongside fields on rainy and sunny afternoons, to catch feathers blowing in the crazy rushing air. She was a kind of sleepwalking beauty. Unlike the butcher, she was a vegetarian.

I just started feeling bad for my friends here on the ranch and thought, I only eat you because I'm the one here not made of meat.

The animals do seem a little out-of-sorts.

So, have you always been a documentary filmmaker?
No . . . this is my honeymoon.

Nodding sweetly, she looked briefly distraught, then her eyes were pulled back to the shrieking game show contestant on her television.

Dead ringer for my sister.

And the ostriches blinked in the snow, always looking for something. They did not stick their heads in the sand; they did the opposite. Peering through a Texas prairie wind, they ducked their heads to look around it, nodded and swayed to look through it. They fluffed, ran, stopped, rigid, and looked for it again. Never saw them find what they were looking for. Africa, I guess. Hope not, but probly. Their lives. While the sea lions on Point Dume felt the sun move across their backs and shut their eyes.

✻ ✻ ✻ ✻

♋ golden ocean

your baby takes your balls and lights a fire in your belly

Back on the island, snow piled up against our back door in a strong wind, as more snow fell, whipped around, and added itself to the pile keeping us inside. Eventually, we could no longer open the door. Friends warned us that the roads were impassable and unplowable. We cheered and high-fived each other: this was our excuse to blow off another goddamn photo shoot in New York and it was a good one. At least I *thought* it was, until I got on the phone with the magazine and told them I couldn't make it due to weather.

Do you want us to send a car?

I have a car. The roads aren't cleared.

We'll send a car.

Confused, I hung up. The man from New York had suspected this.

There isn't any weather there. And when there is? They can't see it.

Really.

Yeah. You know how you're a hick, so you'd live outside if you could?

Uh . . .

Well, New Yorkers are the opposite of redneck, so they don't know what outside is. Closest they get to weather is, like, a breezy hallway with no ceiling and a sidewalk for a floor.

You mean the street?

The temperature in the hallway changes, but that's it.

He looked at me like he was talking sense, but I was *more* confused.

Huh. So, do I have to do this photo shoot or not?

Their town car can drive down a sidewalk hallway, but it's gonna stop being able to drive when it gets to the island. You're cool.

Yay.

I was not a big fan of photo shoots, and they didn't seem to like me either. A photo shoot was, at best, a lousy friend. The polite kind that doesn't remember how you met or why they still have your phone number.

I dressed Doony and we got down to the business of baking. That's what snow is *for*, after all. That and snowmen, and we already had a snowman. Snow octopus, actually, and it wasn't in great shape after this storm. Its icy tentacles grayed as they twisted through shifting drifts and its head looked like a thorax. We'd have to wait until the snow in the air cleared before getting to work on another octopus. So I laid out the cookie cutters, mixed up some dough, and we worked on gingerbread men instead.

Cranberries for eyes ok?

Doony thought hard about this.

Maybe.

Peppermints?

I bit my tongue before it suggested raisins. Mothers get a lot of well-deserved shit for always running up with a box of raisins and spoiling the party.

Chocolate chips!

Do chocolate and ginger get along?

He did not have to think at *all* about this. His pudgy hands flew up in the air.

Of course!

A car horn beeped outside. Doony and I looked at each other in fear as my morning sickness swelled with adrenaline. The man peered out a window and announced thoughtfully that there was a town car outside.

What? How did they do that?

They can't see weather.

The fuck?

I don't know, but you better get out there.

I hugged little Doony and told him to finish making the cookies. That I'd bake them when I got home after he went to bed and he could have a cookie breakfast tomorrow morning. The term "cookie breakfast" seemed to brighten him and he repeated it a few times as I stood him on a chair over the raw gingerbread people.

When I left, he was pressing chocolate chips into their faces and humming. Kissing the man, I promised to escape as soon as possible.

Gonna try and, you know . . . leave early.

I know you will.

And the whole time? Music plays. Somewhere between a crucifix and an albatross, hanging around my neck, breathing into my face. Maybe a noose, but I'd rather not go there. Had a baby and a half to think about and, yeah, there was something amazing about the creature *Song* making noise at all hours. Breathing inspiration and then holding its breath, this weirdo devil created a staccato percussion that fueled it all with excitement. Fear *spun*, I guess.

Song is a mirage, maybe, but I ran up to that mirage like it was a Christmas tree, dazzled.

♋ fortune

you don't seem to need to breathe
unlike us oily flimsy cheap
thick with Wonder Bread

Standing in the overheated hallway at the Chelsea Hotel was a nightmare of old Lysol, mildew, spilled booze, and puked-up booze, all covered with air freshener. And there was no air to freshen, so this didn't work. I swallowed carefully as my throat shut with morning sickness, then said a silent prayer of apology to the human under my rib cage. It's not that I didn't *understand* the grit cred these photoshooty people went for. I knew the Chelsea was a place people took pictures of musicians because they were then allowed into a pile of other people they'd decided were Big Cuz Attention; I just found this irritating. Strike one for my bad attitude.

Opening the cracked door I'd been instructed to knock on, I saw a pile of enormous bones. I mean . . . the room was full of silent, mopey giants who looked half-starved. I backed out and was closing the door when a musician walked up behind me and introduced himself, saying that he was in the same photo shoot. He looked suspiciously at the closed door.

Is this the right room?

I don't think so. I just peeked in. It looks like some kinda support group.

Really?

I dunno. Hungry hugeness.

Oh. Maybe we should just wait out here until we're allowed to leave.

Do you hate this shit?

I hate this shit.

Me too.

The door banged open and two fast women burst through it, carrying fashiony dresses. Spotting us, one shouted back into the room in a thick, unidentifiable European accent.

Here they are! I'm finding them! I have the girl and the boy! The bride and the groom!

We squinted at each other in confusion as she handed her sparkly outfits to the other woman, who raced down the moldy hallway with them and disappeared. The one who remained eyed us carefully through heavy glasses. Suddenly becoming fast and businesslike again, she pulled us into the support-group room.

Okay, you two. We have so much work to do. Come in.

Haunted eyes all watched us as we were hustled past. The other musician smirked and hissed at me.

Kristin, those are models.

Oh. That's what's wrong with them?

The fast woman led us into a chilly, grim room as we dawdled behind her, then told us to strip down before she slammed out. Dutifully taking off his shirt, the boy examined goose bumps spreading across his arms and chest.

It's too cold for this.

We sat on the bed in our underwear and waited to be told what to do, but no one was bursting in and we were fine with that. He sighed.

Lotsa people died here. Nancy Spungen was stabbed and Dylan Thomas caught pneumonia or some shit. I dunno.

As long as they were famous, right? I'd like to see a hotel try to build its reputation on the fact that a buncha poor people you've never heard of died there.

He laughed.

"C'mon in!"

The wind screamed outside and the radiator clanked impotently. He sighed again.

I wanna be a walnut farmer.

I wanna keep bees.

Is that lucrative?

I dunno. I like bees. And honey and candles.

So you're a hippie chick.

Of course I'm a hippie chick; I wanna keep bees. Are walnuts lucrative?

The door banged open again and a different woman—wearing the same glasses as the first but with red frames—led a team in, who all silently stood and stared at us. We stared back.

God, I hope walnuts are lucrative.

They left, murmuring to each other, and we exhaled. Instantly, the team returned with one of the glasses women and an array of equipment. Blow-dryers, makeup kits, hairbrushes, and clothes under dry cleaner bags. We gasped as we were stood up and attacked by arms wielding lights on long cords that they shone in our faces. A woman smeared foundation on my skin and asked me to close my eyes and face the light. The man on my hair whispered something in my ear that was too muffled and buzzy to hear.

What?

He whispered again.

I'm sorry. I love your records.

It's ok. I'm used to it. And thank you.

The glasses woman circled us thoughtfully.

Bride, please? Remove the bra?

Really? I tried to do this without elbowing the hair guy or makeup lady. Let my bra drop to the floor and, eyes still shut, heard the glasses woman address the room.

So, welcome to a rock and roll wedding! A big party but

we are destitute! We are all heroin junkies and drunken poets!
Okay? Very: REAL. *When you hear the music, think about your*
acting!

What the fuck?

I heard the door slam and figured she'd left again. The hair
guy sighed audibly. The makeup woman was drawing new lips
on me, not really where my lips are. When she paused, I called
to the boy.

Are you ok?

Walnuts!

This is not music!

Does it sell records?

Maybe! But to whom?

Did you just say "whom"?

Sorry!

You don't belong here!

Neither do you!

The hair guy laughed and the makeup woman, snickering,
asked me to open my eyes so she could apply more mascara. As
soon as the light seared them, I saw the hair guy holding a can
of hair spray in my face and I jumped. The sticky spray settled
neatly into my eyes. He gasped.

Oh my god, I'm sorry!

Laughing, I told him it was my fault, but the mascara the
makeup lady had already applied melted with the hairspray and
formed a glue. The makeup lady giggled.

Now your eyes are stuck together.

A happy cry from the boy across the room.

Her eyes are stuck together! We have to leave!

The whole team laughed but stopped abruptly when the scary glasses lady stormed back in. The makeup girl asked me to close my eyes again as the guy swept my hair up into a fountain on top of my head. I felt it stick to my lipstick and gluey eyes.

Whoops. We'll have your whole face stuck to itself by the time we're done.

We didn't try hard enough to stifle our laughter this time. The glasses lady was strangely quiet. I guessed that she was circling us menacingly again. Suddenly she clapped her hands and shouted.

Okay, rock and roll, people! Wardrobe! Groom? You have your tuxedo! Bride? Your wedding dress! Now go! Set is ready!

My eyes still closed, I heard a voice ask me to lift my left foot, so I did. Something soft was slipped around my leg.

Okay, now the right.

The voice pulled something up around my waist. The hair guy whispered in my ear.

Just keep your eyes shut. You're gonna hate this.

Aw, geez.

I jumped when someone grabbed my wrist; it felt sharp, like some kind of animal biting me. I opened my eyes in alarm. Red Glasses was trying to chew off my bracelet. She looked up from my wrist, blank.

Take this off, please. It's not in keeping with our aesthetic. How does it unclasp?

Jesus christ.

Ok. Sorry.

The makeup woman rolled her eyes at me and stepped back, hands full of brushes and mascara wands. As I fiddled with the clasp on my bracelet, there was an awkward silence I tried to fill by making friends with Red Glasses, who continued to stare, blank reflections for eyes.

Your job seems tough. You must have to read a lot of magazines.

I smiled at her and then lost my smile instantly as her face shook with hatred, her facade disintegrating into seething melted wax. Her hands lifted like she was gonna choke me and she spat slowly, lingering on each furious word.

I . . . am . . . the MAGAZINES!

She stomped out of the room, slamming the door behind her. The team held its collective breath for a second, then fell apart. In the laughter, I thought: *at least I made magazines hate me as much as I hate them.* I put my bracelet back on.

The makeup woman announced that she was done and the bright light was switched off. Looking down, I saw that over my own underwear, I was wearing white, lacy panties with the word BRIDE written across them in rhinestones. I was still topless. Whoever the voice that dressed me had been was gone. I looked over team heads at the groom, who was dressed pretty much like a groom, he was just shirtless. Looking at me, he threw his hands in the air. I put my sweater back on and stage-whispered across the room to him.

Walnuts.

And he whispered back.

Bees.

That made me homesick for babies and snow octopuses . . . for my guitar waiting patiently in the corner.

♋ vitamins v

home and the contrasting squalor

The set was a velvet easy chair in a slummy hotel room and the starving giants were guests at our wedding. Black Glasses told me I was supposed to sit on the groom's lap and "act."

Act?

Yes! You are a sexy bride who is owned by your groom and you like to be his slave!

She laughed loudly, then stopped suddenly.

I have a model who acts if you can't.

And she left again. I turned to the groom.

I think she might be evil. Are you warm?

Warmer than you. Sit on my lap. They'll shut up and you'll be warmer.

Ok. But this doesn't mean we're married.

Well, not yet.

We sat there, posed, as people fussed with lights and took Polaroids. None of the models had said anything since we'd gotten there. They might as well have been mannequins. Probly too hungry to talk. The groom cleared his throat.

So, did you bring those panties from home?

No, but I have some just like 'em.

What's wrong with these people?

A lot. A whole lot. This shit is so fucking anachronistic.

It needs to become anachronistic.

I guess we call it that because it's always been stupid. What is "acting" in a still shoot, anyway? What do they mean?

Black Glasses reappeared with Red Glasses and they presented us with a lady in a winter coat who began stripping down in front of us. An intake of breath from the groom.

This is getting weird.

This had gotten weird a long time ago. It was just getting weirder. Black Glasses shouted.

Okay, this is the girl model who can act, okay? I know she can, I've seen her. It's good!

The girl model was down to just her shirt, which she removed, businesslike. There are all kinds of bodies, and I'd been in all kinds of locker rooms, but never had I seen breasts like these. They were raw, red, distorted, scarred watermelons; bigger than made any kind of sense. There was no bra that could contain them. They looked painful. She'd been mutilated for porn effect. Now I knew what they meant by "acting."

Red Glasses clapped her hands again and grin-glared at me.

So, first bride! I see you as not so much a bride. You are more like the maid of honor who fucks the groom before the wedding ceremony!

My jaw dropped and she laughed loudly. Jesus fucking christ, what *was* wrong with them?

Is that what the maid of honor does?

Strike two for my bad attitude. She winked at me.

Sometimes girls who aren't so pretty get angry, am I right?

Yeah, I guess I'm feeling pretty angry right now.

Good. So leave the sweater on and give our diamond panties to his new bride, okay? And we'll get you a maid of honor wardrobe!

The model, bored, looked at me, then did a double take.

Oh my fucking god, you're Kristin Hersh. You're fucking fierce, girl. You are fucking fierce.

She addressed the room.

She is fucking fierce!

I smiled and handed her the rhinestone panties. The groom grimaced as I blew him a kiss.

I'm so sorry.

And walked out. Strike three for my bad attitude. Things will change. Someday. There's no way us cerebral animals will allow this to continue; we love each other too much. The groom waved as the new bride was seated on his lap, and I left to put my clothes back on. I was happy; I got to escape. Escape to my clean life in the clean snow. Early, just like I'd promised the man.

The hair guy gave me a thumbs-up as I left. As appalling as wrong can be, its lack of subtlety helps us do the right thing. They leave us with no choice.

✴ ✴ ✴ ✴

My drummer pointed to a cobblestone alley past a creaking dock and we moped toward it on our way to the bus station. Heavy with saltwater and barnacles, the dock sloshed and spattered in a drizzle, its tethers slapping against the surface of the water, mimicking our sulking conversation. He ran a hand over the ski hat he wore balanced on the upper left-hand side of his head and crumpled it up.

Hat trouble.

Moving the hat to the top of his head and pressing it down,

he winced, his dark blond hair sticking out on either side. Then he raised his eyebrows and put a finger to his lips.

. . . then the whole thing catches fire and shit starts blowing up, but our hair stays awesome.

The wind machine'll mess it up.

Oh yeah. Wind makes hair cool but messes it up.

Paradoxically.

Boy, this work is hard.

A gray and golden street lined with crooked colonial houses. Our feet trailing slowly through snow mush.

Also pirates. Sexy ones.

Racing clouds blocked and revealed the sun, the street changing from gray to yellow and back again. Nothing we laugh about is actually funny.

And grog.

Mead.

Rum.

Rum!

Captain Morgan. The Captain. You will dress up as: the Captain.

I stopped in front of the fishermen's deli and pointed at the door as a question mark. He turned to look at me, shoving his hands into his coat pockets. We had had a thirst for music.

♋ gut pageant

that fine fever brought us here

And mead.

You said mead. Are you done?

Cannons.

Pointing at the deli door again.

Do. You. Want. Coffee. For. The. Bus.

Staring into the steamy window of the deli, he paused.

Do you?

Knocked-up chicks can't have coffee.

Oh. You want, like, sardines and ice cream?

I waited. Still queasy, I didn't like thinking about coffee *or* sardines and ice cream. He frowned. He had already been frowning; he frowned more.

Mmmmmm . . . no. I'll get coffee in New York. It's better there.

We won't be in New York for, like, six hours.

He stuck his hands in his pockets and started down the street again. Peering and frowning into late winter sun. A lost ostrich, looking for something.

Coffee's much better there.

Winds coming off the harbor were still penetrating, but every few minutes, you could feel spring coming in the sporadic sunshine. We were preparing ourselves for the goofy sadness to come: directors pitching video ideas at us. They didn't wanna be there and we didn't wanna be there.

I wish they didn't call it "pitching"—feels like we should duck.

When did they decide music should be stupid?

This isn't music.

Yeah. No one is only a zombie.

What they do is a zombie.

He stopped and gasped.

Zombies! In Egypt! With camels and eyeliner and sandals and baskets of dates in an oily marketplace. And we're beggars dressed like Jesus, playing for alms in the dusty street.

And monkeys. Wearing little fezzes. And shit blows up.

Then we're drowning in Malibu but Barbie saves us. And you drowned in Malibu, so it'll be autobiographical.

But this time Barbie saves me?

It's inspired by true events.

Ok. Also pirates.

Genius.

Strike eleventy million for our bad attitude.

Cars slowly bumping down the cobblestones sprayed slush onto the sidewalk. Sometimes a wrecked day'll feel like a wrecked life. Especially when what's wrecking your day is also wrecking your life. Gotta kinda watch that. No day is wholly sacrificed, no life. Probly. I threw my hands up in frustration.

I'm familiar with stupid. I know people buy it cuz they like candy. But when it comes to music, we're not talking M&M's; they're listening to Laffy Taffy. The Halloween shit you throw away before you get home. I mean, not even. They're chewing bees cuz they've been brainwashed to think they like that.

Tell the people. Write a strongly worded letter to the editor explaining that Laffy Taffy doesn't love them and that they eat bees. Break that story. People're dying to hear that they should listen to music they don't like. Wait. A beauty contest. That we all lose. Then we cry and our mascara runs and we look scary.

I'll write the letter in a scolding tone too. People like being scolded. The winner cries, dumbass. The losers all smile.

He looked disappointed. Listless, we willed the bus station to disappear. His hat slipped down over his eyes. Pausing to study this effect, he looked at the world through hat for a moment, then pushed it back up into his hair and pressed down, mashing hat, hair, and skull with an angry hand. I wanted to cheer him up, but all we had to say to each other was the same shit we always said to each other.

Norms say we ruin their fun and we tell them they aren't having any fun and then they say we ruined their fun.

Ad infinitum.

They shouldn't be sold to; they should play their own music. Let's make them.

He laughed. The street was silent, except for hissing wind and patches of melty snow crunching under our feet. We sped up a little, then forgot to. Looking in dark shop windows full of tourist crap, we moseyed like toddlers.

A bus pulled out of the bus station and we squinted down the street; hoped it was ours and we'd missed it. An American joke was being played on us, was playing out in front of us: *you can have your religion as long as it's televangelism cuz money.*

♋ cathedral heat

you have to look close
to see what this disease has done to me

The invading agent proliferating, the terrain reacting symptomatically, healing that hurts. The day you're diagnosed is the day you start fighting. Maybe we're open systems. So what energetic do we let move through us and what do we identify as contagion? It's possible that we just don't understand a kind of parasitic symbiosis.

"Parasitic symbiosis" doesn't make any sense.

Well . . . that'd be why we don't understand it.

Oh.

His big, sunny grin in the sun.

So we're Miss America cuz we WIN.

I nodded.

No losers.

No losers allowed. And . . . our mascara runs?

Pirates wear mascara too. No, eyeliner! Like the Egyptians!

His hat slipped off and he caught it in the air.

Ok, this is getting great. Also our eyeliner runs. And you can be a girl cuz you look like one cuz you are one.

Take that back.

You should thank the lord baby Jesus for that gift, Gidget. And then . . . shit blows up.

Glorious. How do you do it?

Oh, it's not me. It's god working through me.

Oh. How does god do it?

He's really smart.

I laughed.

That dude's not forgiving you your trespasses. You're gonna get smited. Smitten. Smote.

Smoted.

Smoten.

Where'd the zombies go?

They come back in the end when we think we're safe. I don't feel smoten.

Brakes squealed and buses sighed into their parking spots under metal awnings. We found a cold bench. He peered into my eyes.

Could we say no?

* * * *

Dresses are pulled from my suitcase and thrown in a pile on the floor. A bright, wrinkly wad of white trash. The pink flip-flops on my feet are glared at. Not unkindly.

That's not you. Not you, not you, not you.

I look down at my feet and the colorful pile.

I'm so sorry, but this is all very me.

Where do you shop?

Salvation Army.

The photographer sighs and starts throwing my clothes on the floor again.

No, no, no, no, and . . . also no. Whadda you live in a trailer?

Pretty much. It's not that unusual, you know.

My suitcase emptied and rejected, he puts his hands on his hips and stares at me.

Okay. We have to show that you're smart. How 'bout . . . a men's blazer?

I stare back.

Are you implying that intelligence is a masculine trait?

And he laughs.

Abso-fuckin-lutely! Welcome to the entertainment industry.

And the ostriches blink snowflakes out of their lashes, looking for a different world.

✳ ✳ ✳ ✳

INTERVIEW:
Q: Does the band have a unified political orientation?
A: Commie-libertarian.
Q: What?
A: I know, but . . . we believe that people are good.

♋ blurry

you a clean spark or a twisted parody?
well, look at me

The window washer waved and I waved back, touched a spot on the glass and he laughed, swiping at it with his squeegee. Then he mimed dizziness elaborately, as if the squeegee set him off-balance and he was gonna fall. I laughed and was throwing my arms out to catch him from behind the glass when the publicist bustled in, frantic, grinning wildly.

Hello, hello! I am so sorry! Whoo! Oh my god, crazy daaaaaaay!

I smiled back. She carried many binders, which she dropped onto her desk and fluffed down behind, into her bizness chair. Then she rolled from side to side, peering at me through the pile of binder. I sat facing her and waited.

Uh-huh? No, when? Okay, okay, okay. Oh my god! Okay. I know, right? Right?

Baffled, I looked closer and saw a headset under her hair. The window washer waved goodbye and began pulling himself up to the floor above. What a cool job. The publicist turned her brightest smile on me. I pointed at the guy out the window.

You think he's just . . . not afraid of heights? Or is he scared up there?

Headlight smile. Even brighter.

Who?

I pointed again, to the guy's disappearing feet. She still looked confused but hadn't stopped smiling.

Hah! I guess! So let's get started, we kind of have to rush through this. I'm looking forward to hearing your new record; you have a real strong buzz right now. Only problem is, well, I lied; there are two problems. First, the Random Notes of the world have to follow you around and you only appear sometimes. Like, at your own shows! Ha ha! You gotta show yourself off, girl! Follow them around! Let them know you're a force to be reckoned with! And I can help. This is the fun part. I'll get you invited to every party you need to be seen at, tickets to every show, with backstage passes, and your own photographer to follow you around and get you seen being seen with really big people. The magazines won't have to work so hard anymore. You can be a recluse after you're famous!

Yikes.

I'm . . . not a party person. Like, at all. I'm really shy, did they tell you?

Yes! I think that's adorable. But there's nobody big who hasn't done this; success doesn't just happen, you gotta work it!

What are you going to do with your hair this year? I'm seeing a lot of black; that was a good move. What happened?

Hair.

I, uh . . . stopped dyeing it; hard to keep up with dyeing hair on the road.

She was still staring. I laughed.

I mean, I'm a working musician. I live on tour pretty much.

I'm a window washer who's scared of heights, I thought. She shrugged.

So . . . blonde? Blonde always works!

Yeah, I was just gonna keep it natural.

Wincing, she tilted her head.

Ooooh . . . you mean the way it is?

I fought an urge to open the window and join the window washer outside. The publicist smiled sadly at me, concerned.

Yeah, no, I'm not seeing a lot of dirty blonde this year. It's mostly platinum? Which would look great on you.

So they don't like blondes, they like bleach.

Hahaha! I guess! Stylists need to know the look they're working with before the shoot.

Could we maybe not do photo shoots? I work in sound; it's not a visual thing. I thought we could just supply reviewers with the cover art.

She stared.

Wow, you really ARE *shy!*

Her eyes shifted to the wall behind me.

Four o'clock. Four o'clock. Uh-huh! Four. 'K.

Smiling at me, she winked, trying to remember where we'd left off. I prompted her.

You said you had another problem?

She went sober to address her issue, then opened a binder to read something.

So your bio is all over the place? This press kit is a mess: you play indie rock and alt rock, noise rock, art rock and underground rock—I mean, what's the difference?—you make solo records and you play, like, Appalachian folk songs or something? How many bands do you have? Too many, anyway. Like, it's really kind of a mess. I won't know what outlets to go after until we determine a target audience. There's a big word for it: "demographic." But all that means is, what kind of person likes you? Is it straight, young, white women, like you? See what I'm saying? Like, this preview of the last show you played here in New York? "Go if only to witness the bizarre cross-section of humanity that will attend a Kristin Hersh performance." See the problem? You have no genre, no look, and no demographic.

I'd thought that was a good thing. I *knew* that was a good thing. She made the wincing face she'd made about dirty-blonde hair.

Who are your people?

It's music. Listeners don't necessarily have anything else in common. People listen cross-genre and not because of their age, race, or gender. Could we just focus on music publications?

She made an interested face.

Girl? I like what you're saying. And I'm a publicist. So really? My job? Is to make you happy. I bet we could strategize a bit and come up with a really biting, feminist musician presentation for you. You know, take a risk and get our hands dirty—

Her eyes shifted to the wall behind me again.

I'm here. Oh god, what time is it? Ha ha ha ha ha ha! Right? Right?? Hold on.

Standing to get me to leave, she reached out her hand and whispered happily.

Let's follow up right away . . . you've given me a lot to work with! Think about looks we could go with and I'll schedule a photo shoot with my top fashion guy. You'll love him; he'll make you gorgeous and he's hysterical!

Shook her hand, trying to match her smile, then tiptoed out while she laughed into her headset, facing the wall.

Her receptionist was holding half a sandwich at her desk and wearing one neon-yellow running shoe and one burgundy high-heeled pump. She was talking on a headset just like her boss.

He probably has a cold, honey. I'll call the vet, if you want. But maybe he just needs a nap? Coming home as soon as I can. I'm leaving now. I love you.

She threw the half-sandwich down on her desk and, carrying her other running shoe and a backpack, grinned at me and limped down the hall to the elevators.

♋ ether

but beauties few and far between
who knows what you have seen

A photographer moves lights around my face, snapping at his assistant to do the same. He sighs in frustration and hands the assistant a silver reflective circle, holding the assistant's hands and angling it under my chin, then to the side . . . the other side. Takes a Polaroid and studies it. Sighs in frustration again and throws it on the floor with about a dozen others. Paces back and forth on the white paper spread across his studio. He wishes I were a starving giant; it would make his job easier.

The assistant looks like a little kid someone painted with tattoos, smiling at me apologetically as the photographer adjusts his reflector, reminding him that we need it just so. Aiming his camera at me, the frustrated photographer squints at my face in disappointment, then tells me I have a beautiful smile and suggests that I cover it with my hands. This results in a barrage of gunfire as he shoots a thousand pictures in about thirty seconds.

Now cover your whole face.

I do. More pacing and gunfire.

Okay, you can put your hands down. I have an idea. Turn your back to the camera.

The assistant gives me half a sad smile. I turn my back, relieved. Another barrage of gunfire.

Yes! That's it. Beautiful. We got our shot.

♋ spring

I'm grateful to be in this with you

All stories are tiny stories. Unless you overlay all the tiny stories into a hodgepodge decoupage collage . . . when they're at their coolest. We're all god and we're all nothing and we play god and nothing with collective gluey fingers, bright finger paint and stickers. Learn to swim in everything, etc. Cuz the only true big is small.

Anyway. *You Can't Take It with You*, starring Jean Arthur and Jimmy Stewart, on repeat, black and white on a little black-and-white TV in the kitchen. The human being swimming below my rib cage glowed an abundance of nausea and bright and leaves appearing through the mush of melting snow. Spring is an impossibility that sparks awake again and again. Humans are an impossibility who spark awake again and again. We can't *will* that process, though we'll never stop trying; doesn't work unless you throw your arms up in respect/surrender. Spring is hungry.

And after winter's burn? Nothing really catches fire again.

We've had quite a time of it lately, but it seems that the worst of it is over. Course, the fireworks all blew up . . .
—You Can't Take It with You

✺ ✺ ✺ ✺

Kristin?

The nurse was a bleach-blasted, stained-ochre beauty with a heart of gold, like the women who smoked on their porches to burn out the cold. I dropped a magazine on the beat-up coffee table and stood carefully, trying to keep nausea from overtaking my gray matter with gray. I knew I was fully capable of thought and yet this was simply knowledge, not an actual thought; empirical information with which I could not argue. The unborn baby and I slept in a bed, stood on sidewalks, but we were a being in a window's wavy dream: this world plus a wash of heat and gas fumes. Not unbeautiful, just sickening. I was finally in a place where I didn't have to hide my pregnancy and the demon Nausea knew. Let go full tilt and a cloud settled around the two people I was. Hard to see through it. I couldn't think.

The nurse handed me a paper dress and led me to the examination room. The cigarettes in her pocket shifted with every movement, triggering a wave of nausea with each shift. Wasn't sure if it was cigarettes or movement making me sick. *Oh, yeah . . . it's everything.* When she left, I sat, trying to see pukey as holy heat, still thinking about the magazines in the waiting room. The pictures of pain and anger in *U.S. News and World Report* would darken and gray out before you finished the article. The sandwiches we mothers were encouraged to make for our schoolchildren on the cover of *Good Housekeeping* also illustrated the questions of bravery and survival. Mother's Day is an antiwar statement and for that reason, so is every human. Sandwiches grayed out too, though. Children and mothers and their days, plus violence. Babies are life and we're tasked with keeping death at bay. How the hell . . .

No wonder I can't think.

The nurse returned, took blood and more blood, stood us on a cold scale and asked how we were.

♋ cathedral heat

sick as a dog

Smearing goo on the middle the new baby and I shared, the midwife held a wand to my skin and bounced black-and-blue sound pictures onto a TV in the corner of the room; showed me my own home movies. The creature who kicked me out of time and space swallowed and breathed before there was anything to swallow or breathe. He kicked before there was anything to kick except time and space.

Any concerns?

Uh, I can't think.

Don't think.

We watched the universe squabble in its liquid world with nothing to compare liquid to. He quivered and worked at something with his minute hands. He was creating life and he wasn't thinking. Or *I* was creating life and I wasn't thinking. Life just was. And we were dreaming. That's the only way you could ever be this brave. *Life's tough, here's a precious one, fight death, go ahead.* The midwife caught my eye.

He's not thinking.

♋ in shock

pinned by a dream state

She paused the wand and we watched Life breathe.

You going back on the road?

Yeah. Sleep dep and hunger, here we come.

Soy milk boxes. Beef jerky. Dried fruit. Cereal. Bottled water. A suitcase full of food that doesn't go bad.

Ok. Liquid is heavy, though. Heavy as guitars.

You can't carry guitars.

I have to.

Adjusting the slippery magic wand on my belly, she peered into the black-and-blue universe.

I have a pregnant mailman under my care.

Wow, really? A miracle.

She has a heavy life too.

I imagine she does.

The universe sucked its thumb. A miniscule mimicry of a human thumb. A thumb etched onto a grain of rice. A thumb this universe of baby had never seen. A thumb it would take a while to understand when vision kicked in and air threw itself into his lungs. A thumb that would press itself into Play-Doh and Christmas cookies and work toy cars. Maybe play guitar. A thumb none of us had met yet. The midwife smiled sadly.

My baby is gone. Took his own life.

All the tears I'd held back for fear of a lost boy filled my eyes. Universes implode in pain sometimes. Her smile faltered.

I look for him in every baby I deliver. Haven't found him yet.

She watched the unborn child sleep on the black-and-blue monitor. I shook my head in agony for her.

What can I do?

She put away the magic wand.

Be patient with me? I watch babies very carefully.

* * * *

The man crawls across the snow, under cover of pink late winter sun. Doony scrunches down into a snow fort that is no longer what it was, not quite what it should be. His knit hat has settled down over his eyes, its earflaps obscuring everything but his nose and mouth. A crow lands to watch and Doony snaps toward it, worried that it will alert his target. A tiny index finger mashing rosy lips.

Shhhhhhh . . .

My arms are full of snowballs, a few packed pretty hard, could do some damage. The man makes no effort to hide, but serious effort has gone into *looking* like he's trying to hide. He rolls sideways a few feet and pulls himself along with fingers pressed into icy mounds, then "hides" behind bushes much smaller than his body. Doony pushes his hat up so he can make eye contact with me, the snowball keeper. He winks to ask if I'm ready, but little kids can't wink, so he *blinks* to ask if I'm ready. I nod, feeling for the softer snowballs with gloved hands, so that when the man gets whaled on, he doesn't come away with two black eyes.

Slowly, quietly, Doony takes one soft snowball and tiptoes over to the man on the ground, who is actively looking in the opposite direction. The crow takes a few crooked steps, watches.

Standing over the man's still back in snowsuit pudginess, Doony gently drops the handful of snow onto his coat. The man feels nothing. Doony waits.

No one moves.

Raising the front brim of his smudgy hat to look at me, I see him do the one-eyebrow thing as a question mark and I shrug, arms still full of snowballs. Then he bends his snowsuit into a crouch and releases, his toddler body suddenly prone, next to the man's. One mittened hand pats the ground beside him as he gazes up into pink. Ambling clumsily for a moment, the crow then flies off (we've bored it), and I drop my weapons, turning the pile of snowballs into a pile of snow and joining it on the flecked, yellowed grass. Spring is a cool emptiness. Spring is raw. Spring is coming. Spring is winning.

♋ carnival wig

let's just say it crawled across the snow

INTERVIEW:

Q: Give up a body part.

A: Earlobe?

Q: That's cheating.

A: Kidney.

Q: *sigh*

A: Left thumb cuz it's the only digit you don't use to play guitar. Except I do cuz I'm stupid.

Q: Does it have a name?

A: Thumby.

Q: Why do you write so many songs?

A: That's actually true. My little boy named it when I almost cut it off slicing bread for him. I was looking at my son instead of my thumb. Sliced off the top of it. Half the nail. Thumby bled for weeks and I had to go on tour the next morning.

Q: Gross.

A: You know, it actually *was* gross. Kinda takes a lot to gross me out.

Q: Huh. I gross out easy. Why do you write so many songs?

A: So this big, dumb bandage stuck out over the guitar neck for, like, the whole tour. It was *huge* cuz it wouldn't stop bleeding. Doony drew a face on it. Named it Thumby.

Q: Uh-huh. Glad it wasn't the other thumb.

A: Yeah. God. Me too.

Q: Meaning of life?

A: Sound and no sound. Kindness. Music that nobody needs to hear; it just needs to be played. I'll stop now.

Q: No, you're good. Just trying to scribble it down.

A: Please don't.

Q: It's my job.

A: Kind of a hippie chick.

Q: 'S ok. Why do you write so many songs?

A: I don't.

* * * *

Four a.m. buzzing. I watched the ceiling, wishing the buzz would stop. Just this once, go away on its own. *If I don't move, maybe I'll just stay The Lady. I'll be healthy and nice. Not odd.* I don't like strange, like to avoid unsolved mysteries, feel kinda sick. The man jerked awake, his cool bicep against my electrified one.

You have a song.

Ok.

♋ dirty water

hey you
aren't you the lady?
look at the dirty water
look at him
look at the dirty water and swim

Slithered out of bed in what I hoped was a graceful move, wincing as my hot toes touched the cold floor. I was burning.

Ugh.

Electricity is unpredictable, the way it moves around a body, and I was two humans; I had to be careful. Time to jump off a cliff, though, and that's not careful and you're never sure you're coming back. What if you believe the music dream? Cuz it's realer than here, so why would it ever make sense to wake up in this flat black-and-white world again and believe in it? This place is the metaphor and music is hyperreal. You become music when you disappear. The part of you that isn't of this place. Staying in song world, you wouldn't come back, wouldn't undo the cliff dive, run it backward and prop yourself up on this cliff of a plane . . . and where would that leave your loved ones? Cuz here, believing the realer dream is called crazy and people can take your babies away.

I had to be alone. No song comes unless you make yourself alone, but now I was someone else too.

I have to be careful, I have to be alone. I can't be careful, I can't be alone.

The song jangled next door, playing out a window, but it also ran across my skin. Soon, these two stimuli would join up and I'd learn their chords. Meaning, I would learn how their particular vibrations parsed themselves out of a shooting prism of color and bounced off each other. Well . . . fought. Violent and subtle, color would rush, and the marriage of tone would shape a sculpted body, a lifeline. You're looking for a stringent truth and nothing but the truth. The *whole* truth, though? Can go fuck itself. Leave spaces.

We differentiate as minute, realized pieces of the holographic whole. These pieces sound like song bones. Phonetic percussion becomes words-ish and broken melody. You grow a baby, you grow a song. They're both love, they both make you kinda sick, they both have hearts, pulmonary systems, skeletal structure, and idiosyncratic features. Also, your heart goes nutz.

The shit the songs say, my god. I listen and cower and scribble my fingers across the strings. If there was shame in music? I would be ashamed. But really, there's no "I."

And only when the song had a body would electricity call a truce and let me sleep. Would the burning cool. It'd probly be dawn then, anyway. Which is fair. If the sun is up, I should be too. Love and a child. And a half.

Music—an acid trip of technicolor home movies—would not leave me alone, was never going to leave me. Which is also fair. As fair as the sun. Music actually is sun, both of them shining through this window. Sun has no idea there is glass between us, no idea what glass is. Music has no idea either. It wouldn't care if it *did* know. Sunshine does not know solar power. Light doesn't know we break it up into its constituent colors. Music doesn't know this either; the tree just drops another apple.

Synesthesia means that color spills in with the sound. Also kicks in sometimes when people meditate, apparently. Which helps me stick up for it as something other than a confusion of the senses. It's so very alive here within an outline.

The song turns on the path and stares me down. Not unkindly; real is just real real. A baby will stare you down in its searching and babies know *everything*. When you don't lie, you can do no wrong is all. Every wrongdoing is a lie.

The last thing the song says is, *You can go now. We're done.* Which I always took to mean I should die. Like there was no way to escape except to shoot for heaven. To check out. Not sure why I thought that. And now I'm two people, one of them very important to me. For whatever reason, these two people are alive today. And it's quiet in the yard between our house and the neighbors' but for these morning birds and the sound of wet sunshine on a cold tree branch. Leaves are coming; there are tiny, chartreuse buds, each to be born into the biting cold. There is nothing reductive about this outline, nothing errant about a human thumbprint. To see our plane as dead is hell. It's heaven.

And spring is winning again, very slowly. Crawling carefully back into bed, I put the man's sleeping arm around me. He feels my skin for buzzing heat and, finding me cool and still, moves in to whisper good morning.

♋ morning birds

if there was just a little light left

✳ ✳ ✳ ✳

In the studio, the song clangs again, is s'posed to rebirth, if you can breathe life into it.

When you suck, though? And get it wrong, don't respect its *universe is a yes*? Fill it with crap and dress it in stupid frills? Then it fills its lungs with something other than inspiration, and tantrums at you or just drools in the corner. Or worse: struts around like an idiot, shaming you for ever calling yourself a doctor, Ms. Frankenstein. My drummer and I stare at the speakers, baffled.

It was a prayer. I swear.

And you had to go and bring it to church.

I honestly thought it was for the best.

I wanna hide under the desk today, in the cool shade of the mixing console with the engineer's sneakers, and rethink the whole thing. But that would attract more attention than this fail of staring at speakers while they spew. The song was so *walkin' around*. It had brainz and a pounding heart, a few stories.

Normally, patting it on the head and pouring it a bowl of cereal would encourage it to go outside and play, but I dressed it up for picture day and tamed its wild hair, told it not to swear, and now all it felt like doing was sitting in a hard chair, pouting. The engineer waits for an explanation. I shrug.

It just sucks, buddy, I don't know what to tell you.

Suck happens.

I blame myself.

We all blame you.

My drummer ran into a mailbox once when we were kids, playing tag. It was an exceptionally complicated form of tag, so sometimes you'd find yourself slowing, hiding, running down the rules again. Or . . . that was *my* response to complicated. His was to run full force into a mailbox with his face. Not the little residential kind of mailbox either, the *mailman* kind. Looked like a little tank.

Remember when you ran into the mailbox?

He nodded, still staring at the speakers. I stared at him.

Just running and running . . . and then what? Slam?

Yeah, flying. I was winning, but not totally looking where I was going. Still don't know what the mailbox was doing there.

What do you mean, what it was doing there? It was being a mailbox, waiting for mail.

I mean it was never there before.

Like it manifested to teach you a lesson in slam?

Exactly.

He was still staring at the speakers. I watched him watch sound. The engineer turned and squinted at us. I shook my head and went down the list.

The snare is lame. It's snappy and way too loud. My vocals are grating. They're snappy and way too loud. The kick is booming when it should be thudding, the verb on the lead is glossy and the compression is fucking with its dynamics. My distortion sounds like a beer commercial instead of broken static. The bass is punchy and that's stupid. It should be fuzzy here. I don't wanna hear the texture of the bass strings cuz they're playing off that lousy snare bite. The rhythm guitar is chunky and that's almost as dumb as tasty. The hat is sizzling instead of cracking. The rhythm double is in perfect time, so panning them sounds like a chorus pedal. The backing vocals are singing and singing is against the rules. The percussion isn't frantic enough, just clever and too tight. The tracks are all isolated and airy when they should cohere into something tangled and enmeshed. That's really all that's wrong. But that's not what's wrong.

The engineer froze, having no idea what to do. I glanced at my drummer to make sure he agreed and he nodded vaguely.

Murk and not enough murk.

And the song needs an edit; it feels formulaic, even though it isn't. But that's not really what's wrong.

The engineer stayed frozen, hands on the console. These were all the crumminesses that made the big, fat, American record company happy. Crummy is a choice. It's always a choice. No one's essential self wants to impress or fool anyone or be impressed or fooled *by* anyone.

Ugh. It's making me stupid. They'll love this.

Crummy?

Uncrummy is unsalable.

That's it! Let's make it unsalable.

The engineer, still waiting for instructions, smiled, and I smiled back.

We just ran into a mailbox that manifested to teach us a lesson in slam. Scrap it, start over. Let's let it go outside and play.

Suddenly animated, my drummer splayed his hands.

And in the hospital? They told me they'd use butterfly stitches on my face. So I just lay there, waiting for the butterflies.

♋ hope

nobody tells me what to do
I saw hope in my backyard

The park glistened around us as Doony's little hands with their backward knuckles rested tentatively on my stomach. My faded red T-shirt—*Coke Adds Life to America's Junior Miss*—willingly stretched itself pink and tight into a beautiful beach ball of baby. Doony felt no draw to the playground equipment or the other kids. He waited patiently, listening with his fingers through the sound of children playing, which is very much like the sound of children screaming. In fact, it *is* the sound of children screaming.

What's wrong with them, Mom?

They're . . . happy.

They sound angry.

Yeah. They're happy-angry.

Doony was not a screamer. Listened with all his body parts. Pressing, adding an ear to the pressing, trying harder to hear the pressing of a baby body part back against him, he asked if they were two brothers who hadn't met, touching.

Pretty much, baby.

Moving one of his pudgy hands up over my rib cage, I told him he would feel a tiny foot in a minute. His eyes shone. Children on the playground screamed and the sun blazed over the saturated ground.

When the baby kicked, Doony startled and calmed. Oddly calm, actually. I don't think he quite understood or accepted until this moment what it means for people to grow inside each other. Not entirely sure I did, either. Through his eyes, left ear, and fingertips, I briefly grasped the import of rich darkness before it slipped into limbic oblivion with other impressions too bulky to carry around. Some epiphanies are more useful softened by a multitude of days.

Doony's tiny mouth hung open in wonder, then hardened.
Will the baby scream like those kids?
Let's hope he's just happy.
Not angry.
Not angry.

✳ ✳ ✳ ✳

The tour was long and lovely and hard and heavy, trippy and hungry, a blast and a climb. As usual. We crawled all over the world while my middle grew bigger and bigger and my clothes tighter and tighter. I emptied my suitcase throughout the UK and Europe as I outgrew my clothes, started over in Australia, and gave away those clothes when we got to America, where I started over again in actual maternity clothes, hoping the record company just thought I was fat. I swung my guitar to the side and slept between sound check and show. Could not starve, could not drink, asked audiences not to smoke. I felt lucky, having it all, but watched "all" play out so tough sometimes. Sliding down the country back to Texas and its ostriches, we all held each other up; helped each other when it looked like one of us might fall and not get up again. One devastating phone call or injury and tough becomes impossible. It's a hard life, touring. A blissfully bizarre hard life. We called ourselves a family, a circus, and a cult.

♋ power and light

traveling souls like us
the wicked
the carnies

All through the Hill Country, Texas stayed bright and wet. Rain shattered over the bus, drilling through blue clouds, then became a thick, sunny mist, settling a few feet above the road. Odd mornings, too hot for coffee or tea, so we all shared a carton of orange juice carried out of last night's show. Tornadoes spun through a few counties and we watched for them, hoping dust devils on the horizon grew into something more dangerous, a better story to tell later. They did not. The bus did pull over one night and we were told that the safest thing to do would be to get out and lie down in the flooded ditch beside the highway; lightning opening the sky, trash swirling. We looked at each other and out the black windows coursing with rainwater and decided that, yeah, no, the safest thing to do would be to die inside the warm, dry bus. Lightning opened the wet black into a wet blue again.

Loading equipment into a Dallas club under a bumpy, raining sky, we passed each other, reckoning on the likelihood of dinner vs. craziness. We rarely got the first, the second was pretty much a given. A listener might as well be a musician; we're engaged in the same effort. A *fan* is not a listener. A fan—short for fanatic—is just *insert temporary object of worship here and also be bonkers*. They were the record company's, not ours. They were people who liked to like, and like what others like; no love in this equation. They didn't seem to hear the music we played but were wholly fixated on *us*. And not even *us*, really, our clothes or something. Pictures of us. Our records, but not the music on those records; the records were just cardboard to make us sign. I found fans darkly off-putting and oddly mean for people who were trying to kiss up to us. Fine line between sycophant and bully. They want you on a pedestal so they can knock you down.

My bass player pointed out that money is the meat the record company corralled them for.

And we're not into that math.

I knew some musicians who liked that worship shit, but they were never actually musicians, just performers. They offered sound like junk food offers calories, but it wasn't music. They were perfect for the sycophants and vice versa, so I was always recommending them to fans, but it was a pretty transparent attempt to make these shrill people go away.

Kris. Don't say that out loud.

Why? I'm just talking to you.

They love you.

They do not love me and I don't do sycophant. They can go kiss up to somebody who does.

Yeah. Just don't say it out loud.

Ok. I'm gonna think it, though.

I know you are.

A listener sees the work for what it is: a goofy present, sloppily wrapped and thoughtful, a soundtrack for their car, an alive thing, something gifted to them that they now own. The people who play the music they listen to are not their focus, don't matter at all, really. We are their electricians, facilitating currents through their homes; we make an honest dollar and then retreat. I adored and respected listeners, but they always took off after shows, had better things to do than hang out with us. Kinda sad for us lonely ghosts who live on highways. My bass player and I set up our equipment on the dark stage in a thick Texas heat, my baby gut making it even warmer. He plugged his pedals in and sat next to them.

Dinner or crazy people?
I think tonight we'll have dinner but also crazy people.
Aw, Kris, let them love you.
They do not love me. And they won't even like me next year.
A year is a long time. I give 'em six months before they find
somebody who dresses better than you.
I laughed.
Okay. We get dinner and only listeners, no fans.
'S gonna be awesome.

♋ flipside

there's always drooling zombies

Thunder growled somewhere past the city, over prairies and
ostrich heads. Eight feet high, staring into those bumpy, gray
clouds, running toward something that isn't there, freezing
when they realize this.

Dinner was beer again and, pregnant, I could not partake. It
was raining too hard to go looking for a restaurant, so my bass
player brought me an apple and invited me backstage to watch
a man hurl abuse at the opening band from someone's shoulders. I followed him, but the dressing room was reachable only
by rickety ladder and my center of gravity was off. I stared up
at the glow around the top rung as I climbed, each rung warmer
than the last and the noise of rain and band louder. When I
could see into the dressing room, I pushed my swollen middle

over the top rung and could hear a high voice yelling angrily. But sort of happy too. Like a happy, angry schoolyard scream. Gleefully furious.

My bass player knelt in an opening that looked down onto the stage, riveted. I joined him but could see only the opener's bass player, facing the wall, actually pressing himself against it, as far from the yelling as he could get.

Is he ok?

He's achondroplasiaphobic. Dude's kinda pushing his buttons.

What?

Says he's afraid of little-people mojo.

The bass player's hands shook, moving awkwardly against the wall, as he tried to reach the strings.

What? That's awful. Tell him that's awful.

I think he knows.

Craning my neck to see past the stage and into the audience, I saw a man with two heads, one on top of the other. The top head was yelling, but I couldn't hear what it was saying. Looked like bad stuff. Fists waved on either side of it. No, it was a two thumbs-down. I checked the time, hoped the guy'd be yelled out by the time we had to play. The opening band had a good half hour left in their set, but I wasn't sure the bass player was gonna make it. He sweated and shook, played out of time. Looking up at us, he grimaced; the face of nightmares. We waved down at him, concerned, as a voice cut through the noise of the band and the crowd.

YOU SUCK!

Wincing like he'd been hit with something, the bass player ducked, trying to dodge the abuse.

I feel sad for everybody down there.

Have you seen the rest of the audience?

I tried to see through the stage lights and past the monitors and other musicians, into the dark crowd, but I couldn't make out much. I looked at him questioningly and he smiled. A gentle, evil smile, but before I could ask *what the fuck*, the bass player downstairs waved his arms over his head to stop the band and pulled his bass off. His band didn't stop playing, though; they either didn't notice or they were used to him freaking out when little people yelled at him. Leaning into the wings, he disappeared from view.

What's he doing?

I dunno. I think puking.

Jesus.

Whoever was working the lights tried to help by filling the stage with spinning Day-Glo psychedelia, as the band continued with no bass and the angry man yelled that they sucked and should leave.

Is he gonna yell at us too?

No, he likes us. He's trying to get us to play by getting them off the stage.

But we're already gonna play. And he's not making the stage seem like a nice place to be.

Seen the rest of the crowd yet?

Peering down, I saw jumping, but that's it. It just looked like the opposite of pregnant out there.

I'm tired.

Eat your apple. And when we get up there? Hide.

God, if only.

Well. Just melt into the background.

Another evil smile. I took a bite of the apple and watched a
piece of our scared friend's back heave in the wings. The lights
flashed and a chartreuse mandala whirled across the other musicians' faces.

♋ day-glo

then you melt into the background

It took a few minutes to climb down to the stage. I had to back
down the ladder with my belly sticking out in front. Kneeling
by the mic stand, I checked my pedals and plugged in my guitar,
then glanced into the audience and did a quick double take. The
crowd was painted. Like, Woodstock-style hippie face painting, but not just on their faces, up and down their arms and
legs. And not painted *well*, more like covered in scribbles, as if
they'd had a bad run-in with a day care facility. They clapped
for us, but also screamed and whooped and moaned, swaying
unsteadily. I jammed my question-mark face into my bass player's personal space and he shrugged.
    I dunno. They're on something more than beer.
    Ecstasy?
    And . . . acid?
The two-headed man stood directly in front of my microphone. The top head was beautiful, on a kind of fire, still yelling, fists still waving, glasses askew. At least his thumbs were
pointing *up* now. I smiled at him and was met with a clear-eyed

tunnel into Not Zombie. This was vividly apparent, as the man was entirely surrounded by zombies.

When I play, I disappear. That's really the whole point, in an unlikely reversal of drive. The hunger I feel for guitar and for yelling colors pushes me obsessively into a space that is not experienced by the part of me that goes by a name, who suggested it in the first place. And as cool as this plane is, there is no time that I don't want to disappear into sound. Tonight? My disappearing act was exceptionally thorough. Between songs, I could hear the mooing of ecstasy-acid-soaked painted faces, but that just served to fly me into the next song. We wanted this night to end and *soon*. With only seconds between the decay of a last chord and the next count in, we moved through the set quickly, as the audience grew more animated in the kind of groovy free-for-all you usually only see at summer festivals: a muddy groping of glazed eyes and fuzzy communal energy.

The crowd began to take on the appearance of a herd, moving in ripples to one side and then the other, with a constant bellowing. Colorful cows moaned, scooted, and rolled like sea lions, breathing as one to keep an iffy psychedelic fire lit. I could not figure them out, couldn't read what they were all *on* through the haze of scribbly skin and humming. About halfway through the set, I crept to stage left and looked up at my bass player again, dazed.

What. The. Serious. Fuck.

This is where they invented acid.

So they're all on it? Whadda they pass it out at the grocery store?

Maybe they invented something else.

I looked out at all the dazzled, glassy eyes.

. . . and passed it out at the grocery store?

He shook his head, bewildered, as the promoter fought his way through happy zombies and jumped onto the stage. The guy was really into glam rock and sort of . . . celebrated it as a lifestyle. He was shirtless, wearing silver pants that caught the lights and shone like mirrors in all directions.

Are we supposed to keep playing?

Guess he's here to calm them down.

The man perched on his friend's shoulders caught my eye, suspicious, his fire dimmed. As the only audience member not drugged out of his mind, he wasn't painted or mooing, and he could maintain eye contact for longer than a millisecond. Though he did blink and wince when light from the promoter's pants flared into his eyes. I asked him with my face what was happening, and he narrowed his eyes thoughtfully before another silver flash over his glasses shut them again.

We all watched as the promoter climbed the drum riser and pulled a microphone off the floor tom, swaying. My drummer leaned away from him warily. The promoter snuffled and spat into the mic before speaking, raising his free hand to the crowd as a gesture of peace. They mooed quietly.

What beautiful music we've heard tonight! Let's hear it for a beautiful night!

The cows clapped obediently and whooped a bit. The promoter looked unsteady. It wasn't even midnight; we still had about six songs left to play. He then carefully dropped his silver pants, mirrors flashing. My sad drummer leaned further back as the man drawled slowly.

It's a windy, rainy night, folks. And some beautiful musicians worked hard for us. Let's show these beautiful people some Texas hospitality and help them pack up their gear and load out!

What . . .

Instantly, the zombies became animated and, shifting their weight toward the stage, rushed at us, grabbing whatever equipment they could reach. Alarmed, I caught my bass player's eye, but that only distracted him long enough for a cow to grab his set list and push the club doors open, wandering out into the rain with it. I turned to the only sober person in the audience for help. He nodded and yelled over their heads to make them stop. I don't know why I thought he could speak Zombie Cow—cuz he was *from* here, I guess—but his cries were buried; no one could hear him through the driving rain and loving fog. The promoter still had the floor tom mic, but he'd run out of vocabulary except for the word *beautiful.*

Beautiful! Beautiful! Beautiful . . .

He teetered on the drum riser, silver pants around his ankles, as Day-Glo mandalas reappeared, spinning and whirling on us all. I'm sure the lighting dude was trying to help, but. The house music came up: glam rock, as before—as always, I was told. This is when I started having trouble keeping a straight face.

My drummer was on his feet yelling and trying to pull his sticks away from an audience member with a purple and yellow face, but he lost this tug-of-war when a different one knocked him over, pulling his drum stool away. Both friendly zombies wandered out with his equipment and another grabbed his snare, handing the snare stand to his girlfriend. They all took the gear out into the rain, probably wandering home with it. I laughed, couldn't help it, turning to share this moment with the sober man who'd given up yelling at them, but he wasn't laughing; he was looking at my amp behind me, wide-eyed. I turned around and saw two zombie cows carefully pulling the knobs off of it.

What the hell . . .

Hey! Quit it!

At my feet, two others unplugged my pedals as more clambered up onto the stage. There seemed to be way more people at this show now than there were when we were playing. They *surged* onto the stage. The promoter jumped off the drum riser, leaving his mirrored pants behind, and shuffled outside with the floor tom. I couldn't find the sober man in the crowd of beasts pushing around me, so I went looking for the knobs those guys took off my amp. Nothing but hippie hooves down there in the chaos. My bandmates were gone.

I switched from Save Our Shit to *escape* and, gripping my guitar—which was still strapped to me, or it woulda been outside in the rain—pushed my way through the crowd onstage. Found the edge of the stage, but I had to sit down and ease off it gently to keep my guitar from jabbing me in the baby gut. The chaos was more organized down here, as the zombies knew they were all headed toward the exit—and the pouring rain—with our gear in their painted hands. The bellowing, which cut through blasting glam rock, dimmed on the sidewalk, drowned in spattering and splashing. Carefully laid out on the cement was our equipment, broken into pieces and forming a weird mosaic around the entrance to our bus, my bass player's set list smoothed and pressed onto the cement. Song titles dripped and bled Sharpie spiderwebs.

My drummer wrestled his high hat from a swaying hippie chick on the sidewalk, his glasses dotted with raindrops, while our bass player tried to reason with a dripping, green and yellow face. The face stared back at him, interested, gripping a distortion pedal with both hands. I slipped past them and a dozen or so happy, wet forms, then fished for the bus key hanging around my neck and let myself in to the relative quiet of the bus. Taking off my rain-spattered guitar, I rested it carefully on a couch and watched from the window with the lights out.

Without sound, it was kinda slo-mo cool. Zombies are not quick and these were loving ones. They hugged my struggling bandmates and high-fived each other on a job well done, blinking in the rain as they missed each other's hands. I quickly ran down a list of all the other jobs I could have had . . . pretty much anything other than musician.

Fry cook, virologist, shepherd, farmer, mailman.

Doony called from his bunk.

Coming, baby.

The bunks were dark and noisy with rain. Some bodies were asleep back there, so I tiptoed and whispered.

Pretty rain, huh?

A soft, pink night-light shone on his smile.

♋ home

pretty rain makes you smile

Crawling in under the blanket with him, I pulled the bunk curtain closed and we lay there listening to the rain, the yelling, the mooing. Finally, I heard the door creak open and my bandmates climb onto the bus. Kissing Doony on the forehead, I rolled out of the bunk and into the aisle.

Just a minute, sweetie. I'll be right back.

I opened the door to the lounge to ask my bandmates what the hell again—even though they didn't know what the hell—and froze. The lounge was full of painted zombies, leafing through our books and rummaging around in our cabinets. I could see the boys out on the sidewalk in the midnight rain through the window, loading wet equipment into the bay. I must not have locked the door behind me. A hippie with an orange blob painted on her cheek opened a beer and passed it to a skeezixy dude, then opened one for herself. They were no longer bellowing but politely murmuring.

Where'd I leave off? Oh yeah . . . mailman, pet food scientist, baker. Balle-fuckin-rina.

I grabbed my guitar and shoved it into the aisle between the bunks, then backed in myself, locking the door behind me. Doony's little face peeked out, questioning, and I smiled at it.

Just some hippies, baby. They're cool.

Crawling in with him, I began to tell him about the hippies of my childhood. Gardens and goats. The barn in the woods, face painting. Potter's wheel. The parachute we lived under, lentils on the stove. Music. Homemade clothes or no clothes. The hippie chick who saw ostriches with their heads in the sand along the riverbank and how I longed to see what acid made her believe. The love for all creatures, even the rats in our kitchen, who needed to eat just as we did, who needed a home just as we did. The bus began to rock gently back and forth. Which it often did as we drove down the highway, but we were stationary. I groaned and burrowed deeper into the cave of the bunk.

These soft brains fried on ecstatic acid were rocking the bus, as the bandmates I'd abandoned tried to salvage whatever equipment they could find.

Not my problem. Sort of my problem. *Maybe* my problem. Probly my problem but I didn't know what to do about it.

I pictured the loving cows and my loving bandmates, all of them even wetter now and more confused, everyone trying to help. I giggled into Doony's hair and he giggled back, making room for my big belly. The rain sounded so nice.

✴ ✴ ✴ ✴

♋ pretty ugly

you can't see the sky from here

The video was being shot in an enormous warehouse in New York City in a dirty summer heat wave. The tour was hard, but this was harder. There was *music* on tour. My drummer stood beside me watching the passive-aggressive director bitch out a passive-aggressive woman holding a clipboard, who then bitched out the film crew, who then got bitchy. He sighed.

Look out. We're the dog who's about to be kicked.

I know.

Where's our eyeliner? Where's my pipe? I wanna lose a beauty contest. I wanna be a pirate.

I just want shit to blow up.

The director stormed up to me and switched into "frazzled"

mode, which allowed him to still act bitchy but appear to have a sense of humor about it. He assured me that they'd only be filming me from the neck up.

How 'bout not at all? Then I can go home.

My drummer shot me a look and the director explained.

You know, so no one sees how big you are.

Fuckin' wow.

I'm eight months pregnant.

Uh-huh.

He laughed absently and skittered off to frazzle at somebody else. My drummer sighed.

I don't think he knows what the word "pregnant" means.

He knows it means fat.

Musicians can't be fat? Since when?

Since the music business. I goddamn quit this shit. I quit right now. All of this. It's what's wrong with everything.

But he heard none of this, as he was being swept away into a corner of the warehouse and placed behind a prop drum kit. My bass player appeared at my side, grim, and the passive-aggressive clipboard woman sidled up to us flirtatiously.

So let's talk about camera work, okay? So I'm gonna need you guys to be aware of when you're in frame, okay? Always look for the red light. So when you see it? I'm gonna need you to rock out.

He glared at her.

Rock out.

Yeah.

Girlish, she grinned with angry eyes and took him by the arm. I watched as he and his bass were led far, far away, up into the rafters at the very end of the warehouse, and then balanced on a couple two-by-fours about twenty feet in the air. Squinting up at him in alarm, I saw him flip off the woman's back. I guess they thought that since bass is the instrument they didn't notice, bass is the player we shouldn't see, even though he wasn't pregnant. It was, like, ninety degrees on the floor; it must have been over a hundred up in the rafters.

The director used a bullhorn to talk to us.

So when you see the red light? I'm gonna want you to rock out! So if you see the light, the camera sees you and we're gonna need you to rock out, okay? Everybody ready to rock?

Jesus. Shut up and let us go home.

The film crew spat and hissed at each other like pissy cats. I don't know how they were *all* fighting with each other, but each one of them seemed angry. Coulda been the heat, I guess. The first take, the director's assistant was in the shot and everybody yelled at him. The next time, it was the makeup lady. Then a light slipped out of place and everybody yelled at the guy next to it, etc.

You fucking nut jobs.

I stood where they told me to stand and played guitar because the guitar was my only friend. Every now and then, someone would come over and give me a talking-to through gritted teeth.

You're not rocking out. So when the camera sees you, rock out. So you'll know the camera sees you when you see the red light, okay? So that's when you start to rock. Okay?

This lady's walkie-talkie spat and hissed. She rolled her eyes while she waited for it to stop, then pressed a button and spat and hissed into it.

I know. I know. Yeah, I know. I was trying to explain some camera stuff to her.

I wonder if we haven't misunderstood native people who tell us that photographs steal their souls when we call it superstition.

The integration of body and soul hits deeper than suspicion of a machine. A baby born into life *is* life, until we convince it that it must collect trappings that reflect itself back to us as its superficial qualities. We could, instead, gently dissuade each other from buying the emperor's new clothes and become *people* instead of images. Without a photographic version of ourselves, we could become our movement, our sound, our work, and our engagement. In other words, if you believe you are your superficial aspects, you are losing your soul. You are merely a picture of a person, a demographic, one of the zombies.

If rain is the falling and wind is the blowing, then we are the living.

I went back to the guitar. It swung alongside my big stomach so that I could reach it, which was awkward, and I could barely hear the unamplified strings, but it was a way to not look at another angry face or hear another angry voice. The walkie-talkie catfight continued and the flirtatious woman started making noise at me again. I watched her face do it, but as long as I was playing guitar, that's all I heard.

This isn't real. Babies and guitars are real.

Eventually she stopped.

Okay?

Sure.

I looked up at my bass player in the rafters and saw only flying limbs: violent spasms, like an upright seizure. And he was jumping around like . . . well, like a bad music video. Just what these idiots wanted us to do. *What the hell?* The neck of his bass bounced up and down, obscuring his face, sweat droplets flying, as his feet shook the rafters. I laughed, thinking this was for my benefit.

Since I was too fat to make it into the video anyway, I didn't bother to play along, just watched him throw a rawk fit. When the cameras finally panned all the way across the warehouse and pointed directly at him, he froze and slowly removed his bass, placing it at his feet, ruining yet another take. He folded his arms and stood perfectly still. A wail went up as all the mad cats cried at once.

CUT*!!!*

I really did try not to laugh; but hell, you dumbasses.

This is when I knew we were not cut out to be ostriches in the snow.

* * * *

Shutting the door on that lame party, I asked the record company if I could trade them a solo record for our freedom and they accepted. Then I prepared myself for a lifetime of life. Which does nothing for effect, nothing for attention, doesn't lie: the only somebody is a nobody. So sweet there, a sweetness on fire.

Lousy music isn't music; it's an insult and we don't insult each other without lying. We love each other. We *are* each other. We're not our images; we are ourselves.

INTERVIEW:

Q: How does it feel to have your industry turn its back on you?

A: *laughter*

* * * *

♋ flood

you're my bright light

Ryder was born so early that when I went into labor, the man
had not read far enough into the pregnancy books to know anything about it. While I eased myself into the bathtub, he laid out
all the baby books we owned—on the floor, on stacks of towels
and the edge of the sink—and quizzed me on the stages of labor
and vocabulary with which he was unfamiliar.

What's . . . butterfly breathing?

Could you light a candle?

What?

Nothing. Just turn off the light. Sorry, please turn off the
light.

What's butterfly breathing?

It's supposed to help you ride over a contraction.

Ride over . . . ride over it?

It's ok. I do it, not you.

He switched books and flipped to the end.

It says I have to pack a lunch.

No, it doesn't.

It does! Says it right here.

It's ten o'clock at night. A lunch for you or me?

For me. Says I'll get hungry.

Fuck that. You aren't packing yourself a lunch.

Switching books again, he began reading silently, which I
took to be a bad sign. I wished he'd stop.

Hey. Are you ok?

He continued to read silently, so I waved a hand in front of his face to interrupt his terror.

Freaking out? Call the midwife.

He startled and looked at me in mute fear.

I, uh . . . no, this'll be good. I got this. I mean, you got this. We're good. We can call her from the hospital.

I winced in pain and so did he. Took a second before I could breathe again. I felt fine but he looked awful. Really wanted to help him but I didn't know how.

Sure you're ok?

He slammed that book shut and tried another.

Ok. What's transition?

It's when the contractions all come at once and you can't take it, so you get angry.

I get angry?

I get angry.

You never get angry.

No. We'll be fine.

He lit a candle.

The hospital on our island had no deliveries scheduled for that night. The obstetrics wing was dark and empty, unstaffed. We could see this from the sidewalk; holding hands, we slowed, then stopped and looked at each other. The contractions were getting serious and I felt sure the baby was coming very soon.

What do we do?

Stupid island is too small to let us have babies on it?

Let's move to a better island.

Tonight?

Yeah, right now.

We decided to ask the woman we could see sitting at the front desk where we should go. Walking in the front door of the hospital, though, my knees buckled with a difficult contraction and the man put his arms around me. The automatic doors kept clunking open, then shutting and opening again while we stood there, embracing.

The woman at the front desk stood and waved us in, as if we were maybe unfamiliar with automatic doors and were embracing in fear. Then she called out to us, telling us to come into the waiting room, but I couldn't move or speak. The man didn't want to yell in my ear, so he called quietly back to her that it was ok. She heard nothing over the hospital Muzak, and the longer the contraction went on and the doors opened and closed, the more adamant she became that there was nothing for us to be afraid of, that we could just walk into the waiting room like any other room.

The contraction finally faded and I took a breath.

Where could we possibly be from that doors could scare us?

I tried to take a step and lost my balance. The man caught me and the desk woman appeared beside him, ushering us inside. We shuffled in behind her and she went back to her post, facing us with the kind of patient, loving smirk she probly used on toddlers. I was glad. We needed an aunt.

Suddenly, she shouted at us.

WHAT CAN I DO FOR YOU?

The man jumped and looked at me in alarm. He often

thought that I'd be able to explain islanders' baffling behavior, though I've never been able to explain *anyone's* baffling behavior. I was muttering something about her thinking we might be foreign or backwoods or just not that bright, when another contraction began. I moaned quietly as the man began to die.

My wife is pregnant. I mean she's in labor and I think she's having the baby. We need to call our midwife. And we don't know where to go because the—

The woman's kind toddler smirk expanded into a roguish grin.

AND SHE'S JUST A BABY HERSELF! DAHLIN' YER JUST A BABY YERSELF!

I smiled at her but it was really a wince as I fell against the man. He was in agony.

I think we're in a hurry. But we don't know where to go.

The woman laughed.

IT'S GONNA BE A LONG NIGHT! YOU HAVE PLENTY OF TIME!

Shaking my head at the man, I couldn't speak. He crumpled.

Could you help us, please?

Placing a map of the hospital layout on the counter, she circled "Obstetrics" and pointed down a dark hallway to our left.

THIS IS WHERE YOU GO TO HAVE THE BABY, BUT TRUST ME, YOU HAVE TIME!

I slumped into the man's arms, unable to breathe, and she laughed lightly. His arms gripped me as tightly as my midriff was seizing and he spoke through gritted teeth.

It's dark in there, ma'am.

She laughed again. She was very happy.

WE WEREN'T EXPECTING ANY BABIES TONIGHT!

Neither were we.

YOU'LL SEE SOMEONE AT A DESK DOWN THE HALL!

My contraction eased and I took a breath to speak to her while I could.

I think I'm having the baby.

BOY OR GIRL? DO YOU KNOW YET?

Jesus christ.

I mean now.

She shook her head, bemused.

HONEY, TRUST ME, I'VE DONE THIS BEFORE!

Another contraction. I wanted to give up. Bending over, I wheezed at her.

So have I.

The man scooped me up into his arms and took off down the dark hallway as the woman behind the desk waved goodbye.

GOOD LUCK, GUYS!

He panted with exertion and panic.

Why are we always "guys"? They don't call other adults "guys."

I had to wait for the contraction to fade before I could speak.

We aren't adults.

Ignoring me, he kept running.

Someone at a desk, someone at a desk. I don't see a desk.

Taking a corner too fast, he skidded into someone at a desk. But that's all the guy was. Just someone at a desk, reading a book. Wasn't wearing an orderly smock or a name tag or anything. I twisted my head around in the man's arms, looking for some indication that the guy worked here at the hospital, but he just looked up from his paperback, startled.

The man's voice was shrill and his arms shook around me. *Can you help us?*

The guy at the desk closed his book awkwardly.

Um . . .

I could feel the man's racing heart against mine.

Is this obstetrics?

Yes, but . . . there were no deliveries scheduled for tonight. I mean, we weren't expecting any.

I groaned.

Neither were we.

The guy chuckled nervously and, closing my eyes, I gave myself over to another contraction. Tried to remember what butterfly breathing was. Pictured the man reading our pregnancy books a few minutes ago. Riding over . . . riding over a contraction?

My torso froze into marble. Ride over. What the hell does that mean? Breathe really fast? Lightly, the books said. Breathe lightly. *I can't breathe at all. I'm gonna pass out.* An unyielding wall of muscle tightened around the baby and my organs. My body was squeezing us both to death. I tried not to make a sound, but I must have made some kind of noise because there was sudden movement again and the men's voices picked up in volume.

The man and the baby and I were one body. The three of us shook together with running and contraction, then turned another corner and stopped. I heard the sucking sound of a heavy door and a bright light slammed my eyes open, but the light was all I could see. Just a world of fluorescence. More voices, quiet except for the man's heavy breathing.

I was being stood upright in a room full of silver. Silver

railings, silver shower fixtures, a silver drain in the floor, silver sink, silver light switch, all shining in greenish fluorescent light. Somehow, I was standing, but it felt more like balancing. My center of gravity had shifted with torsion and baby density. I looked up and saw a mushroom-shaped nurse in blue scrubs, wearing what looked like an enormous shower cap.

They got me from the ER.

She and the man were both staring at me. I thought I should say something.

Sorry.

I didn't think I could stay upright much longer and said so. The nurse laughed exactly like the woman at the front desk.

It's ok. We're in for a long night. Trust me.

They must say that to everybody. I didn't trust any of them. Not the woman at the front desk or the man reading the paperback or the ER mushroom . . . I began questioning the value of hospitals, of Western medicine, of living on an island where they thought babies were scheduled things. The nurse handed me a hospital johnny, calling it a "nightgown," and told me they'd give me some privacy while I changed into it, then she and the man were gone.

Privacy? I didn't want privacy. Or a nightgown. The man and the baby and I were one animal and she'd just lobbed off a third of us. Feeling another contraction begin, I knew I could no longer speak to say any of this, so I dropped carefully to the floor next to the johnny and blacked out.

♋ fuchsia wall

then suddenly everything I see's a love letter:
oblivion

When I opened my eyes, I was in a hospital bed and the mush-
room's face was inches from mine.
You're having the baby right now!
. . . I know.
There's no doctor here.
Oh. Sorry.
She dissolved and became the man, his face inches from
mine.
They're looking for a doctor.
Ok.
Did you want to butterfly breathe?
I'm good.
The man divided into himself and the mushroom nurse.
Together, they moved me onto a gurney and pushed me out
of the room, then started running, my feet smashing through
doors. *Bam.* As we bumped along, I saw ceiling after ceiling,
then *bam*, another set of swinging doors, until we got to the
dark delivery room. The gurney stopped suddenly and another
contraction squeezed the consciousness out of me until I heard
the man's voice in darkness.
Stop saying that.
I opened my eyes. Another world of fluorescence.
Stop saying what?

The pressure again. I stopped breathing and passed out. Woke to the sound of his voice.

Please stop saying that.

Stop saying what?

Another contraction. Blacked out.

You keep asking me to help you. And I can't help you.

Oh. Sorry.

Passed out again.

Hello.

A child was standing at the foot of the gurney, looking scared. Two long braids, hospital scrubs, and a stethoscope. She wasn't doing anything, just standing there, looking uncomfortable.

I'm a resident. They got me from the ER.

The girl was a baby doctor. I don't mean obstetrician but, like, a baby dressed as a doctor. Could barely see her over my enormous belly. I looked at the man, who was holding my hand. He was sweating but composed.

Thank you for coming.

The girl didn't seem very composed. In fact, she looked really upset. Finally she blurted out:

I've never delivered a baby before!

I started wanting to give up again.

Well . . . I have.

* * * *

Ryder was born blue, a month early, about forty minutes after I stepped out of the bathtub. I had never seen such a beautiful blue creature. Enchanted, I studied his perfect, still features. The mushroom leaned over us to tickle his tiny feet and he flushed lavender, then pink, and opened his space eyes.

Everything was in them. A deep, dark blackness. I tried to learn everything by staring and it felt too easy . . . everything was nothing. These eyes knew they were about to forget that everything is nothing, had to forget, but there was no sadness, only a minor key gravity. That baby was the key of A minor, which is turquoise. He was going to bring space to substance and vice versa, to sculpt a story from active clay, and it was a daunting task. But daunting needs an "I" and he'd only just become one. Color moved over and through him like a cuttle-fish moving across the ocean floor. The closer he got to a blue tinge, the closer he was to space. When pink flushed in, he softened to body. Settling on a lavender dawn, he stayed hovering in between.

For an hour, we gazed into each other in silence, except for a moment when the man spoke and Ryder, having heard the man's voice often, turned his tiny head to look. A crazy few seconds, like a dark blessing. And then, abruptly, he became a baby. A dewy lavender bud. And I knew all that I had to do to worship his simplicity. My role was obsession and earth. Love and cookies and fascination; soft little T-shirts and spotting him on the slide when he finally joined his brother in the glistening park. I turned to the man.

Was there a little girl . . . doctor? Here?
Yeah.
I didn't make that up?
No.
. . . huh.

✱ ✱ ✱ ✱

When Doony met his brother, he looked at him quietly and the baby looked back. He held a tiny hand and studied the thumb I'd seen on the sonogram months ago. Then, gently, he kissed the baby's forehead. Ryder blinked.

Mom. He has black holes for eyes.
Yeah. He does.

♋ dog days

this is life and we didn't miss it

My drummer visits in the afternoons to play with the baby and listen to the songs I've recorded on my four-track. He wears headphones and cradles little Ryder, speaking loudly because he can't hear his own voice through the music.

THEY CAN'T TAKE THIS AWAY FROM US. THEY HAVE NO RIGHT.

The baby jumps, his eyes wide.

I MEAN, THEY'RE JUST TOO STUPID. WE DON'T GIVE A SHIT ABOUT THEIR FUCKING FASHION GAME OR THEIR MONEY, RIGHT?

I nod, eyeing the baby, whose bottom lip is trembling.

I KNOW YOU QUIT THE BUSINESS. BUT DON'T QUIT MUSIC.

He removes his headphones. Ryder watches, his eyes enormous.

I mean, there are good people in this world. Let's find them.

* * * *

Baby Ryder's space eyes blink black in the darkness, shining. The man's tears shine too.

At the end of my life, I'll ask for five more minutes. Just five more minutes of this.

And the whole time? Music plays.

WYATT

♋ god's not a dick

New Orleans is on fire with blue flames and LA flowers

In New Orleans, the mules' hooves mark half-circles on the cobblestones all night. An intermittent, soft clatter. Sometimes a silence will fall, filled with Dopplered, far-off sirens. And then you pray for the suffering folks out there for a second. Cuz you know they're there. I'd wait for the mule carts, lying in bed in a summer burning on the third floor; what used to be the attic of this melting mansion. Wait and wait and finally be soothed by the rataplan I'd grown used to. Hard to sleep without it. Hard to sleep *through* it, it's so pretty.

S'posed to be haunted, this melting mansion. And since everybody here wants to be haunted, we know the story of this ghost: woman set herself on fire. Not much of a story, I guess, now that I type it, but we read a buncha backstory into it . . . her mad pain and the wet swamp heat burned off by fire in the very bed we were lying in. I stared at the ceiling, at a silver-white strip of moonlight, though mist covered the moon, and tried to remember the way I'd heard it. The story part wasn't so much her death but what came after it: she sits on your chest in the night and presses into you with ghost hands while you lie in her bed. The pressure is enough that you can't breathe. You can't scream, either, as you begin to suffocate. Right before you die by a dead hand, she releases you, air rushing into your lungs. And then she's gone and a southern moon, all silver white in your window, like tonight.

You awake?

Yeah.

When she sits on your chest, is she on fire?

Like a ghost fire?

Right. Or is she pre-fire her? Or post. All burned up.

Huh. They would all be cool.

Yeah.

Charmed in the dark for a moment, and then it dissolves into us making exactly the same face. This happens a lot.

Except the only person who actually saw her was standing near the dryer vent, so she mighta just been steam.

Less cool.

Much.

The children slept on makeshift beds behind sheets hung like curtains. They sweated and kicked, dreaming like crazy, then woke early, asking for water. Though the air was filled with water: dew, rain, mist, fog hover, sun held in water molecules drifting over leaf litter. I could keep listing waters for you cuz the place is infused with moisture, built on it. The thing is, water carries sound; a desert's silence speaks to this. So songs live here. People know, and will tell you, there is music in the air in New Orleans. Sounds so lame, is so true. And not just the calliope music that's born in the Bywater, floats over the Marigny, and rains down over the Quarter.

Anyway, the boys were always thirsty. They drank cups of water in the tub every morning under a dewy skylight, watching fish swim in a tank over the grand staircase. Some nights when I couldn't sleep, I did the same; stars foggy through the glass above me, dark fish keeping dark time, and listened to mixes steaming up the stairs like ghosts. But tonight, I just listened for the little boys' sleep talking and heard only breathing as a blanket was kicked off.

You used to set yourself on fire.

Yeah. Sorry about that.

'S ok.

The man was falling asleep again. I turned onto my stomach and leaned out the window to see the moonlit street and the mules I was so grateful for. They looked tired and I wondered about their pursuit of happiness. And what right we have to make a mule to begin with. Horse plus donkey equals can't procreate and then we just . . . clomp it around so we don't have to walk? I dunno. Pretty tattoos, but I bet they didn't ask for them. Same with the flowered hats they wear.

Don't know that it's cool to shame somebody with her own face.

They have names? And that's sweet. Bonded to their owners and vice versa. Smart. Their owners looked pretty tired too, as an early sun pinked up the Quarter. They barely held the reins, the route repeating itself for decades, but still necessary, like breathing. Autonomic mule carting. And the heat, back with

the pink light, which would soon be orange and then yellow
and then a searing white. I felt less guilty lying there hot and
safe, loving the clomping, if they had each other down there,
the mules and their drivers. Coworkers. I did love that clatter
so much.

♋ white suckers

you never disappoint me
you mutilate the morning
shining and yawning

So yeah, the window in the wall between the grand staircase
and the claw-foot tub was a fish tank. In the bath, we watched
fish in their bath, all of us up so high at mansion rooftop level.
The shower was outside on the roof. A beautiful, dangerous
place to be in a thunderstorm. Splashing and dirty and silver
and melting. All of New Orleans was beautiful and dangerous;
splashing and dirty and silver and melting. You could ride an
old rusty bike or an old rusty streetcar all day and get anywhere, get everywhere, get nowhere, in the murder capital of
our country. Cuz with all of its violence, the arrows of the West
were all bent and mocked in New Orleans. Cyclical and wiggly,
mazed and, well . . . soggy. All over the south, time spent on the
porch with thunder cracking overhead gives rise to an element
of dream that never really disengages. The Big Easy is especially
striking in this regard because hard is so hard there and yet

cannot take hold, because gravity and because slippery. Silver mosquito fish, wriggling. Whatever gets you through the night, through the day. Voodoo's only vivid fear: zombification.

Nobody else wanted to be here in the summer, so it was cheap, so it was ours. And, melting like mercury every morning, we slipped from the shower to the rainstorm to the bath. Played records on the third-floor turntable so the little boys could dance. Slipping downstairs to coffee and hazy laughter that melted into margaritas and hazy tears as the day dissolved. To homemade salsa for seven and cloudbursts of stories. Some whispering. Softened by rain and termites, the house itself was crooked, getting crookeder. Good bones, but those good bones slipping down, and then, having grown accustomed to slipping, they slip further. A melting, because once hard, the wood could not maintain. Hard is taught a lesson in New Orleans. Hard fills with water and softness because pliable is the only way to deal until wet eventually wins. Yang burns everywhere, but here? Yin laughs and waits. This was what taking our music back looked like, how no bullshit felt. Then when you care, it's with a deep enthusiasm that kills your bitter. We were so goddamn used to caring with bitterness.

♋ buzz

my limes make a baby healthy and wise
I cut lemons and lemons and limes

People who were dirty and sweating on the outside, with all manner of substances seeping outta their pores—walking hearts of clean—wouldn't walk past without stopping into our studio; always with a story or the ability to sit and listen to one. Always with a song or the ability to sit and listen to one. "Light travelers" ringing the doorbell to ask for bus fare, feathers taped down their backs, as we baked a cake and another song. Always a party cuz what *isn't* a reason to throw one? This particular party, the burritos weren't even started before the salsa was gone. Starting on the guacamole, we got to talking and another round of margaritas went into the blender. Switched to fried okra and redfish. The children played with our silver puppy, Crow. I turned to my bass player, who was cutting limes with me.

What's today?

Isn't it your birthday?

It is?

This is your birthday party.

I glanced around the full kitchen. It looked the same as every night.

Oh, yeah. No, I mean, what day of the week.

Oh. I would never know that.

Yeah. Since when? We've been here how long?

Uh . . . forever?

That's what I was thinking.

We got lost in some stream, got melted. Powerful rain, one eye in music, which is this world clear. Bullshit fell away easily, incrementally, then exponentially. You can become songs. And sound is hyper-life.

So this time didn't end, exactly. Some times never do, because they *spill*, they don't buy into linear measurement; they're too alive. Best you can hope for is that you are forever changed, forever carrying a powerful thunderclap to step into when the buzz calls for it. Not real safe. In any way: economically, psychologically, socially . . . animal is animal, voodoo is voodoo. We got voodoo'd. It was so worth it.

The only vivid fear? Zombification.

♋ Ruthie's knocking

Ruthie's spine is taped with feathers

After dinner, we all tumbled out to the courtyard and slipped into the Roman bath to hold the babies in cool water, where the mosquitoes can't find you. More mercury: slipping, silver water and our engineer smoking a joint under the banana leaves. Following her smoke with twelve eyes, we watch a rat balance on a leaf bigger than a man's torso and leap to another leaf even bigger than that one. The banana leaves bend and shiver as the rat scurries down a stalk and disappears into the darkness. Dark is good for us hiding shy.

New Orleans in the summertime, when it is most itself. We live here dripping and creepy in this old house, me and my bandmates, and record in the living room. We are infused with a dark sleepiness that allows fiery energy to take hold only when playing asks for burning. Dirty and clean, dirty plus clean, dirty loving clean. They balance perfectly in this rat life, shaking down stems of a banana plant in pot smoke.

Songs are apples.

If songs were apples, people would like them.

Is there another six-pack in the back fridge?

Mmm . . . no. Want me to go out?

People like shiny, poisonous apples.

People with teeth.

Don't go out, you're wearing a bathing suit.

People with teeth?

Scary American teeth.

I was gonna put on clothes.

Fuck it, it's too hot.

Well that's what the beer was for.

Our silver puppy has not yet learned to swim or fear the water, so the children throw sticks away from the pool again and again, calling the word *crow* again and again. Crow scrambles and skitters, pudgy and toddling, chasing the sticks, which, thrown by tiny arms, do not land very far away.

Chalk-white American shopping teeth.

Shopping teeth.

Our apples are matte?

Not poisonous, yes. And misshapen plus vitamins and worms and unrecognizable to the shopping public as apples.

Sad.

Nah, just secret.

Secret sad.

I'm getting out. Meet you in the living room.
There might be beer. Check.

♋ gazebo tree

bless my baby eyes

When Crow is snoring and the babies are toweled and
tighty-whitied for bed, I lie between them, read them three
books, then turn out the light. When their breathing slows, I
can go back to work. They know nothing of the lady's ghost or
any ghost. They sleep hard and dream harder, happy to black
out and land in another world and then happy to black out
there and land in this one again. They bless both with their baby
eyes.

They also bless the leaf litter in the mornings with their baby
noses, walking Crow down Esplanade Avenue. Fall leaves in
summer grass are a thing of wrinkled and dewy beauty, with
the mixed scents of growing and dying, wetness and drying. Fall
leaves under water; this place is underwater, below sea level,
and pumping out the excess swamp moisture and rain. Bodies
used to float up out of cemeteries in the mush of bayou earth
before people realized they couldn't bury them. So now they
build them little houses. Cement beds, really. Cats live in the
cities of the dead with the dead; live on rats and rice and beans.
Try to bury something, it moves back in with you. Learn to live
with it and you do just that. Note to self.

♋ city of the dead

I won't stay awake if I can't kiss your fingers
I won't stay married cuz you won't stay buried
stop your talking in my dreams

In the living room, my drummer watches his hands to keep the
sticks from slipping out of his grasp and flying up into his eyes.
Which they often do in this heat. We played all day and he
took a few flying splinters to the face cuzza sweaty fingers. The
AC works a *little*, but the Big Easy isn't so easy when you try
to fight its heat, its greatest strength. The whole point is to go
limp, I guess. And we do. The first run-throughs are heavy with
squalor and laze. The first few takes, a blur of the same. The
snare is rattling and must be tightened before we can record
another take; my bass player noodles in boredom and adds a
melodic fill to his part that changes my guitar part.

That's pretty. May I . . . may I play it too?

If you ask nicely.

May I play it too?

Yes. We'll play it together. Don't tell him.

Our drummer looks up from his snare.

Don't tell me what?

Don't look at me.

Sorry.

The engineer asks if we're ready and we hear the click track
through her voice before we can answer. Falling into it by accident, we realize this take is in color and begin to believe each

measure, forget what we're doing. Forget we're doing *anything*. When a song walks into the room, everybody knows it. It's a body. Yeah, an apple when it falls, but also an alchemical blend of clean fire and dirty water. It rushes past and leaves no footprints and that song ghost has no idea we captured its image. As the last note fades, we remember what we heard, but lightly, as if we could crush the photograph with our minds. If we're dwarfed to invisible, the take is real. If we are bigger than the recording, it's a fail. When we decide we disappeared ourselves, the photograph isn't just for us, but safe to share— publishable—and we're allowed to go to sleep.

What time is it?
It's tomorrow.
Goodnight.
See you today.

♋ bright yellow gun

you leak one apple a week to survive
and you still have to ask if you're alive

The man walks with me in the damp warmth because there is a place down the road that can't pour a lemonade without also pouring a shit ton of vodka. They have fried alligator that's cheap and good and the storefront itself is nothing but linoleum and glass and grime and a fat cat next to some candles. Never black candles because voodoo, but always a new red wax to stack upon the old red wax, so the light is very, very beautiful in there. I'm gonna say it was like stars in a shoebox cuz, sorry, it was.

The others all dug an old bar, an ancient blacksmith's, and the very darkness of it and the time that had moved through it. And yeah, but I never felt the gentle ease there that the shoebox of stars was so good at. I like a storefront that you can slip in and out of without anybody thinking you're shoplifting or should be bothered with. Invisible, that's what I loved about that place; we were invisible there. Hard to get that without music. So cool that the most you can be is nothing. While something wriggled through our grasp like silver, slippery mosquito fish.

Invisibility's not a superpower.

It totally damn well is.

Ok, then we have it everywhere, not just in the alligator lemonade star shoebox.

♋ bywater

a long sidewalk summer
softer than haze on a shrine to the others
harder and harder to find
a red wax pile of kind

Too dreamlike, I guess, and magic folks freak the rest of us out. Some cities bark orders that get lost in their own shouting? But a southern whisper is a hurricane.

Redemption through sin: in that fragility, there's the conviction that cruising through darkness for one more cycle is a freedom. It's an elegant solution to an unsolvable key equation. It is broken *but*. One of the reasons we're here seems to be brokenness. Learn that beast and it spills out into our hands to pour into each other's hands when another one of us is broken and needs help. And then we catch a little broken to make our hearts smarter and it starts all over again.

Alligator lemonade star shoeboxes dirty us up with poison and clean us out with invisibility. Days help and hurt, painkillers help and hurt, we help, we hurt. And truly, we loved the hangovers. Part of the high. The Buddha's drunk is a gentling in the sun, hydration in the air and senses attuned to a sweeter truth. To soften your plans.

I walk the children and Crow through the Marigny and into the Bywater, to watch a tiny Mardi Gras, the floats at knee level. The horn players shuffle in a quiet line and southern whisper into their trumpets. The beads are glass, not plastic, and beautifully small. No hot air in this hot air, no bombast, all precious. Precious is a lesson: feel pain, cause none, and ghost ashes will not haunt you, will not sit on your chest, burning.

♋ vitamins v

the tub's overflowed
I'm still staring through the fish tank

The babies wake thirsty after a long night of music. I put them in the tub so they can watch the fish swim in their own tub over the staircase. Start the kettle, shower on the roof, and then lie down again because they're still splashing and I don't sleep very much. The fact that the tub water is now cold is a good thing this morning. It's so hot already. The carpet underneath the enameled claw-feet is soaked with splashing like it is every morning and stays soaked in the liquid air.

Dressed, but barely, we walk Crow, the silver puppy, enchanted again by the scent of raw grass and decomposing leaves in wet sun. The boys, shirtless, fill the pockets of their shorts with Mardi Gras beads fallen from trees as we walk. They carefully pronounce the names of everything we pass in the hope that Crow might someday speak.

Car.

Squirrel.

Tree.

Band-Aid.

Cigar.

Shiny beads are plucked from the grass and shoved in little pockets. Silver Crow sits, fig-shaped, and listens as the babies cheer him on.

Good, sit!

He's a good boy.

Crow lies down in the grass and dry leaves.

Down, Crow. Lie down.

Good boy!

He's a good boy.

It's really too hot for a dog to do much else, even a puppy.

Mom, he does all the tricks!
I know. He's a good boy.
He is.

Tiny Ryder walks slowly, so we do too. Also, the puppy is so fat and so hot, he just wants to lie in the shade. Stopping and looking down Esplanade, the boys hold hands for a minute, then let go. I don't know why they do this. Because they are puppies themselves, I guess.

♋ cherry candy

the sun shone on the city
harder than it did at home

Doony and Ry walked Crow up the back steps and into the garden, telling each other that the dog was a good boy. A journalist waited in the kitchen, as did the Bee Man, dressed in full apiary garb. We had never seen the Bee Man's face; couldn't see it through the netting spilling from his helmet and over his shoulders. He and the journalist each had a cup of thick, black coffee cooling in front of them on the old enamel kitchen table. It was too hot to drink hot coffee and the coffee was too thick to drink. My bandmates and I called it "silt" and downed it quickly, but a better caffeination came from the Bee Man in the form of pollen. Four jars were lined up on the table. I bought one of them because, as the musician responsible for all overdubs, I couldn't technically stop working long enough to eat or sleep;

we couldn't afford it. And this dude's bee pollen was nature's crack. I poured out a handful of granules and gave half to the journalist, who popped them into his mouth, pressed record on his microcassette recorder, and asked one question that I never answered because Doony ran back in then, panicked.

Baby Ryder doesn't know Santa!

What?

BABY RYDER DOESN'T KNOW SANTA! *I said Santa to him and he didn't know who it was!*

Well . . . did you tell him?

No! You're the mom.

The journalist stared, turned the mic toward me, and wrote something in his notepad. The Bee Man was facing us, but he might have been sleeping for all we could see through his mask. Doony splayed his hands.

Mom, you have to tell Ryder about Christmas. He's a little kid. He needs Christmas.

But . . . it's August.

Doony looked at me the way only a kid with the ability to raise one eyebrow can. I turned to the journalist.

Do you mind?

He was already beaming.

On the record?

Uh . . . I dunno, I guess. Think your readers are maybe fuzzy on the Santa thing?

They could always use a refresher.

Ryder was led in by the hand, ceremoniously. His eyes were huge. Doony tiptoed out of the room, solemn. Lifting Ry onto my lap, I tried to begin but couldn't find the words. Asking the journalist with my eyes didn't help; he just watched. The Bee

Man sat, a white mountain of man-shape, as I whispered at them over Ryder's soft hair.

Baby Jesus?

The journalist shook his head.

I'd go secular.

Right. Still kind of a lot to cover.

Better get started, then.

Ryder sat perfectly still on my lap, watching the Bee Man with gentle fear.

It's ok, honey. Christmas is a good thing.

I looked around for a visual aid, thought maybe I should draw something, but I didn't see any paper. The journalist checked to see that his tape recorder was running. I took a breath.

Ok, I'll just start.

Ryder looked up at me.

Do you remember your birthday, honey? All the presents?

He nodded. I spoke slowly.

Christmas is like that, but it's at night. In the dark, while you're asleep. And a man . . . a fat man . . . a red, fat man . . . in red clothes, I mean, crawls into our house. Down a chimney, and I know you don't know what a chimney is, but that's ok. It's part of a house that's . . . over fire.

The journalist squinted.

But we won't have a fire. And the man's name is Santa. Claus. And his job? Is building toys. No wait. He has small people where he lives. The North Pole. It snows all the time there and the small people—the elves—make toys. And put the toys in a bag and put the bag on a sled that Santa drives. No, flies, the night before Christmas. Actually, all of this is before Christmas. Do you know what a sled is?

Ryder looked back at the Bee Man. I kept going.

A sled is like a tricycle for snow.

The journalist sputtered and I sighed.

It's not, is it? See, he has a tricycle. Anyway. It has a kind of deer attached to it, called reindeer. Do you know what a reindeer is?

Ry looked up at me, baffled.

No. Hmmm . . . it's a reindeer? Which is like a unicorn but it flies. Well, not usually, but Santa Claus has eight? Of them and these special ones fly. And they're not like unicorns, sorry. A unicorn is a horse, right? These are deer. I think maybe they're tiny. Eight tiny reindeer. And Rudolph, the first one, the one in the front, has a red light bulb for a nose.

I stopped.

Would you like something to drink?

The journalist's head dropped a few inches, so he caught it with his hand. Ryder shook his head. A miniature Santa Claus figurine pushed through the purple curtain hanging in the door-way, gripped by Doony's little fingers.

Oh, great! Thank you, baby, where'd you find that? Bring it over here. This is the Santa Man but he's bigger than this. Maybe elves are this big, I dunno. Oh, and hey, jingle bells! You love jingle bells. We have some here. They sound super cool. And Christmas songs. Carols. Not the crappy kinda Christmas song. Gingerbread men.

The journalist rested his forehead on the table and spoke into it.

"The Santa Man." Why don't you just tell him where babies come from?

You know, that'd be easier. Ok, I'll start over. Santa has a wife, Mrs. Claus. Don't want to leave her out; people're always leaving women outta the story.

The journalist picked up his head long enough to roll his eyes, then dropped it again. I laughed.

Gingerbread men and gingerbread women! Ok. Santa finds our house at night because of Rudolph's red nose and lands on the roof in his big sled, called a sleigh. And while all of the special flying deer wait up there, he gets out with the bag of toys that elves made in the North Pole and climbs down the chimney over the fireplace. Without fire. And—

The Bee Man stuck a gloved finger in the air.

Cookies.

He was *alive.* I glanced at him gratefully.

Yes! Inside our house, he eats cookies that we gave him. And milk. And then . . . oh god, there's a tree. I forgot. We get a tree. I mean, before this. We will-have-gotten a pine tree outside in a parking lot, and we'll keep it inside our house. We'll put crooked mints on it and a—

Crooked mints.

The writer was so sad and so happy. I was lost in a haze of Rankin/Bass claymation. Ryder was just lost. The Bee Man had become a still, white mountain again.

Well. I don't think he knows what a cane is. They're called candy canes, honey. They're candy, um . . . hooks. Like minty fishhooks and you hang them on the branches of the pine tree that we carried into our house. Earlier. And. Did I say presents? I did. Like on your birthday. He gives you presents. The, uh . . . fat Santa Man.

The writer looked alarmed.

Minty fishhooks.

Ignoring him, I held the doll up.

And there are lights everywhere! Beautiful lights. That might be the best part of Christmas.

I addressed the room.

Is that the best part of Christmas?

The journalist, Bee Man, and Doony all shook their heads. I shrugged, at a loss. The Bee Man held his finger up again.

Stockings.

My mouth dropped open.

Shit! Stockings! Sorry, honey. God, Christmas is complicated.

Doony's expression froze with an eyebrow raised high on his forehead. I turned to him in desperation.

I have to go back to work. Think you could finish up?

Suddenly remembering that this was an interview, I asked the journalist if he had any actual questions.

Just one: why do you have a southern accent?

Aw, geez. Cuz Southern is my first language and I'm time-tripping right now and don't say that explains a lot, cuz it doesn't.

Yes, it does.

No, it doesn't.

Okay.

He wrote something in his notepad.

Doony? Hold your brother's hand and make sure he has no Christmas shell shock. I'm sorry, Ryder. It's gonna be fun!

Ryder tried to smile but just looked sweetly concerned. The Bee Man's finger went up one more time.

Snow.

I turned to him, amazed, almost wept with gratitude. Clean, beautiful snow was waiting for the babies on the island when we were through learning the hot and dirty melting lesson of New Orleans. I kissed both boys.

Snow, babies. It'll snow.

♋ halfway home

rat banana leaves waving goodbye

When melting itself melts: entropy isn't a badness. We describe process as more than right and wrong, walking crooked lines, landing in lessons until we're swamp-rich and done. Done for now, anyway.

When the killer bees appear on the third floor where we sleep—gradually, over a period of weeks—they hover, making eye contact with us, then drop and dart around the children's ankles. The boys unfazed, unstung. The killer bees store several pounds of killer honey under the floorboards, which the Bee Guy removes, jar by killer jar. Briefly, he lifts the netting over his face to wipe away tears because Africanized bees must be destroyed. This is the first time we've seen his face and it's crying. We tell him, no, leave the bees and we'll leave the house, but it's too late. This is sobering. He drives away, diminished by the afternoon, and we blame ourselves.

Why is it always war between people and animals?

And why do we always gotta win?

We can't handle our animal natures, so we punish the animal outside.

Y'all do the same thing to women, you know.

I know.

✳ ✳ ✳ ✳

When the house becomes electrified, we are shocked by things that don't usually shock you: shower spray, for example, and silverware, the telephone, walls. We're shocked by nearly everything we touch; it's like trying to live with lightning.

Maybe we should let lightning keep the house.

It's a lousy roommate.

What if we're the lousy roommates?

Until an electrician friend willing to slip off his rusty bike and slip under the soggy, old structure—crawl through the rats and the dead rats and the dead everything and the detritus of a couple hundred years—tweaks some wires and we all live. He is an uncomfortable beast made of unimaginableness when he finally pulls himself out on his stomach.

There's a whole city down there.

Is it gross?

Depends on what you think is gross. The rats like it.

Did we fuck with their city?

. . . a little, yeah. They know they aren't safe anymore.

This is also sobering.

✳ ✳ ✳ ✳

When the music business sneaks in—people who don't understand that music is unselfish—we chase it away to go wake up
at home, away from our record. My bandmates and I, pussies
all around, *scare* these people with a badly taxidermied ocelot, a
walleyed and grief-stricken ocelot, a dead-forever ocelot named
Hecubus. We place it in their beds, dress it in their clothes, and
put their headphones on its scruffy ears. It's in their closets, their
cars. We position it outside their doors so that it's the first thing
they see in the morning, or in their showers so that it's the *very*
first thing they see in the morning, or sleeping next to them so
it's even firster. Hecubus gave his life a long time ago and we
honor his hairless, unselfish nature by accepting his help.

Thinking our melting mansion is haunted—having heard
about the ghost on fire many, many times from each of us—
these people leave of their own accord. Our record is then freed
from bad influences and that was maybe mean, but you gotta
do what you gotta do and sometimes you can't, so you do what
you can and you accept help from dead ocelots. Hecubus is
returned to his station on the grand staircase immediately adja-
cent to where we record in the living room. But having played a
role in a dark ritual, he is even less funny; a sobering image of
our species going after another win. We're sure he'd rather be
alive and selfish than stuffed and helpful.

✷ ✷ ✷ ✷

When I put on a shirt with a black widow spider in it, I'm bitten
twice. Wacky things happen when a black widow bites you,
just FYI. I brag that I faced two deadly spiders because I have

two bites, but, really, I just put on a bad shirt, then watched a little, shiny dude scamper away in terror. And called myself a survivor.

Between Piety Street and Desire Street, a Bywater witch doctor tells me she can't treat me because she's arachnophobic. I grimace at her.

Well . . . the spiders are gone. They left. I'm not wearing them. And it was probly just one, but don't tell my bandmates.

Still. I don't think I can help you.

Ok.

But, you know. Spider medicine's powerful.

This is medicine?

Of a sort.

♋ between piety and desire

and we don't like the shit between piety and desire
we don't like the shit cuz we belong in it

When I share four grains of crack bee pollen with my bass player as he's leaving for a run in the French Quarter, he returns with an Elephant Man face, unable to breathe. We are musicians and musicians don't have health insurance, so I stay on the line with Poison Control, checking his vitals and reporting his symptoms, while his head slowly shrinks back to its natural state and oxygen flows reliably through his body again. This takes days. He could have died, but the killer bees *did* die. And they were just as alive as he is. This is sobering.

The bees' revenge.
The bees' revenge.

When you're inescapably sober? It's time to leave New Orleans. The melting lesson learned, it was time to leave anyway. The melting lesson: fall apart.

♋ serene

lose control

When a hurricane hit, we arranged tall ladders around the soggy house and taped up windows. Taped up everything indiscriminately, really. And waited for our flight out, parked in a row on an antique chaise longue, listening to the purple sky crack open and the rain splash as it filled first the rainspouts, then the gutters. The streets filled quickly after that, drowning cars; beautiful and dangerous. Yin laughing.

Twitchy, restless reporters in a war zone, we hugged stiller, more firmly rooted people over rusty bicycles and a grief-frozen ocelot. The dirty lesson: a clean heart.

Then we booked home, promising to come back for Christmas.

♋ secret codes

sorta know how to pray
you just ache with hope 'til it goes away

We did go back for Christmas, just like we promised. All that crazy hurricane water was gone then. Walking in the Marigny on Christmas Day in a thick, cool, floating mist, I stepped off the sidewalk to avoid an enormous puddle of blood that had spilled off the curb and into the street; a prayer of hope for the hopeless repeating itself in my head.

A homeless man shuffled to a stop and joined me, both of us staring down at the spreading red. He sighed into it.

You think that's all blood?

His enormous nature showing itself in his own hope for the hopeless; some story that might play out as . . . what? Spilled paint? Which is unlikely, so, yeah, *some* blood, *some* violence and pain, but also, you know, we were gonna make our mailbox a prettier red and we tripped. So, no, it's not *all* blood. The sweetness. *That's* a prayer. I looked at him, then back down at the red ground.

Huh. I don't know.

Then he sort of tipped his hat like a cowboy in an old movie. Except his cowboy hat was an old fishing cap he probly found in the street. The gesture was beautiful. He smiled sadly.

Well . . . Merry Christmas anyway.

✳ ✳ ✳ ✳

Maybe you oughta go back home.

—*Bachelor Mother*

Our island is dry, clean, alert and waiting. We dry out there, sober up there, live clean, wake up. And try not to forget dirty melting.

Bachelor Mother, with Ginger Rogers and David Niven, plays on the tiny black-and-white TV I've had since I was a teenager, stuck in the kitchen wall. Doesn't show TV, only old movies; this one on repeat cuz Ginger Rogers *invented* backward-in-high-heels. Talking about it, anyway. A family of squirrels knocks softly on the kitchen door every morning, asking for breakfast. With very, very tiny knuckles. If they get no response, they scratch with tiny claws. And *chit* in distress.

We live in a small, broken house with our babies and Crow. A house we painted obnoxious cartoon colors because we couldn't handle paint swatches. They were all white but claimed not to be.

Ivory, bone, eggshell.
Ecru, off-white, origami white.
White heron, light beige, snow.
Windfresh, eider, rose white.
Cream, white mint, polar.
Frost, paper white, ice.
Swiss. Swiss?
Probly the same as snow.

The man sleeping next to me in our Matisse Green room with Orange Gay trim. Fun fact: "orange gay" is bright yellow. So, the man sleeping next to me, I see a sad, strange boy by the window who asks if he can curl up on my stomach. I know I'm dreaming but I also know I haven't fallen asleep yet. In the morning, the man tells me he dreamt a sad ghost boy was in our room; a ghost boy who curled up on my stomach. Leaving the room to vomit, I pray the prayer of hope for the hopeless that the ghost baby will be ok.

✳ ✳ ✳ ✳

INTERVIEW:

Q: How do you juggle music and motherhood?

A: I don't juggle anything, I just hold the balls that were handed to me. Songs and babies are the same. They grow themselves if I keep them safe and don't get in their way. So I put sweaters on songs and pour their cereal, you know. If you start thinking songs and babies are *yours*—your creations that belong to you? And tell them what to do, what to say . . . you've missed the point.

Q: Do you sleep?

A: Sometimes. And the sleep-deprived keep a foot in dreams anyway, so it's nothing to whine about. Shark sleeping is one of the most spiritual acts we got going.

♋ shark

your eyes aren't too clear

New York, in the greenroom before doing a late-night TV show I had never seen. I watched dress rehearsal on the monitor: a slanted shot of a man at a desk, slumped over, as if he and the cameraman had both passed out. This static image remained on the fuzzy, greenish TV for long enough to keep me frowning and staring at it. I grabbed an orange out of the fruit bowl and peeled it, watching. Slight movement *around* the slumped-over guy as a stagehand adjusted something and left.

They cut to footage of twin boys holding baseball bats in front of a green-screen forest fire. The kids didn't speak, just stood there grinning awkwardly. The fire disappeared and they remained in the shot, giggling over green. Back to the guy slumped over at his desk. Then a shot of a list of TV shows. Two of our two and a half children jumped off a couch and landed on the floor, then did it again—the only possible game to play in a greenroom—as I squinted up at the man.

What the hell . . .

Is this a popular show?

I dunno.

Well, it's challenging anyway. Pretty fuckin' arty.

Yeah, they're trying something.

That guy ok?

The slumped-over guy suddenly sat upright, yelling, and he was a crazy color: ash pink. His hair stuck straight up and his long arms flailed.

THAT'S NOT FUNNY!

Screaming seemed to take it out of him. His body dropped like a dead puppet; his limp torso just a lumpy extension of the desk again. The twin boys were reintroduced, with their forest fire. The dead puppet screamed from his slumped over position.

GODDAMN IT, THAT'S NOT FUNNY!

This was dress rehearsal? Like, this is the camera angle they chose for this shot?

That's cool, I guess. Kinda postapocalyptic.

Have you ever seen this show?

No. Television's changed a lot since we last saw it.

I whispered to the man that he should maybe take the boys out into the city for lunch because, while jumping is cool, it doesn't *stay* cool; it quickly lapses into wanting to climb out windows or lying on the floor making weird plans. There were no windows in this room, but still. The babies heard the word "lunch" and stopped jumping to look expectantly at their father. But when the man opened the dressing room door, a tense woman with a headset and clipboard was standing there, already talking to him.

Yes? Can I help you?

He almost shut the door, but the boys were waiting for him to help them leave.

No, thanks. I'm just taking our kids out for a while.

Her tenseness got tenser.

We'll have a runner get you whatever you need.

Oh, we don't need anything.

He pointed at me.

She's the guest; we're her family. I'm just taking our kids out, like for lunch or something.

More tense.

I'll have someone bring you takeout menus.

I, uh . . . that's ok. I'm just taking our children outside. She's staying here. She's the guest.

The children watched as the woman spoke into her headset, then addressed the man again.

I'll be right back.

The door making a sucking noise, then vacuum sealing shut.

We can't leave.

It's not her fault.

Should I get takeout?

Lie on the floor, boys. Make weird plans.

On the monitor, the camera briefly righted itself. The dead puppet was back up and yelling.

NOOOOOOOOOOO!

I turned to the man.

I've been treated like a freak for my whole career. I can't wait to be the straight man.

Yeah. You'll bore these people.

The dead puppet stood unsteadily and walked off-screen. He appeared to be about eight feet tall. As soon as he was out of the shot, the camera slowly tipped until the puppet's desk was completely sideways.

What a strange show.

When the door opened again, the headset woman stuck her headset face in and addressed me.

Ready for you. Just a sound check, you don't need stage clothes.

I looked down at what I was wearing. "Stage clothes." Even this crazy show wants me better dressed. Fuck 'em. You don't learn the dirty melting lesson just to be clean.

♋ cleaner light

in a cleaner light
it's ok

The dead puppet turned out to be the host himself, which I had suspected, but . . . I just wondered how he'd gotten his own show. All I knew was that he was a writer—a good one—and angry and slumped over was definitely like other writers I knew. Just didn't realize there was an audience for ash-pink yelling. I mean, godspeed, you know. Crack it open.

But in the interview, the host was a polished, charming creature. Strangely unhuman, but his hair was neatly combed, his expression sweet and intelligent, his pallor American tan. He was quick and articulate. Appeared to be a pretty upbeat guy. The only thing he had in common with the dead puppet at dress rehearsal was that he did seem to be about eight feet tall.

As the last guest, I was instructed to stay on the couch until the closing credits were completely over. While the audience clapped, waiting for the "CLAP" sign to be turned off, the host thanked me for being there and said something nice about my record. But I wanted to know *what the fuck*, so I interrupted him.

I saw dress rehearsal on the monitor.

For a moment, the dead puppet flitted across the man's eyes.

Oh yeah?

Yeah. You ok?

Kristin? I wake up every morning wanting to kill myself.

Jesus.

He looked stricken.

The pressure. You can't be funny every day; it's not possible.

So . . . are you ok?

I am right now because the show's over. And I'll be ok when I go home and I'll go to bed ok tonight, but in the morning? I'll wake up wanting to die. I always wake up wanting to die.

I stared at this nice giant who was gonna want to off himself tomorrow.

Life's not always funny, huh?

No. And I'm a comedian. That's tragic.

♋ gin

I know it makes you swallow hard
here's the plan: don't leave your backyard

Driving home from New York, I saw this bright giant's stricken face through the windshield, like the broken, white fireworks over the same highway years ago . . . that were actually breaking bodies up there, falling in their exploding airplane. Our American joke isn't funny; the host's ash-pink screaming still in my head, *Goddamn it, that's not funny!* Taken from other cautionary tales and inflated to a degree that has left us convinced that we are without depth.

We could write our culture with our *lives*: flick pretty out, so ugly and beautiful shine. See each other clearly but with love. It's a tightrope.

There is a perfect ludicrous that hits so deep, we feel each other's pain. Real music balances in this sweet spot, and real laughter. Musicians and comedians walk a line when they monetize this spontaneity. The fact that we ever put art and entertainment in the same sentence may say something about who we once were—inclusive and fundamentally giving—but having been taken from *people* and placed in the hands of corporate beehives, these two disciplines are opposed. The bees become killer, the honey, poison. The term "art" is synonymous with privilege, while "entertainment" is for imaginary dummies. Neither is real.

Why wouldn't art entertain us when life is the highest art form? Richness is in inspired moments of enthusiasm and kindness; personal and interpersonal. Work that reflects this hits deep. If it doesn't? It's not work *or* life, just a misapprehension.

Here's a rant. Totally phase out if you want.

Walking into the spotlight is walking away from the work we were meant to do for each other in our small worlds. Like kids with lousy parents—*We're so proud of the attention you got!*—we earn only a distortion of love. The spotlight is bought and paid for; the conceit is that the audience shares an opinion.

You *can* write jokes that aren't funny, write songs that aren't music. But forced laughter dies away, is not substantive, and you forget the bad joke, so it doesn't become a part of you. You will never be made of candy because it doesn't feed you, in other words. You will not grow. A fake song is selfish, a showing off. It was never a part of *anyone*, so it will never be a part of *you*. And dancing to candy makes your teeth fall out.

The journalist adjusted his glasses.

Q: "Dancing to candy"?
A: You know what I mean.
Q: *I* know what you mean. But . . . you want me to write that down?
A: No . . . don't write anything down. Let's just talk.
Q: My editor'd love that.
   (I laughed.)
A: Our goal should be resonance. Told you it was a rant.
Q: Yeah, but elaborate.
A: I can sound a little didactic.
Q: Go for it.
A: 'K, but be kind. It'll be another rant.
Q: Rant away.
A: The only true cultural shifts are small fish, small pond. After that, an honest movement is an organic snowballing effect:

an idea spreads when its time has come. It has become necessary and therefore beautiful. What an opportunity for that kind of growth America is, as a melting pot; politically, artistically, socioeconomically. But the word "culture" is a misnomer here. We aren't a culture, we're an economy. We mimic an impression of cultures we've heard of, but our system is a pickpocket talking at your face while it reaches behind you for your wallet. It views invention with suspicion, it has no patience for organic shifts that make no one money, bring no one attention.

Some of us don't like having our faces talked at, so the populace looks crazy to us, just absorbing marketing and trying to be like everyone else when there *is* no everyone else.

But if that's all you know, you adopt marketing spiels as your own opinions, believing that it's what everyone else is doing. Advertisers call it bandwagon appeal. The marketers know there was never really anyone in the wagon to begin with; they're just buying attention for their product with the threat of isolation. Or: *this is what better people are doing . . . would you like to be one of them?* Snob appeal is even worse. Fear and greed. To them, everything is potentially a product: politics, food, sex, safety, art, information, travel, medicine, news, education, home, spirituality, clothing, parenting, books, health, film, music.

They co-opt Maslow's hierarchy and sell it back to us . . . and then some. Nobody cashes in when we sleep with people we love, play our own music, move our bodies to help others: live our idiosyncratic lives and keep an internal monologue going, you know?

Q: Right. So where is music in this equation?

A: Everywhere, like it always was.

Q: Everywhere . . .

A: Except the music business.

Q: This is your opinion? That there's no music in the music business.

A: Well, yeah, it's my opinion; it's not empirical information. There's maybe a little music in the music business, not much. Cuz they want product. And this is *my* interview, I can say what I want.

Q: Okay if I write it down?

A: I think I . . . don't care. Is *that* okay?
   (He laughs.)

Q: Yeah. That's okay.

A: But I also didn't make it up. Anyone who's ever experienced an actual song knows this.

Q: I get that they want to keep people dumb because it's easy money. But . . . why is there so *much* dumb?

A: You know what? There isn't *any*. That is the first lie they tell us and the most important hurdle we gotta pull each other over. We're born with the will to cooperate, not compete, and to offer something. That's it. Love, work, and bodies. Give with these things. It's *great* here. Wake up to that.

Q: You really *are* a hippie.

A: Duh-uh.

The music writer I was speaking with'd moved into our slanted little cartoon house for a while; I guess to write down everything we said and did, though I rarely caught him writing. Writers are cool that way. The real ones.

A touring musician crashed on our couch for a few days of this and joined the conversation. Yawning over his coffee, he spat elaborately and fluttered his fingers in the air to illustrate the confetti shower of appeal for our wallets and the denigration of substance.

We've just been sold to so consistently that value is associated with selling. And nothing of value is ever sold. Hardly ever, anyway.

This is true, this is true, this is true.

It's not okay.

How is it ever gonna be okay?

It's not.

It has to be.

So we go to the beach. And I try to tell them about the spicy olives I'm picking up for dinner at a salty little shop on the water, but baby nausea chokes me on the word "olive" and I leave the thought hanging. The ghost baby doesn't like us to eat. The men stare after my hanging phrase and the writer squeezes my arm, mistaking sickness for darkness.

It's gonna be okay. We will win. Mission first. Don't be one of the soldiers we lose.

The other musician shifts his squint to the gray waves. We all know that we will lose him.

On the cold beach, my children scatter and return to each other, leaving footprints and line drawings in the sand. They draw seaweed people and make them talk. Watching them, we grow silent. Nausea colors my world while removing color from my world, the way a cave dive might. The colors are there, I guess; we just can't see them, which alters our concept of light. There are more important things to do in caves deep underwater and in the process of growing other humans under a rib cage than enamor oneself of saturation: focus requires having few distractions. My muted color wheel gives me a granular perspective I need for the ghost baby, but I am in no position to help him. He is already drawing this.

* * * *

The ghost boy began drawing before he was born. Quiet Wyatt, the baby who didn't cry, had it all storyboarded by the time he eased himself into life. His version of cellular will had a foot in this plane and a foot in the other. Any half-ghost lives an orientation like that. At his birth—after seventy-two hours of labor—his father slipped down the wall, unconscious. But Wyatt would *always* be conscious, staring with ocean eyes. And always in a dream, staring with ocean eyes.

He drew and drew and drew and we walked into his scenes. Before he could walk, Quiet Wyatt was drawing us a world. Sage green. He drew a desertscape movie set that we obediently moved in to as characters in his cartoon. Pioneertown, California, a town in the Mojave Desert of a few dozen people and a few dozen movie facades, on a dirt road up above Joshua Tree. Way up, like four thousand feet up. So high that snow could settle gently on the green sage and cactus in winter. So dry that the road could be blocked by fire wall in summer. Coyotes and roadrunners. All senses engaged, one of the coolest things you can be is a cartoon: unpretentious, obstreperous, and fundamentally sweet.

Cartoons will save us.

Music stopped in that place. For the first time in my life since my skull had cracked open and let it in when I was a kid,

I heard nothing but wind through the whispering pines; god's harmonica or something, I guess, but after a life of noise it was strikingly muted. A thunderclap of silence, like a memory of sound. An echo. Wyatt taught me quiet.

♋ echo

can you hear the loudest sound and you and me in the echo?

Baby Wy liked to watch bats drink from a corrugated metal cattle watering tank on our land. We had no cattle, so we swam in it and told ourselves we had a pool, but were careful to hop out at sunset when clouds of bats came to drink. Gliding down sideways, they skimmed the surface, lifted instantly and circled, again and again. Young and clumsy bats miscalculated and had to be rescued, landing like ducks instead of escaping the pull of surface tension. Bats aren't great swimmers. Wyatt pointed helpfully when another bat went down and then the man would grab a skimmer and gently place the fuzzy wetness on the deck to dry out. The bat, eyeing us—maybe suspiciously, maybe gratefully, we never figured out which—would flop around a little, slow and goofy.

We loved the bats. When they were wet, we all hung out on the deck together and watched the sun set. A bat on pause is a precious thing. The tiny, flickering mark of dark on a wide sky finally calmed, eye to eye, vulnerable and charming. Lifting one wing at a time, they dried quickly, though. And then they were gone. A bat flies like a swallow, quivering and swooping. Beautiful to watch, but we liked them best soggy and visiting. We were selfish. Wanted to *keep* them.

You don't sweat in the desert, not visibly; movies are wrong. Like, five percent humidity or something. Bread I made the boys' sandwiches on'd go stale before they could eat more than half, but bags of tortilla chips stayed open and fresh for months. Just as an experiment, really, but it was cool. Couldn't keep enough salsa in the house for chips that never went stale.

People in town lived in cowboy facades—saloons and brothels—but our movie set was an elaborate Moroccan lean-to. A dusty fantasy a friend built on sixty acres and handed over to us one night under a hypnosis of a kind; a beery generosity spell.

Pay me a dollar a day, I dunno. Just bring the boys and move in.

A dollar a day? For your house?

It's your house. I built it for you.

You did?

Well. I didn't know it at the time, just now realized. Plus, I got a house I wanna build next door and I like to know who my neighbors are.

Your neighbors are sixty acres away.

Still. I don't like to drink alone.

So we did. We brought the boys and moved into a life shell, like all the other hermit crabs in Pioneertown. Had no idea Quiet Wyatt was the one writing this script, moving the chess pieces around. Had I known it was ghost baby magic, well . . . I would've moved in sooner. Ghost babies know what's up, can see the whole chessboard from above: black and white pieces graying out, past and future moves. The concepts that tend to wriggle out of our grasp, fate's mosquito fish. Might've been a burden, now that I think about it. The world is a cartoonist's oyster and that oyster demands care and respect. A balancing act to overlook pearls for funnier pearls. They need the land of sleep to speak over the land of things. So you look into Wyatt's ocean eyes and catch a glimpse of heavy spiral. It must have been lonely.

New Orleans's saturated melting learned, the sage-green will in him determined our next lesson: stripped to bones and seared by sun with a touch of snowflake on cactus and goofy coyote medicine. The sun is an odd master; bodies require careful handling in that terrain. And while I did sometimes wonder who was writing this, who was drawing this, I can't say it ever occurred to me that it might be the baby. You can't watch anyone twenty-four seven, even though I tried. His reaching paintbrush fingers, stretching past my arms in the dark, groping for a picture of this.

His first word: moon. Wy said, "Moon," while pointing straight up into that desert forever of a billion and one spinning stars.

And later:

We're painting this.

✴ ✴ ✴ ✴

INTERVIEW:

Q: I saw you on TV the other night. You were introduced as a housewife.

A: I *am* a housewife.

Q: Aren't you a musician?

A: Sure, but everybody's a musician. Potentially, anyway. A housewife creates and facilitates *lives*. Fuckin' scary.

Q: Scary.

A: Yeah. Scary as shit. And fun as hell.

✻ ✻ ✻ ✻

♋ milk at mcdonald's

every coyote in the freezer

The dude who built our house played along, following Wyatt's script, grateful for the chance to become neighborly. The beery spell remained unbroken, in other words, and he became another character in Wy's desert cartoon. Baby Wy floated above the dream, moving us action figures around to suit his cartoon about it, and this desert dude didn't fight it, was happy coming over in the evenings to play checkers with Ryder.

Little man . . . up for a game?

His checkerboard under his arm. And Ryder's little face, grave.

Come into the playroom. That's where we play.

Every night at sunset, pretty much. Ry's little sneakers kicking back and forth a few feet above the ground, as he beat the shit outta the desert dude. Who once called Ry "a mean checker player" and meant it as a compliment, but gentle Ryder wept at the idea of being mean and from then on let the desert dude win every game. To thank Ry, the dude brought us rosy boas to play with. Sweetest snake there is: pink and green and curious. Then he put them back where he found them.

Beautiful snakes there, my god. California kings, gopher snakes, rattlers, coachwhips. The man once caught a four-foot gopher snake that immediately bit him. A sizzling bite. Literally, the fang marks bubbled and burned. I asked him to maybe not pass out and he promised it was nothing, a little embarrassed. The gopher snake huffed away into the sage, pissed.

We'd find rattlers in the hills, under boulders, and at the base of Joshua trees. In shadow at noon, sunshine morning and evening. The dog'd run into them first and stop short, wagging his tail and smiling at us. Rattlers find your eyes, hold their ground, shy and aware.

Bafflingly, the desert dude left a coyote in the freezer for us. A coyote pelt. Wasn't sure what to think about it or do with it. Just didn't buy ice cream for a while and left the coyote alone in its deep freeze out of respect. And fear. Every now and then, I'd forget and, in Pioneertown's arid searing, go looking for ice cubes. Then make the same scared face again at the tawny fur in a Hefty bag, before letting the freezer door close by itself. The coyote had not died of natural causes but had been roadkill as yet undiscovered by vultures; pristine and glossy. So the desert dude thought: *taxidermy*. Which isn't what would occur to everyone. Or me. But yeah, this coyote was run down and waiting in our freezer for a zombification that was not kicking in. A Hecubus in limbo.

One morning, I carried Baby Wy into the kitchen to find a visiting musician friend staring into our freezer. I stood behind him and stared too. He looked at me with haunted eyes.

Is it ok?

Mmmm . . . I wouldn't think so.
What was it?
Coyote.
Roadrunner?
Car.
Oh. Sad.

This kind man found a shovel in the garage and laid the pelt
to rest behind a stone wall. Dug through terra-cotta sand and
chocolate mud to give the coyote back to the desert. I thanked
him and went out for ice cream to take its place. We're all garbage. In a good way. Wildflowers covered the mound he left,
patted down with the back of the shovel. I'm sure vultures eventually found the skin, and that's as it should be, but the coyote
had a funeral of sorts, was not zombified. Went home.

♋ home

you are some swell trash

Wyatt drew blue birds in the sage green and we discovered a
closet off the side porch that held a bin full of birdseed. Every
morning before the sun came up, I'd fill a silver scoop with millet
and sunflower seeds and scatter it in a clearing between a cluster
of barrel cactus and jumping cholla. My theory was: *birds like
me cuz I'm Snow White*. Not: *birds like birdseed cuz they're
hungry*. A shining royal-blue beauty with half a beak would
perch on the windowsill and wait for me to shower in order
to be the first bird to breakfast. Then, on the gritty, sparkling

sand, I spun in a circle and made spirals of seed around me as scrub jays and cactus thrashers yelled and dive-bombed my feet. I think they didn't love me as much as I loved them, in other words. A journalist watched from the window.

I think they don't love you as much as you love them.
I know. They think they steal my breakfast every day.
Uh-huh. And what do you think?
I think I'm Snow White.

INTERVIEW:

Q: Let's talk about birds. Why do you live out here in the middle of nowhere?

A: This is the middle of *some*where.

Q: Why do you live out here in the middle of somewhere?

A: We're learning desert.

Q: You don't want to keep up?

A: I keep up with children, music, animals, and the phases of the moon. What else is there to keep up with?

Q: Your industry?

A: It's not *my* industry. What it does to music is not harmless.

Q: It hurts music?

A: It hurts *people*, I guess. It can only hurt music as much as televangelism hurts spirituality. A perversion of a valuable aspect of humanity. Everyone knows a Grammy is an award for a marketing department, but they don't always see that their opinions are too. Marketing warps their response.

Q: Uh-huh. Why listen?

A: Desperation to keep up? Fear of . . . falling off the world. Cuz we're sweetly social. Imagine how much money they'd stop making if we all played our own music, lived our own lives.

Q: Industries would collapse. My concern is that . . . no one will hear what you do.

A: I don't need anyone to hear what I do. I just want them to become musically literate so they can't be lied to anymore. They've been lied to for so long.

Q: So how come people like lies?

A: They don't. They're just comfortable with the script. Lousy music is an insult. Everyone is born a focused musician and an attuned listener. Some of us choose to forget this.

Q: Why?

A: Love vs. like. Love is not for sale.

Q: But which survives?

A: Depends on your definition of survival, of a full life. If you like *rich* or *famous* in yourself or others, do better and you'll do better. They're the two most significant indicators of having missed the point. You don't want those people writing your soundtrack.

Q: No . . .

A: I used to want the business to do better; now I think the only art is life and so's the only entertainment. I'm just wholly enthusiastic about real. It's such a nice place.

Q: 'Til you starve.

A: Yes. Until we starve.

Q: Let's talk about birds.

✳ ✳ ✳ ✳

It rained. And I don't say this lightly. Rain in the desert is a godding anomaly. A hard rain too; muddying eddies swirling

and silver bullets pounding our metal roof. The noise was over-
whelming. I took the boys outside and we swung on the porch
swing, watching a water wall land on the fire wall's territory.
Watched the water try to clean mud. Wyatt toddled to the edge
of the porch and stood staring. Stood until the ghost fire sur-
rendered and the dirt was clean and the water won. "Rain," he
said. And then, much later:

I was born for rain on sage.

♋ lavender

```
I watch the muddy eddies swirl
I swing and swing and watch the water clean
```

Let's talk about birds.

A neighbor who lived out in the hills offered to teach us
how to feed roadrunners. She said it'd be easy as long as we
weren't afraid of beaks. The boys and I looked at each other. We
didn't *feel* afraid of beaks, but these were essentially dinosaur
beaks. Apparently, the reason roadrunners never showed up for
breakfast was that they're carnivorous; something I should have
known from seeing the little dinosaurs run down roads. They
always had lizards—littler dinosaurs—in their mouths. I didn't
feel like sacrificing any lizards, though, and I wasn't sure how
cool throwing raw meat around in a desert spiral like I did with
seeds woulda been, so we didn't get to hang with roadrunners
and the boys felt that we were missing out.

Our neighbor said they were bold, that we could feed them
by hand, and I figured, yeah, you gotta dinosaur when given the

chance. Then she said the beak thing again and I glanced at my boys' beautiful little fingers. Shot them a *yikes* look, but they were determined to dinosaur.

Holding out a dusty red frisbee full of raw hamburger, our neighbor made some clacking noises and shuffled her feet in the sand. Her bloody meat frisbee shone glossy in the white sunlight. Then she made some more noises and tossed the meat in the air, catching a little bit of it in the frisbee. The rest landed in the dirt; some of it splashing blood onto her sneakers. I looked around. Nothing. Well, there was a vulture if you looked straight up, but we weren't looking for vultures.

No roadrunners appeared. She clacked and shuffled. Five, ten, fifteen minutes passed. Ryder sat down. The woman pointed.

There's a roadrunner!

She was pointing at nothing. Well, at a stone wall. The boys and I looked at each other. Our neighbor was gleeful.

There it is!

She tossed her frisbee meat in the air again and dropped the rest of it. We squinted at the wall, then at her. Ryder whispered something and Doony shushed him. I shifted Wy to the other hip and the neighbor lady called to the wall.

Come and git it, baby!

Then she pitched a fistful of sandy hamburger at the empty wall. The boys ducked and looked at me. I shrugged. More meat flew through the air. Some caught on a barren tree branch. There was no roadrunner anywhere.

Doony kicked some dirt. The woman clacked and called an invisible roadrunner "baby" again. We waited. I stared into the middle distance, hoping for a glimpse of something that'd make this moment less awkward. *Come on roadrunners . . . or any-one looking for bloody meat. Help this lady out.* Ryder found a stick and started drawing in the sand with it. Putting Wyatt down, I held his hand as he toddled over to his brothers.

Suddenly, two roadrunners tore past the children and circled the meat on the ground. The boys froze. The birds were beauti-ful, crazy dinosaurs, but . . . they were also us. Strikingly so. This grouping of species did not negate the other. The roadrunners ran around the meat and each other until they decided it was safe to gobble it up.

It was over in a few seconds. Wy, Ry, and Doony and the roadrunners all had the same bewildered expression. Birds and meat and a searing landscape: we were dinosauring.

The roadrunners looked up at us when they were done and then took off running again. Holding her bloody frisbee, the woman had the same expression as the boys.

I never get sick of that.

♋ teeth

I could get a piece of meat from a barren tree

✹ ✹ ✹ ✹

Wyatt began waking at dawn. I'd carry him to the porch then and we'd greet the morning. A cold high desert night morphed quickly into the white thing we knew as our days. Wy watched studiously, carefully. He watched watchfully, I guess.

When day *was*, he reached up to be carried inside. Where he'd begin drawing. I think he was waiting for the light to be right.

❋ ❋ ❋ ❋

♋ white trash moon

the neighbors' gun won't let you sleep

An enormous owl wants to eat our dog. It sits outside my window at night, fluffing, spinning its head, shifting up and down a cable, and hoots in wait. This is a moan-scoot-rolling, an airy bellow of wind moving through a deep chest cavity. Hooting is not quiet.

Coyotes sit in a semicircle in our driveway. Silently gather as a village and then scream en masse at midnight. We jolt awake, our wide eyes lit by moonlight, staring. Screaming is not quiet.

Guns go off in the neighbors' horse corral. They tell us that they shoot into the air to scare the coyotes who scare their horses, insisting that guns don't scare horses. Shooting is not quiet.

❋ ❋ ❋ ❋

Though I no longer hear music, I am still a musician, still must pay bills, still must travel for a living. I record songs I wrote before silence fell, I tour these, and I discuss music with writers, but . . . all in a deep quiet. My universe has tilted on its axis. Not unpleasantly. Just getting the feel of un-noise.

On a winter promo tour, Wyatt falls asleep drawing, every night. He is with me because young children need their mothers, but it's a tough call in a tough life. It is dark, it is drizzly, it is lonely. Every night on the pillow rests: one boy head, one pencil, and one pad of paper. I wake him in the dark for early morning flights and he wordlessly lifts the pencil to pick up where he left off and finish last night's drawing. He draws while I dress him and draws in the taxi to the airport; draws at the gate while I feed him whatever food we can find. Or, if we've found nothing, he doesn't eat breakfast and doesn't complain. He draws on the plane and in the taxi from the airport. In Spain, Italy, France, Germany, England, Holland, Ireland . . . wherever we go, there is a desk waiting for him with a stack of paper and sharpened pencils. A wastebasket for rejected work and a corkboard covered in his drawings from the last promo tour. Journalists speak quietly, respectful of his work. I do interviews for hours while Wy draws silently, his sandwiches getting warm and his hot chocolates getting cold.

At the end of our workday, there are new drawings pinned to the board and many, many more in the wastebasket and tossed *around* the wastebasket, over Wy's little shoulder. He keeps nothing. It's drawing that he values, not drawings. This is instructive.

✳ ✳ ✳ ✳

INTERVIEW:

Q: How will this industry survive?

A: The recording industry was about copies. That model is now obsolete. So we're discussing copies only because we need a physical analog for what comes after inspiration.

Q: Which is?

A: Sharing. This is where my understanding of the process breaks down. If it's medicine, we're tasked with finding others who need it. How hard do we have to fight, though? It's all uphill. Even the sick people who need this medicine don't know that; snake oil is everywhere, filling their ears and emptying their wallets.

Q: If you care, you will continue to fight.

A: You know what? That's true. And I care less and less every day.

We try to emulate Wyatts, we music people. Try to draw a world that is right. Not pretty, just ugly and beautiful and necessary. The question of whether or not *we* are necessary? Goes unanswered.

✳ ✳ ✳ ✳

I hope to myself that Wyatt isn't hiding, creating a safer world than this dark and hungry one. He looks pale. I do too. Months of urban darkness and bright people-noise are eating away at us. We stay close. It's all we can do. It's not music; it's just the life of a musician. And I've inflicted it on a raw soul who is

ill-suited to the barrage of people and the noise of cities. Sometimes the only clarity is in escape.

INTERVIEW:

Q: Do you ever feel guilty making your children live a musician's life? I imagine the road does not always feel like a
home.

A: Yes, I feel guilty. And no, the road is not always home.

♋ power and light

medicine rush or clarifier?
dangerous candy or safe fire?

We come back to the desert too tired to be confused.

✱ ✱ ✱ ✱

The American promo tour is also months of bright noise and a
barrage of people. But . . . wider. There are prairies between the
cities. There are silences and mountains and beaches and animals. And there is snow. Snow that sticks around and becomes
the landscape. Cities are a very small part of this land and we
hunger for the land, so that's what we see. The man drives and
I deejay. Wy's brothers are with us, carrying animal-face paper
plates in the elevator to motel breakfast rooms, carrying back

oddnesses for their TV picnics on the staticky carpets. We bring the dog. The sun comes out in a mushy, glistening way, through steamy motel windows in the heartland. We take the boys to grocery stores with lobster tanks in lieu of zoos.

Is this bad?

No, just sad.

We aren't bad parents?

Of course not.

Just sad ones?

I don't feel sad.

Neither do I.

One lobster does not wrestle the others in the tank, doesn't wave his rubber-banded claws around in panic and aggression. He looks calmly out the glass at the boys, who press their fingertips against his waving antennae.

Can we take him home?

Home?

To the van. He's the best one.

He is. Be like him.

People at record store signings don't know that I lack sound now. I *play* music, but I don't hear it. Trying not to lie, I just get very quiet. The children gather around me, gripping Sharpies, drawing pictures on the paper tablecloths and signing their names on kind listeners' records.

You look weird on the poster, Mom.

Well . . . yeah. It's a poster.

Do you like all these people?

I'm sure I would like them if I knew them.
Maybe you need to meet them one at a time.
I wonder if this is how wandering off begins. Seems ok.

♋ bug

one more somnambulistic year

Wyatt begins to wake up and tan up and move. We all swim together in motel pools, admiring the snowy prairie through steamy windows, and we watch cartoons. Animation where nothing happens is our favorite; textures, seasons. Pouring three bowls of cereal and passing them out to pajamaed babies is a beautiful way of life. Driving every day, we see the space out there. It's an emptiness that is very much alive and I still get to play songs sometimes. Music as day job is pretty exquisite. A grounded walking away: you know the ground and its swell. Just need the gas station in New Mexico to hire me. *Live donuts bait.*

Wy talks more, hides less. He is a kid, after all. We find more food, sleep more hours. Lighten, as we make our way slowly back to the desert.

I loved the silence. It's music somehow, but it isn't records. I could finally look at music in the quiet and I stalled between selling and not selling. A kind of dust bowl had started in the recording industry: *records don't sell anymore.* Started as a dust devil and rumors and then real fear and the first farmers falling. No more low-hanging fruit. The desperate can get pretty desperate. Some musicians chose to suck in order to make money. Some close to me had wandered off and even died from the hunger of left-behind, offing themselves.

Commerce over art is a sickness and the healing gets dark when we go into hiding to put art over commerce and there is no longer any meat on the trees. Cannot change that. Wouldn't if we could, but . . . what the hell is music, anyway? Maybe too sacred to sell.

INTERVIEW:
Q: I think you guys're some of the most underrated musicians in the business.
A: Huh. That's good, right?
Q: How is that good?
A: Well . . . the business only rates how lousy you are.

✳ ✳ ✳ ✳

A newspaper headline: JELLYFISH APOCALYPSE NOT COMING.
Well, that's a relief.
What the hell is a jellyfish apocalypse?
Doesn't matter now, I guess.
Are they sure it's not coming?
Hope not. I'd kinda like to see the jellyfish win.
Maybe the apocalypse is for the jellyfish and they lose. Maybe it's that kind of jellyfish apocalypse.
Oh. Crap.
In the motel room, I pour a boy another bowl of cereal. The pad of paper from the hotel nightstand is placed carefully in front of Wyatt's little pajama legs on the staticky bedsheets,

ready. I glance at it. It's a multiple choice checklist. The motel is asking its guests if they're traveling for business, tourism, or "other."

One of my sons—not sure who—has checked "other" and written in the blank space next to it: REVENGE.

✳ ✳ ✳ ✳

I'd heard that the sea called. And don't believe everything you read, but it *does*. Once you speak ocean, you hear it spoken forever. Sometimes even through whispering pines.

The desert lesson learned, the desert years over for now, a jellyfish apocalypse was blowing up the coyote and roadrunner cartoon that was the only home Wyatt had ever known. I wanted to say goodbye to music, but it was already gone; buried in the sand with the coyote pelt. Wyatt said nothing. And since Wy says nothing lightly, I listened. The desert lesson: quiet.

The boys and I muscled our way through the land, trying to have it all, climbing up the rocky hillsides to the monastery at the top of the mountain, past rattlesnakes in the foothills. Long-hugged the dude who built our house and the house next door so that he could play checkers with a child and know who his drinking buddies were. He smile-squinted in shadow.

Don't worry, Ryder. Some checker games never end.

This turned out to be true.

We took pictures of the crazy-ass boulders and pointy, reaching Joshua trees, blackened by the last fire wall, so that we'd never forget the color of the sky there. Wyatt drew a pie flying through the air over barrel cactus, so we gave a cherry pie to coyotes who didn't give a shit about pie.

It's kind of a lousy pie.

Yeah. I feel guilty for trying to sell it to cool people like coyotes.
Let's make them a better pie before we go.
I don't think they'd eat it unless we put jackrabbits in it.
Oh. Huh.

The boys perched on a stone fireplace, watching, looking calm, looking sepia-toned. Orange light shone across their shirtless smallness.

* * * *

Wy did say one thing. As he sat cross-legged on the deck by the bat watering tank and gazed out into pink hills.

Where the lizards are? Is my house.

* * * *

♋ bright yellow gun

with your bright silver grin
you own sin
and I think I need a little poison

New York City: a baby chimpanzee wearing pajamas races through the freezing warehouse, dodging legs and lights and drag queens. He is chased by a woman wearing a bulky winter coat and a bigger chimp the woman holds by the hand, her coat flapping in its face. This chimp keeps pushing the woman's coat aside to see where it's going, but it's wearing a cheap suit and has trouble running. It trips on its trouser legs and slows the woman down, while the younger chimp slips away again and again. Drag queens stumble on their heels as the little chimp circles them, spinning, and then takes off again. The woman tells us it's time for the baby to change out of his pajamas and he doesn't like wearing suits, so he took off. She and the older chimp try walking calmly up to the baby, but he baits them with a grin and spins away again.

We have no bright-yellow guns because you know: guns. But we found you a bright-yellow guitar pick.

Well, that was nice of you.

You can pretend to shoot me with it.

I'm good.

A painter friend of mine told me he could direct a video for us; paint a song. Make it color-funny and gross like us. I still heard no music, but there was work to be done, born song-children to raise. I didn't want to make any more videos, had become mistrustful, and I told him that. He nodded and considered this. Then said that the world was ours and music was ours-er. He didn't know I couldn't hear it anymore, but that's ok. He thought we could take it all back: the beautiful, the ugly, even the *pretty*, our dirtiest word. Then we'd have it all and fuck 'em. We earned *fun*, our other dirtiest word. He grinned.

I'm having fun. Are you?

You know what? I'm always having fun.

Don't forget that.

This was really good advice. So was this:

The chimps can play poker.

They can? Do they win?

If you let 'em. And I'd let 'em if I were you.

So our song was being painted in front of us and it was dirty. Good dirty, with a clean heart. Some silver redemption through sin, like New Orleans. Some space and sage green, like the Mojave. And a splash of salty, blue ocean. Real dark shadow, technicolor bursting through. I love freakin' technicolor . . . always bring color to the view, it's how to see. Saturated with humanity. *So fake-a-listic,* as Wyatt says.

The little chimp circled us, then paused, having completed another circuit of the warehouse.

God, is he sweet.

He could rip your arms off.

Yeah?

If he wanted to. That's really all I know about chimps and I learned it this morning.

Both arms at once or just one at a time?

We watched the little chimp get his bearings as the woman in the coat caught up with him, pulling the other chimp along. This one was still having trouble trying to run in a business suit. Calmly, the baby acquiesced and allowed a jacket and square trousers to be pulled over his pajamas. Then he took off again and climbed onto a stage holding our equipment. People scattered. My guitar went over as the little chimp jumped up on the drum kit and grabbed a drumstick. Pausing to put it in his mouth, he crawled up a camera and climbed down the tripod beneath it. A few drag queens cheered. My drummer and bass player, dressed in pink and powder-blue tuxedos, laughed from side of stage.

I wonder if he's gonna rip somebody's arms off.

He really doesn't seem the type, does he?

The furry baby jumped off the stage and into the woman's arms.

My children would get the chimps' costumes as hand-me-downs as soon as we were finished lip-syncing and trashing a hotel room. It was like Christmas. Beautiful lights and new, little clothes, smiling faces.

I know this isn't music, Kris.

You know what? It might as well be.

The baby chimp kissed me while we were playing poker—unprompted—and together we trashed the holy heck out of a hotel room.

He won't remember you tomorrow.

How do you know that? He kissed me.

He was just trying to see your cards.

You think?

Yeah. So don't, like, get a monkey or anything.

I'm not gonna get a monkey. And don't call him a monkey. He kissed me.

I heard.

Driving back to the island with my bandmates, we wondered what that particular baby saw. Day to day, was his biology at war with his life? Not all that different from us then. Did he look for the same thing the ostriches looked for in the snow and never found? Was he embedded in our culture? Cuz *we* aren't. And, you know, maybe not deeply, but he deserved America as much as any other kid; as much as a coyote deserves a palace. Not a need certainly, but a playground aspiring to comfort.

He's trapped, though.

All kids are trapped.

He's a kid who's a pet, so he'll be trapped forever. Our kids have a future of freedom.

And exposure. They aren't safe.

I saw him staring out the window.

Oh god, how sad.

I saw him watching TV.

What does he see?

Good question. Can he draw?

Why, was he watching cartoons?

Yeah, it was cartoons.

He deserved cartoons. Maybe he didn't need them; maybe he needed something very, very different. But the next morning, watching the boys race around in a chimpanzee's bathrobe and business suit, I felt like the best I could do was raise humans a little trapped, with some windows, some exposure, some freedom, some pajamas. And some cartoons.

♋ cartoons

I was just looking far away

And all this time? Music doesn't play.

A journalist who moved in with us for a few days brought a photographer with him and, as always, we tried our best to treat them like family. Ryder, in a chimpanzee's business suit:

Can I get you guys anything? Margaritas?

They looked at me, shocked and impressed.

Can he really make a margarita?

No, the kid can't make a margarita! I don't know why he said that.

I shot Ry a glance and the photographer shrugged.

Can't believe he can even say "margarita."

Well . . . maybe on the rocks. He's not allowed to use the blender.

In the recording studio, the photographer shot stills and took some video while I worked.

I hope I'm not bothering you.

If I'm playing? I can't see you.

Perfect.

I was recording in a horse stable. Recording quiet, old songs. Still had a pile of leftovers I was reheating and calling it dinner, in other words. Hadn't cooked a song since Quiet Wyatt. So I shrugged and heated up leftovers again. The children played outside the studio until they were breathless, then slammed into the kitchen outside the control room, pink-cheeked and chattering. Having grown up in recording studios, however, they tiptoed silently into the room itself, suspicious; knowing anything they said or did could be picked up by a microphone and captured forever.

Piled up like puppies on an overstuffed pink velvet couch, music blasting through the speakers, they calmed and slept. *Mom is the most boring creature that ever happened. She soothes with boring, and we sleep.* Though Wyatt always woke up briefly to draw something.

Q: What does Wyatt draw?
A: Everything. The dream version of everything.
Q: Would he draw me if I asked him to?
A: I'm sure he already has.
Q: The dream version of me?
A: Probly . . . that's all Wyatt sees.

* * * *

The road is the road is the road, but we always know where we are. It's a myth that the touring musician is not attuned to geographical subtlety. Yeah, our ever-widening view would blur if we didn't study its nuances hungrily, but we *do*. I mean, what else is there to do? We wake up in a Montana field surrounded by antelope and buy breakfast in a gas station, all of us agreeing that there was an alchemical reaction between the presence of the antelope and the crappy gas station coffee, creating a demon drink of . . . well, maybe not *all* gods, but one particularly cool antelope god who hung out for that morning and turned chlorinated water into caffeinated wine. The kids claim the same of their chocolate milk:

It's smart.

When New Mexico pulls up in front of the van, it does so in a deep, dry cold with a scattering of snowflakes that clear the land as they fall. Arid water. The same snow that swirled around us in our early days, in the attacks, in the fireball, in the courtrooms, the lawyers' offices, and in the plane crash, in the repeating image of the cop standing on the front porch. Flashes of Baby Doony, of losing him, and I grow raw as the hauntings begin again. The baby is gone, I drive all night, it is summer in the unmelting snow.

I'm used to these pain angels, I live with them, but I don't yet know that it is PTSD giving me an allergy to the markers that describe a trauma. This particular snow seems dangerous, deadly. PTSD fucks with time, so triggers like weather will throw you back to the event, to a spiral time, and now becomes then, forever. The life event you can't incorporate broke you, you are broken: you and time are the same broken thing. The man picks me up when I fall off the world, out of this day and into shell shock: there is always a cop standing on the front porch.

Doony is alive.

You don't understand.

No, no one does, but time passed. This isn't happening. You're dreaming the past.

I'm awake.

Just not all the way.

Many years from now, someone will tell me that if an earthquake happens before you're ready for it, you will store the event for future use. When it comes back, it's because it knows best. The crashing sweat spills in through cracks in your head, as an external experience that happens inside you this time: a rememory. It builds itself in sound, color, texture, movement, weather, fight and flight. We don't ever feel ready, but a life seizure plays a role in your story if you live. And even if you don't. If you die, loved ones tell the story after the fact. But it's still yours.

♋ mississippi kite

sweat seeps in through a crack in your head

Tequila. Herradura Silver.
I can't. The babies.
Just soften.
The man and the boys and I're staying in a cottage on a wide
path, in an enclave of tiled casitas. Each cottage has a fireplace
with an actual fire burning in it. Something to stare at together.
Like a song: to flirt you into blurting out what you mean, confuse your daydreams. After living in a van for so long, we can
barely pull ourselves away from this fire. It brings us even closer,
the semicircle of us growing tighter: bright, dry voodoo. Unlike
the dark, wet stuff in New Orleans. And we're beginning to feel
just how tired we all actually are. Night fell a while ago, and
babies *have* to sleep. Fishing around in backpacks for stuffed
animals and toothbrushes, half firelit.
  I never want to leave them, never ever want to leave them. I
don't stop counting heads, and when I leave, I come up short.
A limbic bird's nest without enough chicks in it. The man waits
in the snow outside the casita, his back to me. It isn't just the
stars that are different in New Mexico; the moon glows brighter
too, illuminating surrounding clouds like lightning. Unsettling
to look up, really, so I focus on the blue snow and the lit candles
in paper bags placed along the walkway, which make me wonder if we should have put the fire out before we left.
  The boys'd be so sad.
  Sad and safe.

I think that's why it's called a fireplace. The place you put fire where it's okay to have fire burn.

The man takes me out to a dinner neither of us can remember post-margaritas. Not the tequila so much as the flares between us. Fireworks and plane crashes look similar from below, where the children watch us; feel very different from above, where we watch each *other*. We were the place we put fire where it was okay to have fire burn. And that night, fire pulled and cleared, then our gentle waiter's tequila burned up the dry snowflakes. I will always be losing a baby, but New Mexico lights that strikingly, snows on it. We were right.

We are fluid creatures, Kris, change is a constant. Your oobleck hurricane. Don't get stuck on the particulate, you know?

I do know this. I can do better.

You're already better. The happy ending.

Without an ending. Yeah.

I was right about all those fires I set myself on when we were first together. And that is what it is, but on a clear, cold night in New Mexico, the tequila and bright flashes do our math for us, do it wrong, and we stiff our beloved waiter; only realizing on the snowy walk to our casita that we didn't tip him. Racing back to the restaurant, we count out our cash and pledge it to the dude who helped me shake off shell shock. But when we get there, outstretched hands full of money, he has left for the evening, they don't have his home number and won't let us leave him cash.

The tequila and snow moon still talking, still doing fucked-up math, we decide that it is most right and just to call everyone

with this guy's name in the Santa Fe phone book and tell them
that we owe them money. Whispering so as not to wake the children, I call two dozen baffled men in the middle of the night—
none of whom are waiters—and we go to sleep heartsick, the
fire dying off to sleep too.

⌒ jacklighted

all this time you were right

In the morning, we take the kids to a sun-splashed diner in the
snow outside of town. They're bright and hungry, we're still
mopey and kinda hungover, so we let a beautiful, fried-and-a-
half waitress grandmother them with pancakes and milk. The
boys giggle us back to cheerful and we leave waving our thanks,
the babies carrying crayons and thanking their new sun-kissed
grandma. It's not until we're over a hundred miles away that the
man asks me how much I tipped her for her kindness.
You paid the bill, remember? You tipped her.
I didn't pay the bill, you did.
I didn't pay the bill.
I didn't pay the bill either.
Our choices were either to drive into a tree because we're
terrible people and don't deserve to live; turn the car around
and add four hours to the trip, missing sound check and risking
car-wide mutiny; or calling everyone in the Santa Fe phone book
with our waitress's name and telling them that we owe them
money. Which works great, as we found out the night before.

Or driving to the show and commencing the life of crime we'd already begun. Which got more and more interesting the faster we drove away from karma, the more diner coffee caffeinated our veins and brainz.

I think the key is to be friendly and boring, so you don't arouse any suspicion and no one remembers you after the fact.

And we're both of those things already.

Oh, totally. It's not like we'd have to train for this or even lie.

So we eat free forever.

Don't think small. We could stiff hotels, steal clothes . . . gas up the car. Forever. The kids are friendly and boring too.

Definitely. I had no idea we were such a talented family.

Sometimes talents stay hidden until you need them. Like picking up a car with a burst of adrenaline or something.

The superpower boring. Maybe our waiter and our waitress will meet at a support group for stiffed waitpeople and fall in love.

And then we're . . . good people?

And then we're good people.

That night, I played a quiet show. Played quietly and people listened quietly. Not *nice* or anything, but passion can wear all kinds of volume. The quiet in my head was so different from the last two decades of sound . . . I had become a low-hum musician. The next morning, the boys had quiet bowls of cereal in another hotel room—so fucking hard to score milk that hasn't gone bad sometimes, but I did it that morning—and then we walked Crow and piled back into the van. Silence speaks eloquently, but to a synesthetic, music is color and without songs, a graying numb had settled over me.

℧ power and light

silence is eloquent, too
and kind

Sleepy shows drive us to more sleepy shows, morph through nights into mornings owned by others. Owned by families with homes, with real jobs. Our homeschoolers diligently workbook their way across the country, pencils lost under car seats with boxes of raisins. And we slip quietly out of town before the children catch a glimpse of real life. I worry that they will look up one day and see that they are gypsies. A marginalized subculture, belonging nowhere. When their little hearts are so open to connection and peace.

In capturing all of America in their oddly photographic memories, they forfeit an American life, which they will always crave. In their schoolbooks are pictures of what they see out the car window. They hear so many languages spoken in America that, overseas, they have no idea they aren't in their own country. It would make no sense to overlay borders on their experience of people, which is all-encompassing and warm. A beautiful and lonely orientation.

But through the whole state of New Mexico, a snow moon blues down on the red dirt, reminds us that earth can be an unearthly place. It disappears us to the extent that we can no longer feel lonely. Who would feel the loneliness? Music as a day job is indeed bewitching. It's just that somehow, I had lost music.

Stopping in a café to warm up, we gathered at the counter and let the man order. He is tall and loud, so people tend to (1)

Notice him, (2) Look at him, (3) Listen to him. Sounds like a no-brainer, but when you fight for invisibility, embodying the "drab female" we see in other species, it can be a challenge to have *any* of those things happen. I counted children absent-mindedly, as I always did. When you come up short, you start looking under tables right before you panic. When you count more children than are rightfully yours, it's either because they move around a lot or some other mother is counting heads across the room and coming up short. You catch her eye and push her child across the room right before she panics.

All the hot chocolates ordered, the man looked down to ask me what I wanted and froze, staring at me. I was frozen too. Tears were pouring down my cheeks. Choking, I couldn't breathe, and color was spilling all over me with the tears. I stared at the black speakers over the barista's head, under an array of plastic flowers and chili peppers, while the man stared at *me*.

What's wrong?

I could see music climbing out of the speakers and into the air and it was falling on me. I remembered the sense I had lost in the desert: songs. A desert as quiet as this one, where sound is not played by people but by coyotes, owls, and wind harmonica'd through whispering pines. In this place? *People* had made something physically real out of the essence of color, sculpted from sound waves. I thought I was gonna pass out. Leaned on the man.

I can see music.

Jesus. I knew how dumb that sounded, like a stoner roommate. But I was seriously caught by sound color. My throat shut and gray static blotted my vision. I tried to think, couldn't, tears were blurring out the room; saltwater superimposed on wooden tables, shoes, and faces. A sudden and elaborate flood. Very much like drowning in Malibu. And the children watching . . . little beach monkeys. I half-thought the man's hand could cut through the surface of this water, but only half-wanted it to.

Synesthesia took over completely, so color spilling wasn't a visual element but an essential one. Like the essence of something that I was usually too small and clunky to grasp. Something you'd have to close your eyes to see-hear. I sound like a stoner roommate just *typing* this. Anyway, the man, alarmed, grabbed me and spun me around so that I was facing away from the children.

What happened to you?

I shook my head, splaying my hands at him, and three men sitting at a table behind us looked up. A young man rested his hands on a guitar, as two older men burned a bundle of herbs over its strings. My throat relaxed and I took a deep breath into my constricted lungs, flushing with something like aesthetic arrest. I could remember music, was hearing it for the first time since Quiet Wyatt brought me home to silence.

The man walked over to the table and studied the smoking herbs.

My wife is crying about music.

One of the older men, deeply still, spoke slowly, moving only his lips.

Oh. Sorry.

The three of them looked at me and then angled the guitar and herbs away from me, toward the door, the young man blowing smoke into the sound hole. I was too busy remembering why I was born to follow exactly what was happening.

My husband held out his hand to shake theirs and they paused before reaching out with theirs. His voice was conversational but kinda high-pitched.

Did you do this to her?

The stillness. Like mountains or stones. I wiped the tears off my face and joined them. The children's hot chocolates were placed on the counter and the barista sprayed whipped cream on top of them while they watched. I could hear music again.

Yeah, we're doing a music blessing. Must have missed the guitar and hit your wife in the back of the head. Sorry.

That's ok. So . . . what?

The younger man introduced himself to me.

My name's Crow Dog. I bought this blessing and it missed the guitar. Hit you, I guess.

He looked unhappy. I didn't know what to say.

I have a dog named Crow.

He looked at me. Didn't seem surprised.

Oh yeah?

I shrugged.

Yeah. I'm sorry I took your blessing.

That's ok, I just . . .

He sighed.

. . . paid for it, you know? Been fasting.

Still wasn't sure what to say. This was the third thing I'd stolen in one state.

Oh, wow. That's a bitch.

He looked up at me hopefully.

Think you could play my guitar for a little while? Maybe some of it'll rub off.

The café had a performance space in the next room that

Crow Dog led me into while the children and their drinks were corralled by their bewildered father. The older men sat, friendly and intense and still as stones: plain. Smoke rose from the bundle of herbs on their table. I gestured to the man that he should shoo the kids away from the smoke and then sat with Crow Dog on the stage, admiring his guitar. It was just beat up enough to look loved, just polished enough to look cared for. And it played raw and cracked. Heavy strings and dark wood bring about a certain kind of song and I had forgotten this. I had forgotten so much. Like a baker's hands altering bread dough, the player's hands have to respond to the substance to facilitate a process. The worst thing you can do is interfere, the second worst thing you can do is wander off. The goal is invisibility with muscles. Playing Crow Dog's guitar, I tried to keep up our awkward conversation, but most of my brain was occupied by the garden of wild wildflowers that was this particular guitar's language. He listened while I played, then pointed at my left hand on the fretboard.

You like B-flat?

Your guitar likes B-flat. B-flat minor, actually. It's a heavy key.

It's got an F in it. I don't like F much.

Sounds bright green to me.

I played a sweet classical piece I learned as a kid, something I didn't know I remembered. I played a few of my own songs, then let my hands do whatever they wanted for a while and, honestly, forgot that Crow Dog was there. When I looked up, I handed him his guitar, embarrassed to have lost myself in it. He nodded thoughtfully.

Cool. Hope something rubbed off. Did you just start playing guitar?

You mean today? No.

He laughed.

I was gonna say, you know. That's some music blessing . . .

Sorry. It's a nice guitar, didn't wanna give it back.

F is green?

I dunno. I always thought so. F minor has some aqua.

You a composer?

I thought about this.

I suppose. But not in a good way.

Crow Dog studied me.

So you have a crow dog?

I do. He's in the car. We live on the road, so he lives on the road. Would you like to meet him?

Sure. Does he like living on the road?

Not much. But he doesn't complain because he can't speak English.

My dog complains all the time and he doesn't speak English.

This is when Quiet Wyatt's silence ends. As we walk outside together, I look past Crow Dog to catch Wyatt's eye and see if he drew this, and he stares back at me with ocean eyes over whipped cream.

BODHI

I dream I see a bear cub in a Bodhi tree and when I reach out to it, it falls into my arms, a Bodhi boy. I look over a pillow at the man.

What's a Bodhi tree?

♋ silver sun

only sweetness
that's all
to shake off the bitter

My hippie dad tells me that the Bodhi tree is the tree the Buddha was enlightened under.
   Which totally makes you a hippie too. Sorry.

It does not. I didn't even know what it was.

That's the coolest part.

My due date was Bodhi Day, the Buddhist holiday, of all things. Bodhi would have ocean eyes, the same odd color as Wyatt's, and his first word, like Wyatt's, would be "moon."

❋ ❋ ❋ ❋

Some running:

The Columbus police had only accounted for one of the two lions wandering the city and no one was actually missing any lions. Big cats are not indigenous to the state of Ohio, so there was some confusion, but not quite enough, if you ask me. Residents seemed to take it in stride that, you know, these things happen. Which they don't. After the show, wary audience members walked each other to their cars or took cabs home. Seemed like death by lion'd be a cool way to go, especially Ohio lion: definitely, right fuckin' now, it is your time. But when it came down to it, nobody was really sure how quick and painless it'd be and most of us thought, *not at all either one of those things.*

Carrying hot meat down the sidewalk at two in the morning on a White Castle tour bus run, it occurred to us that we maybe took things too much in stride as well.

What is the very last thing you should do when being stalked by a lion?

Two lions.

. . . by two lions.

Picking up the pace.

I'd say . . . disguise yourself as a sick or elderly wildebeest.

Okay. Cool. What's the penultimate thing one shouldn't do?
Running.
Carry hot meat in a bag and run.
Running faster.
That's what I was thinking.

Later, safe on the bus:
You don't even eat White Castle, Kris.
Yeah, well . . . this is how much I love y'all. And being chased by invisible lions is cool.
Another couple sliders in the bag.
Save 'em for the lion.
Lions.
Lions.

♋ fever few

four red horses

In Brussels, a football match ends in riots that don't end, but take to the streets. Walking to dinner from the club, my bandmates and I are surrounded by hot yelling and breaking glass. Men lift garbage cans over their heads and throw them into shop windows, then set stuff on fire. Which'd be hard for *me* to do under the best of circumstances: just taking out the garbage is hard, and I don't lift the can over my head or anything. Coaxing flames from the driest wood with all manner of pokers and matches and wadded-up newspaper wasn't a slam dunk either. I was impressed with their rioting. The fact that it was for no reason was even more impressive. I could've probly lifted a garbage can over my head for social unrest, but for a game? That you didn't even play?

I was enjoying the riot, hands resting on my pregnant belly, watching the tumult. Didn't realize I was *in* it. None of us did really; it looked like improv. A plein air school play about a riot. And yeah, they were awfully close, but we were the audience, right? Not *our* football.

Turns out, no. If burning and shattering are in front of you, you are considered to *be* the burning and the shattering and, also, it's your fault. My bass player grabbed my hand and pulled me out of the path of four red, shimmering horses clattering on the cobblestones. But *fuck*, not New Orleans mule clattering. These "horses" were powerful, huge, fast machines. The horses I knew at my studio stood quietly in misty sun and let you pet their noses, feed them hay they already had, which was just lying on the ground. *Those* were horses. Farm horses. Day horses. These Belgian night-cop horses were . . . hippo trains. They made me dizzy.

Hippo trains?

They're too big, too fast.

You'll have to run. Can you run?

So we ran. Ran down the cobblestones, away from the melee, which followed us, so we ran faster, also clattering on the cobblestones, in our boots. Then, turning a corner, I saw my drummer crying behind a glass wall, his fingertips pressed against the glass, calling us silently. We stopped and stared.

I haven't had this dream yet.

Does he need our help?

We felt with our fingertips across the glass wall until we found a seam and pushed. When a door opened, my drummer's voice opened too, but it was raw and squeaky.

Tear gas. We have to hide somewhere. It's already in here.

Let's go to Toone.

Toone was an underground puppet theater and bar/café. There would be no tear gas down there.

I was starting to have trouble seeing and breathing, as if I were trying to run through a fiberglass cloud. Toone was still a few blocks away, but the club was miles away. Safest place to go while the chaos died down and the air cleared. We struggled down the sidewalk, no longer running, more like stumbling. Shouting men ran past us, followed by night-cops on hippo train horseback.

Are we gonna miss the show?

The puppet show?

Our show. I forgot about the puppet show . . . hope we don't miss it.

Down the cool, wet alley to Toone, the sounds of breaking glass, hooves, and rolling metal echoed, muffled. We knocked and were hustled inside where the light was a dim gold. Seeing that I was pregnant, a waiter shook his head in dismay and brought me a glass of water.

Has the air damaged you?

I shook my head and smiled at him. But I thought I should maybe call my midwife and ask *her* if I was air-damaged. The kind waiter sat us down at an ancient wooden table, then led me to a phone in the kitchen. My throat and lungs were on fire and fiberglass tears still poured down my cheeks as I listened to an American ringtone. Finally, she answered and I heard her accept the collect call. When I asked her about tear gas and unborn children, there was a silence.

To be honest, I really haven't seen this before.

I sighed, could hear typing on a keyboard. More typing. A waiter squeezed by me, carrying a tray of coffee and Framboise Lambic.

Normally, what I would do is get you into the office to check you out.

Right. I might be late for my appointment.

Can you get to a hospital?

Well . . . not without getting tear gassed again.

More typing. Billie Holiday played scratchily through the tumble of kitchen noise.

Okay. The next thing I would do is tell you that it's gonna be okay.

Really?

What else can I do?

Well . . . could you do that now?

It's gonna be okay.

Great.

When I got back to the heavy, carved-up block of wood my bandmates were sitting at, I recognized the drinks I'd just seen walk past me while I was on the phone. My bass player pointed at my drummer with the beer.

Behind glass was a nice touch. And crying? Beautiful.

Think so?

Dude. I'm a big fan of your work.

There was no room for my pregnant gut at the solid medieval table, so I sat down sideways in front of my glass of water.

That was very . . . war.
Yeah. War movie, anyway.
We watched people glowing rosy and drunk.
Did we miss the puppet show?

✱ ✱ ✱ ✱

While we're on tour, my house floods in a wild storm: two floors
fill with water and the ceiling collapses. Neighbors break in and
rescue floating guitars and suitcases full of family photos, but
we lose everything else. And then our savings, when the insurance company refuses to cover the loss due to a glut of losses in
the storm. The adjuster breaks the news to us gently.

*You have a case against the insurance company. You may
be in debt for the rest of your lives because of this. I'll testify
on your behalf, but I'm leaving to work in construction. I can't
hurt good people anymore. I wish I could help. All I can do is
stop hurting people.*

So he did. Because people are so good. Corporate beehives
do things that no bee would ever do. Like many people, we
couldn't stomach a lawsuit, not even against a beehive. Had
done that before and it's too ugly.

So we tried to stay. And then we began to know mold. Mold
grew everywhere; on and in everything we owned. The children's baby clothes and storybooks, my guitar inputs, our curtains, clothes, and furniture. *We* smelled so much like mold that
we could no longer smell it. We scraped, sprayed, and washed
everything, as if we could dig back through the mold to our pre-
flood lives, but it just grew back, a more successful organism
than us.

One morning, workmen who came to help undo flood damage set fire to the garage. Holding mildewed sheets and blankets we thought we could save and children's drawings we knew we couldn't, the man and I stood by the window, quietly watching the fire spread from the garage roof to our soggy, wet house. The workmen ran around yelling and waving tools, but we couldn't hear what they were saying through the glass.

How is that even possible?

Yeah . . . physics.

Mm-hm. I remember physics.

The man pointed to a frantic workman on the roof of the garage, trying to shut off a blowtorch.

He does too.

We gave up, lost the house, went back on the road. Loaded moldy guitars into the car with the boys and some grocery bags. Some mildewed Lynda Barry comic books and a few damp CDs. Wyatt's drawing materials and the boys' schoolbooks. Clothes I'd washed and rewashed, trying to coax a laundry scent out of moldy cotton.

The babies didn't feel the bump. Like, at *all*. They sunshined through the car windows as the sun shone back at them.

This is home, anyway, Mom.

Yeah, Mom. Motels have pools. We didn't have a pool.

This is where our friends live. On the road.

I thanked them, watching our town disappear through the windshield.

It is, boys. I promise I'll work until we can live somewhere again.

Ryder leaned up between the car seats.

When you go home to a house, you miss out on everywhere else.

I turned around, baffled by the angels yet again. I was used to songs telling me how to feel. I strongly considered switching to baby logic. Ryder grinned. Wyatt looked up from his drawing.

If you live in a house, you can't live in a igloo. Or sleep in a field. Remember antelopes?

Yeah, I remember antelopes . . . do you guys know what just happened?

They giggled.

Our house died.

It drowned.

It melted and burned.

They laughed helplessly. I squinted at the man while he drove. He was both smiling and frowning. And then I looked again at our boys in the rearview mirror.

Are you guys trying to cheer us up?

Their eyes were wide.

Why would we do that?

Suddenly, I realized I was on the wrong side of this. That I had grown up in spite of myself. That *they* could still see clearly. Ryder gazing mildly at the trees passing, smiling from the back seat:

Mom. It's just a house.

✳ ✳ ✳ ✳

By MLK Day, we'd made it to Atlanta and Atlanta was blue. Thick mist holds color in water molecules and that day's thick mist held blue. Dawn was a robin's egg blue, then the noon sky swelled with, well . . . sky blue. Wyatt, holding my hand, looked up.

It's not actually sky blue, Mom.

I'm sure you're right. That would be silly. What is it?

It's periwinkle. See the lavender?

And by afternoon, it was powder blue. I told the babies I was born in Atlanta and had spent my early years there; walked them through my old neighborhood. Then I walked them down a handful of streets named "Peachtree." Not all seventy, but enough to make my point. And the blue kept up with us.

♋ loudmouth

just south of here sirens blare

After the show, the air, the city, the houses, the peach trees and the Peachtrees, were still blue. Standing on a moonlit sidewalk in front of Martin Luther King's childhood home, we told the boys who the man was that asked us to live above and look beneath the superficial. That they had learned this lesson easily, traveling the world and clarifying their interactions through a lens of real. What else are you gonna go on? And therefore not to be afraid; that they were never truly alone.

Doing the right thing is a different kind of easy. It isn't safe, but it's good.

You guys were born good. We're all born good. Don't forget what you were born knowing.

The boys stared solemnly into a home, into a life that no longer was. We spoke slowly, hoping they got it.

Sometimes pain and fear make people selfish; sometimes pain and fear help people evolve. Evolve, ok?

They nodded. A moment of silence while we imagined the story of a life playing out in this misty blue front yard, on that misty blue porch, in that misty blue driveway. The boys, on pause, stared into the windows and asked who lived there now. But there was no plaque, no museum visiting hours.

The man pointed next door.

There's a plaque over there.

As a group, we shuffled over to the neighbor's house. The man read the plaque.

Birthplace of Dr. Martin Luther King Jr. Whoops.

We looked at the plaque. Then up at the house. It just looked like a house after bonding with the place next door.

Well, boys. Lesson still stands.

Wyatt reached into his tiny pocket for his pad and pencil; had some trouble with his overalls, so Ryder helped him. Doony cleared his throat and looked down the street as headlights appeared.

The man and I looked at each other.

Fail?

Wyatt began to draw in the dim blue light from a streetlamp.

Nah . . . even better: it's just a house.

✴ ✴ ✴ ✴

Ryder finds a baby squirrel in the street, dying under a parked car, having fallen from her nest. I tell him not to name her.

Just call her baby squirrel. Warm milk, salt, egg, and honey in an eyedropper.

So she'll live?

No, baby. Help her die.

She lived, and Baby Squirrel watched *us* live, riding in the van with us, on our shoulders, chewing seeds in our ears. Watching with her beautiful eyes.

She lived. It's a good omen.

She's a good omen. The whole thing of her is awesome.

Little frantic maybe.

Yeah, but. So are we.

We lived in front of her; TV to our squirrel.

✷ ✷ ✷ ✷

Bodhi was born into laughter. Literally, while we were laughing. In Palm Springs, California, a community based loosely around the past's impression of the future. The Jetsons grounded. Plus grapefruit trees and mountain goats, liquor stores, humming-birds, and trailers. We didn't settle down, really, as much as settle *in* and take a breath. A place to breathe when we didn't know how to keep moving and breathing at the same time.

Clean and dusty, Palm Springs does light and shadow like nowhere else; a breathtaking place to breathe. Also, a commu-nity of gay men and retirees, so not a place where many babies were born. For the second time in our lives, in hard labor at two o'clock in the morning, we were told that there were no babies expected that night. The nurse on duty seemed twitchy, avoided eye contact, said she'd never delivered a baby before. I sighed on the inside, smiled on the outside, and told her I'd delivered three, maybe I could help.

My labor plan was to act passed out during contractions so that I didn't actually pass out. I told the man I wouldn't *be* unconscious, I would just *look* unconscious, so he shouldn't try to talk about me behind my back. He frowned.

Does that work?

What, pretend passing out? We'll see. Did you have any other ideas? I'm so open to anything right now.

Um.

It's ok.

Uh.

Not drugs.

. . . did you pack a lunch?

The nurse weighed me, offered me drugs, sat me in a chair to take some blood, offered me drugs, filled out forms, took my temperature, offered me drugs . . . trying to stay busy, I guess. And then watched me pretend pass out. I just went silently limp cuz I couldn't think of anything else to do; lost in a semipermanent blackness of shutting down. A woman's voice.

Is that ok?

When I opened my eyes, the nurse was elaborately placing a wad of gauze over the needle she pulled out of my arm.

Don't worry, it's not painkillers. Unless you want that. Do you want that?

She secured the gauze with a Band-Aid and looked hopefully at me.

Shut my eyes. I lived through this three times *how*? The nurse asked if the Band-Aid she'd put on my arm was bothering me.

What?

Yeah, is that Band-Aid bothering you?

I opened my eyes long enough to look at my arm again.

The, uh . . . the Band-Aid isn't bothering me, no. It's fine.

Another contraction started and the man suggested a bed and a hospital room.

I just think she's probly gonna have a baby soon.

The nurse's face lit up. I guess she'd forgotten about that part. *Something to do!* Immediately, another contraction began and I was lost, spinning through an inner tornado. Pretend passed out. Fine line between pretend passed out and real passed out, I guess, though. Cuz when the contraction lifted and I came back to our shared brightness, I was lying on a gurney with the nurse's and man's worried eyes on me. There was a long silence. The man—who had turned a cool shade of purplish-gray— spoke first.

We thought you were dead.

Dead? Why?

You looked dead.

I told you I was gonna look dead.

I didn't think you'd look that dead.

The nurse interrupted.

I can remove that Band-Aid now if it's bothering you.

I looked at her.

It's, uh . . . it's ok.

Did you feel that last contraction?

Did I feel it?

. . . yeah. I did.

I jumped and winced as another began. I wasn't ready for it and hadn't had time to turn dead. She paled and gasped.

Let me get that Band-Aid for you.

This time I didn't surface. Fake-passed-out walked over to actual-passed-out and introduced itself, and I was still there hangin' out with both of them, limper and limper, deader and deader. While the tornado spun itself bigger and bigger. And all I'd done wrong was get sucked into its ever-widening chaos. How the fuck was *this* what having a baby is? Babies were so cool and this was so *medieval*; didn't make sense. Evolution could go fuck itself; wasn't working. No normal creature would evolve to have giant things grow inside them. Grow too big to get *out.*

So, yeah, I was gettin' real whiny in there. And who knows what was going on in the hospital room; if they'd found a doctor or a little girl with a stethoscope or anyone who'd ever even *seen* a baby delivered before. Maybe on TV? Other than the baby's father, who, from the looks of it, was about to *actual* pass out. Again. His voice in the dark.

Kris, you need to be present for this.

I'm here, honey. I'm really, really, really here.

Light flooded into my eyes when I opened them. I was pretty damn sure my pretend dead would become real dead if I had so much as one more contraction. And it was beginning. The big one: the earthquake that makes a joke of its precursory tremors. I opened my mouth in what would have been a scream if there was any way left to breathe and the man whispered into my ear:

Is that Band-Aid bothering you?

So, yeah, Baby Bodhi was born into laughter.

♋ in stitches

we just drove away
into the day

in stitches

INTERVIEW:

Q: What's life on the road like?

A: As hard and fun as that sounds, I guess. Nomadic is enshrined
in this subculture.

Q: But you have kids.

A: Well, they don't really know they're kids. They're just alive
things I gotta keep alive.

Q: This is my point.

A: Right. Circumstances dictate which muscles you build, but
that doesn't make your skeletal structure any different from
someone else's, huh? I would like to go home. We would like
to have a permanent home to go to. But honestly? We might
not know what to do there.

* * * *

How do lemons get away with calling themselves fruit?
  They don't, baby. Nobody's fooled.
    I looked over Bodhi's soft head, up at Doony and Ry, who
were posing carefully in a pointy, spiky lemon tree over a pointy,
spiky cactus Wyatt was carefully drawing. The pointy, spiky
black mountains that surrounded Palm Springs moved with racing clouds and a scattering of mountain goats.

So please stop eating lemons.

Okay.

You're not going to come across a sweet one.

Okay.

The crow who had taken up with a flock of wild parrots that lived on this corner squawked his distinctive imitation of a parrot. Ry called down to his little brother.

Hey, Wy! Draw us!

Wyatt dutifully turned a page in his drawing pad and began drawing his brothers surrounded by spikes and lemons. I covered the baby's eyes with a blanket against the white sun.

Boys, could you please not be in pointy spikes?

Okay. Want us to drop into the cactus?

They looked down at me blankly, balanced delicately in the lemon tree.

How long do we have to wait for Dad?

No idea.

What if it's forever and we live in a tree now?

That'd be cool. Hope you like lemons.

Doony pointed down the street.

What's that?

We all looked. A whirring mirage of blocky, blue metal shone, working its way toward us, slowly growing larger as it passed the gas station, the mountains, the trailer park. The unsteady gloss of moving objects in the sun cleared as it came closer. My boys and I stared. The wild parrots and crow-parrot took off together in a whir. Wyatt looked up.

What are plastic flowers for?

Uh . . .

Ryder eased himself past thorns and lemons to join us on the sidewalk.

He's probly right.
He's right?
When Wyatt talks, listen. It's always worth it.
Okay.

It was a bus. A blue bus. And the blue bus was growing; getting bigger, clearer, and closer. We squinted at it and Wyatt grabbed my hand. Plastic flowers . . . a fabrication of beauty, controlled beauty, perfect and ugly, can't die, never lived. Not perfect at all. Zombies for sale. Some effort, some saddening. *Huh.*

Standing in a row on the sidewalk, we watched as a massive windshield glinted in the sun, hissing up next to us. A freakin' blue ghost of a bus, dusty and creaking. It slowed, pulling its fat self to the curb, and groaned to a stop in front of us, cut its engine. The boys were silent, I was silent, the bus was silent, the mountains were silent. Pulling Wyatt closer, I glanced at his drawing pad. He had drawn a sky view of a bus driving down a snaking highway past scattered cactus. Suddenly, the bus door slammed open, our dog staring out, the man smiling in the driver's seat.

Welcome home!

✱ ✱ ✱ ✱

♋ god's not a dick

it's all over you
it's riveting

This is how we came to battle plastic flowers:

An oversized pickle jar containing four goldfish knocked and
rattled in the bus sink. Bracing himself against the fridge, Ryder
reached out with his goldfish hand to steady the jar as the highway curved. The dog lay at his feet, Baby Squirrel rode on his
shoulder, and in his popsicle hand were four popsicles he held
for himself and his brothers. His life had become balancing,
had become brothers and popsicles, but, as he put it, that's a
life goal some of us would never achieve and it had just been
handed to him.

My bass player sat at the table, one hand catching a coffee
cup as it slid past his newspaper, the other pressing the newspaper onto the table so it didn't blow away in the air rushing
through the bus window.

Why do we read newspapers?

We don't. You do.

Why do I read newspapers?

I dunno. Boredom?

That can't be it. News is boring.

*Yeah. And they do it every day. Those're people. Feel bad
for them.*

*"News." The new stuff. The important new stuff. The
important new stuff we all have to know.*

Follow the money. Want a popsicle?

Ryder handed him one, then passed his brothers theirs. I
pointed into the back lounge, where the beds were.

Bring Bo his, ok, Ry? He's watching fish.

We could no longer keep our beloved old black-and-white

movies on repeat because two-year-old Bodhi had brought a
visual aid with him when he joined the family and woke into
himself: a burst of blue on every screen. So while Bo's first
word was *moon*, like Wyatt's, it was followed immediately by
a life dive underwater. He'd glanced at the sky, then turned
away forever, finding his own outer space underwater. Marine
biology documentaries had been playing as long as he could
point. He watched them, splayed toddler-style, in the back of
the bus, wearing a wet suit and breathing through a snorkel,
surrounded by hundreds of lifelike fish and marine mammal
figurines. Sometimes we thought this was sad, sometimes funny,
sometimes amazing. The sound of splashing water and snorkel
breath was the sound of Baby Bo.

You probly read the paper cuz other people read the paper.
It's the same every day. I'm not doing it anymore.

Wyatt looked at him over his popsicle.

Maybe you like paper. I like paper.

My bass player froze for a moment, his face lit up. Suddenly,
he attacked the newspaper with enthusiasm, frantically. He tore
pieces of it into strips and handed them to Wy, who watched
quietly.

Those are feathers.

Wyatt nodded as if he understood and began coloring the
feathers with crayons from a plastic cup wedged between the
table and the window. My bass player then folded individual
sheets into complex triangles and wedges.

These are hats.

Wyatt smiled and rested his popsicle in the crayon cup in
order to address the feathers and the hats and how they should
come together. Soon, the two of them had matching Robin

Hood hats slipping down over their eyes, their popsicles were bright, sticky puddles, and they both looked very happy.

It occurred to me that you could maybe love people too much, to the point of pain. My bass player lifted his hat to smile at Wyatt.

I like paper too, Wy.

* * * *

Little Bo fishes in a motel pool, placing a lure on his hook and casting out. Sits patiently, humming, waiting happily for nothing.

* * * *

A journalist leaves the club and climbs onto the bus to join us for dinner, carrying a six-pack and a backstage pass.

This is your dressing room?

This is our everything room.

The man and I roll rice paper wrappers into summer rolls while my drummer drinks the journalist's beer and answers his questions.

Q: Three people need help crossing the street. One very young, one very old, and one very sick. What do you do?

A: Nothing. I just got a ticket for jaywalking. I don't think I'm allowed to cross the street.

Q: Do you believe in ghosts?

A: Yes.

Q: Five bands get to live, five will be erased from existence. Go.
A: The bands who live have never been recorded . . . the bands
　who never will be are the ones who sold the most records.
Q: You live in a mobile yurt.
A: Yeah.
Q: Old people do that.
A: We're ahead of our time.

Interrupting with dinner, I serve my children rice and carrot
sticks with their summer rolls. The journalist watches in silence.
The children watch in silence. It'd be awkward if my children
weren't *always* silent, which weirds some people out. They tell
me there's no evidence of children except the children themselves; their physical presence. No noise, no plastic paraphalia-
lia, no fun. When I try to explain that they don't *want* noise and
plastic—that that would not be fun, just noisy and plasticky—it
doesn't sit well with people who have preconceived notions of
children as less intelligent humans, hyperactive and acquisitive.
I mean, kids're goofy, but so are *we* if we're honest.

Anyway: silence. But when a car honks its horn outside, it
slams the silence shut and Doony and Ryder jolt, then look at
each other.

Customers!

Excusing themselves, they race off the bus, the journalist
gently raising his eyebrows at me. I sigh.

Don't write that down. I honestly think they're just sick of
summer rolls. We make 'em a lot.

He nods and gazes out the window at the boys, who are
thanking the door guy for a box of colored chalk. This bouncer

remembered them from the last tour and showed up for work with boxes of raisins, a Winnie the Pooh book, and, evidently, colored chalk. I call to them out the window.

You guys want brownies?

Three blank stares. My drummer clears his throat.

A: So . . . mobile yurt?

But the journalist is still looking out the window, so we do too. The kids have begun drawing, the sidewalk leaving its gray behind in a swell of faded pink, blue, green, orange, and yellow; in faces and sharks and math problems and roses and spirals. It cleans a whole lot.

♋ st. christopher

unmoved by unlived futures
the streets run with soap

The interview having faded, my drummer wanders away and the journalist turns to me.

Q: Okay to talk?

A: Okay to talk *slow*? I'm sleepy.

Q: You're southern, you always talk slow. Are you a good cook?

A: Uh.

Q: Okay.

A: No, it's just that I had this idea that we could make food that didn't, you know . . . kill the children.

Q: Sounds like a plan.

A: Cuz look at what they shove into kids. We gotta teach their cells to live better than Froot Loops and chicken fingers. That's bad music.

Q: Music again.

A: Sorry, can't stop yawning. I'll shut up. But also? Yes, music again. And not *gourmet*, just real. Not foie gras *or* fast food, just apples. We're all born musically literate and we're born predisposed to eating things that don't break down our cells. So we look for fruit and get Loops, we look for music and get fashion, you know?

Q: You really hate Froot Loops.

A: I don't blame the Froot Loops. I've known some wild, awake people who can transmute poison cuz they know this illusory deal here. They *live* on Froot Loops cuz they can.

Q: In America?

A: *Way*. Look small, look trailer park and hard weather. Look very young and very old. Look poor. Look down.

Q: I dunno. I'll have to trust you on that one.

A: Excuse me.

Raising the window, I call down to the boys, who are now lying on the sidewalk, pointing up.

What're you doing?

Ryder startles.

Clouds, Mom.

Cool. Is that a . . . clean sidewalk?

Blank stares.

Okay. I really do have brownies in here for you.

A beat. Ry gives me a thumbs-up. Closing the window, I try to remember what we were talking about.

Q: Did your sons just turn down brownies? You sure you're a good cook?

A: I never said I was a good cook. But they're just suspicious of brownies.

Q: Suspicious of brownies?

A: Well . . . all brownies gotta be is brown and square. I could hide *anything* in there. Wheat germ, yoghurt, bee pollen, dates. Never let a hippie cook for you.

Q: Do you make people suspicious of music too?

A: Wow. I guess. But if I do, I'm not alone in that. Music wants to be timeless and inventive. Timelessness and invention are suspect in all spheres. If you don't play by their rules, they think it's cuz you didn't get the norm memo—*How come you don't do it like everybody else? Because you don't know how? Because you aren't as good as everybody else?*—but you know what, we *all* got the freakin' memo.

Q: In triplicate.

A: Every goddamn day, we all see how the norms do it and what'd they come up with? Top 40. *New York Times* bestsellers. McDonald's and celebrity chefs. You could pick an apple and hold it up to their blank eyes and they wouldn't know what it was. *This* is the zombie apocalypse. Sorry, I can't stop yawning. I'm really tired.

Q: I know you don't sleep. Are you mixing metaphors?

A: Just disciplines. Every work, every love, should be an apple and not a poison one. A flower and not a plastic one. Organic and idiosyncratic.

Q: Are you pissed?

A: A little? Sometimes. When people play along instead of waking up. And sleepwalk through the insult; buy it. Or show off, sell it for money, for attention. Mostly I'm just enthusiastic about real. I love it here.

Q: It looks like heaven.

A: Really? Would you like a brownie?

♋ frosting

in heaven maybe
they don't call you crazy

Later, I stop doing dishes to open a bus window and eavesdrop on the journalist trying to get my two older boys to speak. He is mild and sober, rather than cutesy and condescending, so, dismayingly, they open right up. Standing on the sidewalk over their drawings, holding broken pieces of chalk, they recite for him advice that I've apparently given them.

"Good things come to those who steal them."

"Be yourself. Unless you're a dork. Dorks get beat up."

"Half-assed counts."

"Bad is good. And so is good."

The boys giggle and so does the journalist.

"Clothes are a waste of time."

"There's no such thing as big."
"Y'all's hats."
"He's never met a potato."
"If it's hard, it's not worth doing."
Calling down to them, I splay my soapy hands.
I can explain all of that.
Three blank faces look up at me. I roll my eyes.
And "Y'all's hats" isn't advice, anyway . . .
They're all just looking at me, so I shake my head and close
the window, but I can still hear Ryder chirping through the glass.
Mom loves washing dishes! She does it all the time.

* * * *

Baby Squirrel runs skittery laps through the bus kitchen, leaping
from counter to couch to shoulder while I clean up. When my
bandmates come back onto the bus to write set lists, the jour-
nalist follows them up the steps and, placing himself between
my two younger boys, tries to get *them* to talk too. Sinking
inside, I look at him.
Really?
He grins.
Indie rock gold!
Wyatt draws, his pad of paper spread across his pajama
knees. Bo bounces a toy fish on the back of the couch, still wear-
ing a mask and snorkel. The journalist starts slowly.
Nice pajamas. You guys match. Are those lizards?
The boys glance at him and nod.
What kind of lizard is this one? An iguana?
Bo turns to him, removing his snorkel.

It's a blue-tongued skink.

Is it?

Mm-hm.

Replacing his snorkel, Bo goes back to the fish. I start writing set lists with a Sharpie while my drummer digs around in his suitcase for a clean T-shirt. Bo's snorkel breathing is the only sound. When the journalist points at Wyatt's drawing and asks what it is, Wy stops, his pencil in the air.

Well. This guy is a woman who left her money inside the house behind this tree. But in the tree is a family of squirrels. See in here? And their money is these acorns, which all have a tree inside them. Like a memory of their future. So the guy-lady's memory of the future becomes no hiding places, only a Before Tree. Which, you know, is probly better. If you're a squirrel.

Baby Squirrel watches from the back of the couch, my Sharpie squeaks over the set lists, Bo snorkel-breathes loudly, and the journalist stares at the drawing, saying nothing. Wy looks up at him.

Want me to draw a blue-tongued skink?

✴ ✴ ✴ ✴

A bear is spotted by three different people, lumbering through the California neighborhood where we're playing, digging through garbage cans and kicking around backyards. Because three different people saw it, the county decides that there must be three bears, so officials call in a bear wrangler to come handle the bear problem. That evening, we stand in the club bar, watching him do his thing on the local news.

"Bear wrangler"?

Watch, he'll only find one bear.

Duh-uh.

People on the screen scatter behind a man who stands in the middle of the street holding a metal garbage can lid and a stick, tentatively approaching a tiny bear. "Bad bear!" he yells in a shaky voice, hitting the lid with his stick. The men at the bar squint over their beers.

"Bad bear"?

The bear pauses, watching the bear wrangler jump out of its way like he's being attacked, hitting his garbage can lid again. "Go away! You're a bad bear!" My bandmates and I look at each other.

Is this the best bear wrangler around?

It's not a bad bear. It's just a hungry bear.

I wanna be a bear wrangler. How much would something like that pay?

✳ ✳ ✳ ✳

Colors and noise wake me at four a.m. I tiptoe out past the sleepers to the front of the bus and play my Les Paul in the driver's seat, watching morning birds gather to ready themselves for the sun through the windshield. A dumpster, a tree, a softening in the air over dewy dead grass and litter. Songs are an infinite now. The only way I understand infinity, the only way I understand now.

Whatta they do, shine? Something like that.

✱ ✱ ✱ ✱

The children discover our movie camera and begin making films. With wardrobe, props, special effects, and a deep insight into the world of: *these adults we're supposed to become? Are out of their minds.*

They film in empty lots, in closets, at grocery stores, in trees and motel pools, on planes, in dressing rooms, under tables, on the bus, at restaurants, in offices, on club stages, in parks, at truck stops, and on the sidewalk, engaging with pedestrians only when it suits their unpredictable interest in grown-up craziness. Otherwise, the world that is not pretend can't capture their attention. But when a child races past, followed by another, and they're wearing hats and ties? Move, cuz you're in the shot. If Baby Bo is not wearing a mask and snorkel? He's not Baby Bo; he's playing a role, and you should get outta the way cuz you're in the shot. If a kid asks you pointedly to say something, ask no questions; speak loudly, enunciate, and try not to be backlit. Then get outta the way.

If a dressing room fills with bubbles, also ask no questions. If a plastic shark appears on a pool table or a pillow suddenly has a face and is wearing a wig or the brownies you just struggled to make in a tiny bus kitchen are enshrined with mustaches and incense and your coffee has a drink umbrella and the dog is wearing a saddle? Know that you don't understand because you *will*. After editing.

Just keep the flight attendant away, Mom. So she doesn't start that career options conversation with us.

How? Career options?

I don't know, create a diversion. Yeah, career options: "You a little cowboy? You wanna be Batman? Are you a pirate?"

Oh. Yeah. And in Dallas, "cowboy cheerleader."

Yeah, they always think we're girls in Texas. Are we flying to Texas?

I don't think so. You know none of those are real jobs, right? Especially not Batman.

I just need the shot clear. Whatever you can do to help.

The flight attendant interferes anyway. Her only line in the film, improvised and cut in afterward:

I eat everything.

✳ ✳ ✳ ✳

Light pollution and headlights created a sulfurous haze over the highway as the blue bus cut through Cowschwitz; the dead land of feedlot hell between San Francisco and LA, no smell like it. We'd just seen a naked woman doing donuts in the parking lot of In-N-Out Burger—around and around and around, dust flying—and were hypnotized by the spinning cartoon. Stayed to watch. When the cops came, she revved then cut the engine, greeting them with wonder, as friends.

Lady Godiva is an American hero.

It's true. I think she was wearing a tube top, though.

Whatever. She's my hero.

Our songs are her cops.

And that was also true. They came to arrest us and we greeted them with wonder, as friends.

♋ lady godiva

falling off the deep end
calling the cops her friends

falling off the deep end
calling the songs our friends

That night, a sudden spray of sparks across the windshield and the body of an enormous owl smashed against it for a second. Then the owl is thrown off into a feedlot, leaving an intricate pattern of spidery broken glass superimposed onto the nuclear-greenish highway in front of us.

We take this as a bad sign.

* * * *

Our bass player, balancing on the racing, careening bus, held up my cell phone as the flashing sun and shadows played across his face and hands. I made him answer my phone so I could finish a scene for the boys where I finally get to play a villain. I call this "playing against type," but Wy tells me to use my repression.

Repressed what?

Everything! I mean, repress 'til you die, right? Then who's it gonna hurt? You said that!

I said that?

The owl-broken bus windshield breathed with passing cars, sucking in and puffing out. We didn't know how long it would maintain its integrity, so close to shattered like that. My bass player, blank:

Fashion magazine . . . it's your two o'clock interview.
I'd rather chew bees.
What do I tell them?
Tell them I'd rather chew bees.
What else can I tell them?
That you'll talk to them.
But . . . I'm a dude.
Perfect.

INTERVIEW:

Q: What are your musical influences?
A: Truth and the manipulation of time.
Q: The what?
A: A *facility with time*. Seeing it clearly, allowing it to fluctuate. When you hear between notes and beats, you see between atoms and moments.
Q: You do?
A: Sure. Fucking with time is important.

He gives a good interview. And he was so right about that.

✳ ✳ ✳ ✳

With Bo's entrance into personhood came a biological imperative to go to every aquarium in the whole goddamn world. It could not happen that there were sea creatures within driving distance that we did not peer at through glass. Food that wasn't yet moldy could be hard to come by, sleep disrupted, showers and laundromats few and far between, but every member of the bus family knew aquariums must happen. The man and I took it in stride, having walked three other souls onto this plane and attended to their every quirk. But my bandmates ate it up, celebrated ocean life, lived partially underwater with Bo, learning the names and habits of different shark species, the secret consciousness of jellyfish and anemones, and the preferred diets of kuhli loaches and glass cats.

At the Tennessee Aquarium in Chattanooga, we lay underneath the big tank, on a viewing platform, and watched sharks swim over us. Bodhi rattled off their Latin names, then went quiet. I elbowed the man.

How does the kid speak Latin and still go fishing in pools?
Well, he doesn't speak Latin exactly. He just says Latin.

Bo had no snorkel on, which had taken some work. I wasn't big on getting stared at in public. Also a little concerned that he breathed so much of his air through plastic. He did have a little shark in each tiny fist, which he held up under the glass, swimming them around, as if they might Pinocchio into real sharks.

When a school field trip screamed and echoed its way into the room—chattering and footsteps and bouncing laughter—he looked at me.

Do we have to go?
I think they're just walking past.
I mean ever.

What do you do when you can't give a child something

beautiful? Or fundamental? Something he wants deeply, so close to need.

Climbing out from under the shark tank, I grabbed the man by his sleeve.

Who do we see about a lease?

We took Bo to the top of the shark tank so he could look directly down into the water, which he seemed to believe was more real than the water behind glass. Silver fins cut across mercury ripples and the whole place echoed, metallic with water. Little Bodhi rested his chin on the security bar surrounding the tank and peered down at the circling sharks for about two and a half seconds. Then in one fluid move, swung a leg over the bar, hoisted himself over it, and dropped.

♋ glass cats

so leave the bottom feeders to their old shrines
we'll hang in heaven with our own kind

I caught him in the air, his tiny, round sneakers inches over the surface of the shark-filled water, and turned him around to face me. Eye to eye, we studied each other.

We're going to the butterfly room.

✳ ✳ ✳ ✳

The butterfly room was a lovely, steamy jungle of rainforest flowers and thick vines. All colors and flutters of flying stained glass. Checking the baby for toddler wonder, I threw him my best Mom smile, but he was tight-lipped and wary. He and a shark toy gripped my hand as his steps slowed.

The first butterfly that landed on Bo released a louder sound than I had ever heard from him: a high-pitched whining squeal that built to a scream and didn't stop. I couldn't talk to him over the noise of his open mouth and traumatized psychology, so I waited, but it kept going, became a keening. Another butterfly landed on his arm and the wail soared. People stared, shocked and concerned. I imagined that he'd need to breathe soon and I would use that moment to interrupt him with maternal soothing and maybe some kinda science lecture on butterflies and caterpillars and . . . the *silence* of cocoons, I dunno. The exhalation lived, however, and didn't fade until the butterflies were removed from the boy and the boy was removed from the butterflies, unhurt but severely shaken.

He gripped his toy sharks, white-knuckled and panicked, as he was led away from the butterfly room and offered ice cream, which he declined. I was also pretty shaken and ready to leave. We studied each other again, eye to eye.

Would you like to go home?

Home?

Gently prying one of the sharks from his hand, I made it talk to him.

I want to go back to the blue bus, Bodhi. Will you take me there?

Bo nodded at the shark, grim, and spoke quietly.

Ok. We can go home.

* * * *

In Detroit, the children stare out the bus windshield at a costume shop with dead clowns hanging by their necks in the window, masks grimacing.

Can we look at them?

You're looking at them.

Can we look at them closer?

I sighed. We don't play in the good part of town, not ever. We play in the part of town where it's ok to make your shitty noise at shitty people, according to most cities. I looked down at my clean boys, then squinted out the window at the dirty clowns. Wyatt was holding the movie camera, which meant that the squalor had already written itself into a script, at least in his head. So I marched them off the bus, holding all of their hands—two in each one of mine—to protect them from . . . what? Pollution, violence. Acts of God. The snarl of people.

Up close, the clown costumes looked moldy, their primary-colored ruffles edged in greenish-gray. I pulled the boys back from the smudgy glass to keep their noses from touching it.

Yikes.

They aren't even smiling. I thought clowns smiled.

Not when you hang them.

Sirens, too many sirens, building in volume way too quickly, coming too fast. I glanced over my shoulder in slow motion and saw a van swerving wildly up to the intersection next to us, behind a line of cars waiting at a traffic light, with many police cars in pursuit.

In one move, I swept the children back onto the bus as the speeding van plowed into a car waiting at the light, pushing it up onto the sidewalk and through the plate glass window of the costume shop, straight into the dead clowns. Shattered glass sprayed everywhere and the car horn moaned. Four police cars appeared, sirens still going, emptying cops onto the sidewalk. The driver of the car was clearly dead. The driver of the van, who'd rammed the other guy into dead clowns, into *his* death, struggled to open his door, finally pushing himself through the window, then ran past the bus. Two policemen shot at him. I pulled my children down.

On the floor, boys. Now crawl to the back of the bus and wait in the bedroom.

They obeyed. More gunfire. Again, I ran down the list of all the jobs I could have had other than musician, following the children down the length of the bus on my hands and knees.

Milkman, herpetologist . . .

The boys sat on the floor at the foot of the bed, wide-eyed. I crawled up to them.

Was that scary?

Ry shrugged.

The clowns were scarier.

♋ bywater

midnight's falling down on the party

Glasses flew out of the cabinet and shattered on the floor. Doony grabbed Wyatt, pulling him onto his lap. The engine and the wind and the world blended in a rushing blur.

Don't let go.

Ok, Mom.

My drummer's arms reached for the baby and I fell into them both. They hugged each other as a wash of coniferous trees swirled past through the bus window behind them. The man fought to control the steering wheel and navigate turns down this mountain pass, but he shouted that he was failing and so were the brakes.

Just hold on! Everybody hold on!

Smoke billowed from the back bedroom where Ryder was. My bass player and I looked at each other and ran back. The man saw us running in the rearview mirror.

Don't go back there!

He didn't know that one of the babies was in the back. All I could feel was heat, all I could see was gray. I felt in front of me, felt on the bed, against the rumbling walls, and finally found Ry on the floor. Together we pulled him into the front lounge, coughing, as the bus swerved and built speed. My bass player yelled to get down on the floor. He braced himself against the table and held us both. With every turn, more glass smashed around us. A shock of flame in the back bedroom.

♋ 37 hours

I don't want this to be over

When the man was faced with driving off the side of the mountain or into the woods, he stood and pulled with all of his bodyweight against the dragging wheel and metalweight of the speeding bus, jerking us sideways as we rushed into the woods. My bass player and I flew into the air and across the bus kitchen, into each other, both reaching for Ryder. I checked to see that my drummer still held the baby in his arms, that Doony still had Wyatt. More crashing around us as everything we owned slid and fell and broke. I waited to hit a tree and explode. There were trees all around us; no way could we miss them all. The bus leaned and bumped, whistle-screaming and gradually slowing, then quieted. It sighed and stopped, leaning at a crazy angle.

Pulling myself up to the sink, I saw that it was full of broken glass. The goldfish pickle jar had shattered.

Ry? Help the fish.

✳ ✳ ✳ ✳

There was no cell service in the woods. The man walked for help. And on a dark bus, the rest of us picked up shattered glass and foraged for life pieces. We found marshmallows and matches in a cabinet and built a fire in the woods. Holding children, we toasted marshmallows and talked about cartoons.

Speed Racer.

Didn't he have a chimp?

I think so. Hyperactive sorta.

Who? Speed? Or the chimp?

"Speedy." And the chimp.

My bass player pulled a burnt marshmallow off a stick and gave half to Bodhi. Sparks flew past their faces. Ryder read a Lynda Barry comic book, Wyatt drew in the firelight. I didn't want to look at the picture, but I was glad he was drawing. We were so lucky. We were so, so, so lucky.

Drawing can help us stand to be there.
—*Lynda Barry, What It Is*

The man came back slow and sad and we waited for a tow truck, which had at least a day's drive to do before it reached us. A day and a night passed. I was used to my triggers and nightmares. But the more raw life became, the emptier it was, the more space the monsters had to grow. Summer, the bus crash, and crying children trigger flashbacks and I lose time in a wash of PTSD.

Where've you been?
Gone.

I cut my hair in a dark, crooked bus mirror.

The goldfish swam in a blue plastic bowl.

We shared picnic food, keeping each other company whenever someone was hungry. The bus was dark and quiet. No colorful fish movies.

We walked in the woods and took turns reading stories to Bodhi and Wyatt.

Opening the bus fridge, we realized mold had already taken it. Shades of our flood. We drank what we could and threw away the rest, with a lot of broken glass.

The man took me aside.

We tried, Kris. It's over.

I know.

I didn't cry then, and I didn't cry when I told my bandmates that I would cancel the rest of the tour and send them home and that it had all been very beautiful, this life of music, but we can't be musicians anymore; that our career had literally gone up in flames. They shrugged.

No.

What do you mean?

No.

And then hugged me.

Kris. If we pool our money, we can afford to finish the tour.

I don't have any money. And I put your lives in danger. You're cold and hungry.

And dirty. And we're gonna finish this tour.

Then I cried.

Wyatt found one of the goldfish belly-up, floating on the surface of the water; asked what he could do for him.

Send him good vibes, honey.

Walking away with the blue plastic bowl, Wyatt stared down into it, then settled on the ground cross-legged. Pets are good, clean practice deaths for the complex grief that follows in our lives, but this seemed unfair. A distraction maybe? More likely a compounding of sadness. I gave him some time before I started any death walking speech.

When the tow truck driver came for the blue bus, we unloaded gear from the storage bay and emptied the cabinets into a few paper bags. The last thing I saw as I stepped off was

Wyatt's drawing from years ago of a bus winding past cactus down a highway. I stopped and took it off the bulletin board, put it in my pocket. He was outside, still studying the goldfish.

Ryder and Bodhi cried as their home was towed away; a big, kind dead animal. *Not* just a house. It gave us the way we lived. Watching the children, my drummer swore he would put this right.

Somehow. If not me, then some higher power.
I dunno. I think music was a bad idea.
You mean good music was a bad idea.
Yeah.
Uh-huh. But that can't be true.
It is in this world.
Yeah. But it still can't be true.

☺ no shade in shadow

you're supposed to be the first to go
not the last one standing

Joining Wyatt by the blue plastic bowl of fish, I told him that everything ends, at least as far as humans know, and that saying goodbye is a useful skill. He continued to stare at the floating fish.

I waited.

Think you could be okay with an ending, if something else must be beginning?

The dead fish twitched and the surface of the water rippled. Its tail flipped up and back as it jumped, turned itself over and joined its goldfish buddies in circling the bowl. I blinked and moved closer. It was swimming, all right. The dead fish was swimming around, alive. Wyatt and I looked at each other and he smiled.

Good.

The tow truck driver helped us get to a motel and we split a room, started making phone calls. The next morning, we pooled our money and rented a car, filling it with gear and bus family and dog and fish. By the time we got to the club, word had gotten out that we'd lost our bus and the club'd been inundated with calls from people asking how they could help.

Opening the man's laptop in the dressing room, we saw that we had hundreds of emails asking the same thing: how can I help?

You can't stop making music.
Take my bass.
Please accept this donation.
I need this soundtrack.
You can have my amp.
These songs are my therapy.
Stay at my house.
Take this drum kit.
Don't stop making music.
Eat free at my restaurant.
Stay free at my hotel.
Where can I send this guitar?

Record free in my studio.
Take my van and finish the tour.
House show. Come do a house show.
How much do you need to keep working?
Please don't stop making music.

I checked the blue plastic bowl on the coffee table next to Wyatt's little sneakers. Yep: dead fish, alive.

✻ ✻ ✻ ✻

There's always the lesson of the gas station in New Mexico. Pay your bills and your music doesn't have to suck.

Music is nature, is our nature. The god in the math. Maybe you don't wanna charge people for nature. But if together, you'd like to keep your church open and share the pieces of humanity you find for each other—musicians and listeners on the same side of the stage—are you allowed to accept help then? Listener-supported, could a dead fish really keep swimming?

I could finally give music away.

All I know is, if you live an honest life, you will never have to lie.

♋ strange angels

strange angels made this planet glow

The listeners declare themselves to be Strange Angels, a loosely associated band of givers who pay my recording costs in exchange for the music itself. When I thank them, they say: it's not about you. Which is true. Never liked putting a dollar sign next to songs, anyway.

No one else in the way, no one else paying attention. Music. My dream job.

♋ fox point

your new adventure will be mind blowing

Behind the recording studio was an abandoned apartment building called the Coyote Palace, where coyotes lived with human detritus like mattresses, teapots, and posters on the walls. It was postapocalyptic and beautiful. Wyatt and I explored it tirelessly. He filmed and drew it as I walked ahead and checked for signs of rotting wood or falling girders. Spiders watched us drift from room to room in the snow that blew in broken windows, growing into mini-drifts over the shattered glass on the floor. Which was a puzzle of carpet remnants, torn books, and splintered legs of long-gone furniture. Sometimes the iron fire escape steps were dotted with coyote prints and blood.

In the spring, flowering vines crawled in the same broken windows, along with squirrels, birds, and many more spiders. Butterflies and bees. Tall bright-green grass quivered around the base of the building. Air whipped through the structure, settled inside it. Still cold.

I'm glad the coyotes have some cover.

Are they okay here with all this people stuff?

I don't know. Kinda the least we can do after taking their habitat.

A lot of broken glass.

True.

Let's bake them a pie.

Every day that I worked in the studio, Wyatt worked in the Coyote Palace, flushed with purpose. The feel of the place intrigued him, he said, and he wanted to discern which elements spoke the most vividly. Old paint or bird shit? Magazines or mattresses? Blood or fur? Silver or sage? The visual themes in his small world/big picture were often deceptively simple elements that, when captured, articulated a sculpture that fell out of the sky. No one really sculpting it, but it has a heart or it wouldn't have fallen from Eden. He was just looking for its heart and hoping nobody got hurt. And he did that with his senses. In this way, he was no different from any other organism.

I don't think I really believed in art before I met Wy. And he convinced me that it's just life.

INTERVIEW:

Q: Do I want to see Wyatt's drawing of me?

A: Maybe. It won't be nice though, it'll just be kind.

We walked a photographer through the best parts of the Coyote Palace.

This is a tough world to capture.

I guess that's why we keep coming back.
He paused in front of a cracked, dingy alarm clock.
Who is the invader here? Humans or animals?
Yeah, we go back and forth on that one.
What's the answer?
The answer is that humans are animals.
Garbage is the beauty here. The photographer took a picture of Wyatt taking a picture of graffiti over the coyotes' bed.
I imagine the rabbit population has been a little shifted around here too. Who's the invader again?
Wyatt, listening, turned away from the graffiti and shrugged.
People are animals and animals are here.

♋ moths

moths can feel no shame
and such a lovely flame

Soon after this, Wyatt stopped going to the Coyote Palace. Actually, refused to go. I was gutted.
We learned so much in there.
Wyatt smiled.
Yeah. We learned it.
My drummer told me not to worry about it, that Wyatt's outline of the place was just complete.
You'll see it again, in his cartoons. He knows nothing exists here without measuring the finite.
I guess. I like infinity.

Well, you're a mother . . . infinity's a given, anyway.

And soon after that? The roof caved in. I'm not kidding and I don't mean metaphorically or anything; the fuckin' roof fell *down*. So yeah, I'm a mother but not a good one. Thank god babies know how to take care of babies. I didn't want to tell Wyatt. The Coyote Palace had been his everything for a time. When I finally met his gaze in the kitchen on a sunny morning and told him that the building had fallen, its constituent parts carted away by men with enormous noise machines, raking the land and chasing that world away—no more blood on snow on no more iron fire escapes—he grinned brighter sunshine than the sun splashing in the windows and across his ocean eyes and said exactly what he said about the alive dead fish.

Good!

♋ reflections on the motive power of fire

my dirty wings not what they were

It takes years.

Staring out at another ocean; the beach where the kids played when they were little. None of them are playing today. Instead, we stand in a line, squinting at the sea, and wonder what a family is when the man leaves.

Some families never had a father to begin with.

They call this broken, though, and that's how it feels.

Maybe you can't make a new shape without breaking something.

Atmospheric pressure is 14.7 pounds per square inch at sea level. Only a rise in altitude is concurrent with a decrease in pressure. With increased intracranial pressure, we first lose the concept of time. Only after that do we lose location or people. Pressure has its own beauty. Can't feel it without a body and we're bodies. Black widow medicine—a comforting poison—doesn't feel so good either, but like that Bywater witch doctor told me in New Orleans, it's a powerful force and forces alter inertia. You don't necessarily have a mountaintop with which to relieve the pressure in your near future, is all. Not until you learn how to climb. And some valleys shake with true disaster. Air drowning.

Really, we're just connecting the dots, so we needed some dots. Buckshot at a map.

I think we should stay here for a little while.

Cool.

We'll just have to ride this one out. Living through doesn't mean making it . . . it means living.

So no fist bumping.

I'll bump any fist you got. You still have fists?

I got two of 'em.

Right on.

✱ ✱ ✱ ✱

It is spring, and the children and I have come home, wild-eyed and panicked, to the island where most of them were born. We begin living in circles.

I've done this before, boys. Here, on the island. Circles are actually spirals. It'll be ok.

We rent a furnished house near the water, from a loving Indian chef who is uncomfortable charging us rent and so sometimes comes back to her kitchen to make curries for the boys. The beach, saltwater. Tears and heartbreak soup and dousing for songs. I begin to record a listener-funded collection of an unimaginable number of doused songs. A Scheherazade of material, to be addressed one day at a goddamn time. *Are you breathing? Then you should be working. Are you working? Then hell, you must be breathing.* The songs say terrible, sweet things in sleepy noise. Comfortable poison.

* * * *

Summer, and mosquitoes stop biting for a whole season. We figure it's because we are now toxic, but it's possible that the air itself has been made toxic. A town trying to kill its own mosquitoes so it can breathe air that doesn't bite: comfortable poison. Or maybe the mosquitoes are just giving us a break. They can probly smell overwhelm.

* * * *

Wyatt and Bodhi and I watch a rabbit out the window at the top of the stairs, our three chins on the sill. A midnight rabbit, the most tentative kind, and it's sort of moping around in the street. The boys stage-whisper down to it.

Dude . . . get out of the street.

Yer gonna die.

Then there are only two chins on the windowsill, as Bo and I watch Wyatt career off the front porch and into the street silently. The rabbit watches too, doesn't move. Wyatt stops careening and stares at the rabbit, who stares back. Wy calls up to us.

Why isn't he running away?

We say nothing. Wy's arms lift gently and he circles the rabbit, helicoptering it to safety. The rabbit allows himself to be herded gently onto the sidewalk in an odd, yellow moonlight.

Bo's chin bounces on the sill as he speaks.

Never let me forget Wy helicoptering a rabbit.

Wy standing in the dark yard and looking up at us, his thumbs in the air, eyes yellow moons.

◔ upstairs dan

    helicoptering rabbits
    the street cold as its mist
    omnipotence of boy

I record in the horse stable where most of my records were born and in the fall, the children and I gather firewood in the street to stay warm. Cheaper than buying it. We play cards to stay warm. We curse some memories and laugh at others. We pile into the car to see the giant hog at the harvest fair across the island. It cannot be the same enormous pig I remember; I mean, years have passed. He's more like a pig god, an homage to porcine bigness, an island king, and we love him. Sitting on a flatbed, he looks at us looking at him. He's really big.

In winter, we bake endlessly and work ceaselessly, struggling to pay the bills together. Ryder and I check the oil tank in the basement with cell phone flashlights, and we say nothing to the other boys about how low the level has fallen.

* * * *

LA takes Wyatt. He is still a child—not yet eighteen—but hired by Disney, he disappears in a sudden wash of forms, IDs, flights, interviews, applications, and leases. It feels ungodly wrong to send him into an urban, corporate world I worked so hard to escape. Little Bo and I sit at the kitchen table about this.

We live stories so that our children don't have to, right?
I don't know, Mom. I'm children.
I know you are.
Stop biting your nails, Mom.
Ok.
Let's follow him.
Ok.

So I book a recording session in LA and bring Bodhi with me to chase Wyatt. Sort of splashing into a session at the deep end, without rehearsal, without anything but maternal drive, I find myself recording an elaborate noise, a glare of sound, a loud comfort. No longer suited to the glare of Los Angeles, oddly suited to its comforts, Bo and I freeze into a suspended animation of this . . . what? Power of pain.

The studio is grim but begins to glow with church heat. You can pray, or you can pray together. My bandmates join me and this becomes the together kind. I breathe this music like I've never done before and we spin a cacophony that shines. No pride, no shame. A record of continuous music, I know this is the best noise we've ever made. Bo watches from couches and lemon trees.

Mom. This is the best thing you've ever done.

It sounds like a party. Like a really intense party. One you wouldn't wanna be invited to.

Yeah, but . . . if it just showed up at your house? You'd probly be cool with it.

♋ power and light

soft and low
a pilot light burning

In a Thai restaurant with a friend, who is an animator like Wyatt, Bo and I catch each other's scared eyes. Wyatt is an hour late, then another hour late. I text and call dozens of times and get no response. Bodhi and I leave the restaurant abruptly and begin racing around LA, looking for Wy, a missing baby. He is nowhere. I begin to feel an empty car seat behind me, a life-freeze fucking with time.

At midnight, I get a neon-bright text from our animator friend who's been calling hospitals since we left. He tells me where Wyatt is, says he'll meet me in the emergency room, that they won't tell him what happened. I call the hospital as I run outside to meet a cab and tell the bored man who answers the phone that I'm Wyatt's mother, demanding to know what happened.

Was it a car accident?

Ma'am, all we can tell you is that he's breathing on his own for now.

Looking down at little Bodhi, who cannot see what I'm about to see.

I'll come back as soon as I can.

Mom, I'm coming with you.

No. I don't want you to have this memory.

Eyes yellow moonlight, he shrugs.

I'm coming with you.

In the hospital, the animator takes Bodhi's hand and leads him to a waiting room full of burns, blood, and fear. Wyatt is on a gurney behind a curtain in the emergency room, alone. I stare into his unseeing ocean eyes. He is in there, but just barely. In there deep, deep down. I chant into that ocean.

No more pain, Wyatt. No more pain, no more pain.

I want him to know that if he has chosen to leave this plane, it is with my blessing because my baby will be free of pain. And I want him to know that he is my baby; on this plane, I protect him from pain. And if he can stay, I will fight for his life. A painless life. This is not a promise I can keep, but it's one I make with every pulse of my will.

Hours go by. No one has any idea what happened to him. All they know is that he collapsed in a cab on the way to the restaurant and the cab driver called an ambulance. I grab a doctor and ask her to help. Unresponsive, she looks at me, then walks away. Wyatt is moved to the ICU and we're left alone in a dark room.

A seizure. He chokes, I scream for a doctor who doesn't come, mashing my hand into the call button, my arms around Wy. Then I scream for nurses who don't come. Then I just scream. He stops breathing and fades. I freeze, watching. An orderly leans in the doorway and murmurs something into a walkie-talkie. Eight people swell into the room then, and work to bring Wyatt's lifeless body back to life. I am told I must leave. I refuse. Two ex–gang member orderlies—hospital bouncers— try to forcibly remove me but are unable to. A nurse tells me under her breath that she is also a mother.

Don't leave him for a second. He won't live through the night, do you understand? He'll be dead by morning. I tell you this because as a mother, I would want to know.

I thank her. Instantly, my gratitude for each moment I have spent with my ghost baby becomes an infinity.

♋ bug

I'll see you on the light side of the darkness we're so
    scared of

Wyatt stays here. Somehow, he doesn't die, stays warm. His seizing soul a barometer, he is not yet Wyatt's mind. There is no way to know if that mind still exists, but his soul is very present, like a newborn baby's. He makes eye contact when he is conscious. Resting his cell phone on his hospital pillow, I play him his own compositions until the phone quiets and goes dark. I don't know what he can hear. I don't know if he can think or move in any way other than seizing. He needs the pressure of my hands on him or he seizes; no other hands can keep his seizures away. We CAT scan together, we toxicology lab together, we x-ray together. We are oddly at home in the hospital. No tests reveal anything about his collapse.

Squeezing into his hospital bed, I don't leave him. Because each night is one he may not live through, because he seizes when I remove my hands, because I don't know if I will ever again speak with that brilliant mind or if his body will ever helicopter rabbits to make his little brother laugh; because each night is dark, because once we were one person, and because we are oddly at home in the hospital.

Doctors decide to airlift him to another hospital. That day, he starts talking again.

♋ cathedral heat

arrest the boy
warm between the eyes
as he jackknifes

Because he can speak, Wy is eventually released into my care and we come home. His brothers gather around to help bring him back to Wyatt, back to life, back to drawing our lives, back to the gift and curse of straddling this plane and another. This takes years.

* * * *

In winter, I walk to the studio past the Beautiful Cows: shining and brown with shining, brown eyes. I love the Beautiful Cows. And they love me, because they love everyone.

Stomping through rain and ice, I drag my boots through the snow and on the way, walk directly into an electric cattle fence. Staring up at the sky from the icy ground, I draw a nice fuzzy blank. Then I pick myself up and stumble the rest of the way to the studio to play drums until two in the morning, pretending that I haven't yet gotten a good take so that I can keep playing drums. I do this every day but all I have are drum parts. The songs won't speak beyond this, so once the drums are done, I have to face the not-music.

That was great, Kris. You got it.

Please don't make me stop.

Kris. It'll be ok.

Walking home in the dark, staring down at my bright phone, I walk straight into the cattle fence again.

✳ ✳ ✳ ✳

Buckshot at a map: we keep moving, a grinding restlessness. But also a playful pile of boys who love movement. In the spring, we spill back down to New Orleans. If any city can help carry you through a darkness, it is this rich, soaked, warm, green one. Music in the air.

Maybe it'll help me finish these songs.

Nature encroaches and you are in it, wholly accepted and at its mercy. The streetcar brakes and the whistling ducks, both gently screaming: music.

We find a place and begin filling it with books and animals;

softened warmth filtering in with southern light through the Spanish moss, but before any life can begin, a doctor tells me I have cancer. I tell her I don't. A team of five doctors tell me I do; I maintain that I don't.

I can't afford it.

Nature encroaches and you are in it.

℥ your dirty answer

you know how it feels when the real world encroaches

I don't tell the children, but eventually I must leave the older brothers in charge of the younger ones, to become one of those bodies in a hospital bed that can't even remember movement. A nurse sees how much pain I'm in and fights to help numb it.

You been cut up, shot up. Seven stab wounds. Only thing is, doctors did this to you, didn't happen on the street.

No doctor answers her calls, so she risks her job to kill my pain. A heavy opiate that finally releases me from the grinding restlessness: comfortable poison. A week later, I am released and I tell her I have to take a cab or I won't get home. She eyes me flatly.

We're not allowed to do that. Where is your husband? Your boyfriend? You got friends? Family?

I look back at her and she grows dark.

You ain't got nobody, do you, baby?

I shake my head. Darker, she shakes her head too.

You ain't got nobody.

And drives me home to the children. Standing on the sidewalk, I reconsider, lean down and speak through her car window.

I got somebody. I got the babies and they need me.

So you got everything.

There are all kinds of gods. She was kindness: balls and humanity.

I tell the boys only when I feel it winding down, so that I can say it's gonna be over soon. Three surgeries later, the same five doctors tell me I don't have cancer. And I smile at Bodhi's open face across the room.

I know.

✳ ✳ ✳ ✳

We're living in circles.

You said they were spirals.

They will be.

✳ ✳ ✳ ✳

One very early summer morning, our beloved dog shakes down to the basement and dies between goodbyes. I have wasted away; so thin and weak that I can't lift the body I lifted so easily when there was life in it. So I cry in a basement with my dead dog while the children sleep.

My drummer tells me dead weight is a real thing.

So it's not your fault.

And the children wake and cry through a brighter sunshine than we have ever known. We curse some memories, laugh at others. We are so very grateful for that person who wasn't human.

* * * *

Texting with my drummer at midnight, I ask him to finish my record for me if I'm unable to, then shut off my phone and go to bed. In the morning, after a run, I hear sirens and know immediately that they're coming for me, though I don't know what that means.

I wait. The cop knock, like a battering ram. There is a cop standing on the front porch.

May I speak with your son?

Which son?

Doesn't matter.

Rousing Wyatt, he blinks and focuses mildly.

I don't know what he wants, baby.

It's ok, Mom.

The policeman is enormous. He towers over Wyatt, who looks calmly up at him.

Has your mother given you any reason to worry about her health or safety?

I know the answer to this is *yes*, so we both wait. The cop shifts his weight and rephrases the question.

Do you think your mother is capable of self-harm?

Wyatt thinks.

Given the circumstances, I think she has shown more strength than fragility.

The cop studies him. Wyatt looks at me. This is exactly what he needs to say to tell the truth but not get me carted away. The policeman nods and looks down to write something. When he looks up, there are tears in his eyes.

My wife left me with four children. Every breath will hurt until it doesn't anymore.

I'm so sorry.

Turn on your phone.

On my phone are thirty texts and calls from my drummer. The policeman looks grim.

Tears rush down my face.

This is what New Orleans cops do? How do I thank you?

The cop lets me hug him and pulls Wyatt into his enormous arms too.

Y'all are gonna be ok. But it takes years.

❋ ❋ ❋ ❋

INTERVIEW:

Q: Do you *have* to play music?

A: Yeah.

Q: I think that's really the only delineation.

A: That and unselfconsciousness.

Q: What tripped that wire?

A: A car accident I now see as a car *on purpose.*

Q: Really.

A: Cracked open my skull so I could hear real music.

Q: It did?

A: It's not as uncommon as you'd think.

Q: Where does real music come from?

A: It just *is.*

❋ ❋ ❋ ❋

Songs suddenly flower out of control, building mercurially, embracing shattered. A backing vocal will become a twenty-second freestanding instrumental and then reappear in another song's bridge. They bridge each other's broken and broken, they ask only to appear as such. Lyrics are fluid staccato sandpaper, what sea glass is made of: sand and water and violence and patience and strange. We pack up and go back to the island so I can finish my record, put its pieces together into a shattered whole. Strange Angel listener-supporters facilitate every moment of hearing this out loud.

When I get home, a silhouette is standing on the front porch, holding a six-pack on the top step, a darkness in the dark. My bass player. His silhouette *is* him except for the clean eye light. Like an indigo snake. Been looking for one my whole life.

Shoots me back in time to the boy in the truck parked outside my apartment, waiting to take me to band practice, making me laugh while I rested my chin on my guitar case. A thousand limbic photographs, caught in an updraft, flutter around me. I realize I've been blind for thirty years.

* * * *

I run and run and run. Cycling miles to a nature preserve, I run the perimeter, then jump into the ocean, swim, then run again, and cycle back. An odd triathlon, hyperactive. I never get tired; I only stop cuz I've got shit to do. I mean, the studio is always waiting. Crazy how I can't exhaust myself. Really, I just can't exhaust the *pain* and that's all I am; pain is what I have become. I wonder what I have to offer on this plane, bringing only hurt to it. Seems like there's already enough hurt here.

Sometimes it's just me and seagulls and a brain cracking open with broken heart and withdrawal from a drug that was supposed to numb that broken heart. I run into a god/soul, devil/ego equation, seeing ghosts of the living, hearing voices that aren't speaking. This is a truth: God *is* soul and the devil *is* ego and all is forgiven, but, you know, maybe do better.

Withdrawal is a phenomenon, a re-unbalancing, waiting for a correction that slips through your fingers again and again; silver, slippery mosquito fish. I don't sleep.

Just not being the best custodian of this system.

Maybe do better.

✽ ✽ ✽ ✽

I ask the silhouette of my bass player what he thinks a soul is.

✽ ✽ ✽ ✽

Ryder decides he will be the one to keep us all here.

I saw life in my brothers' eyes and now I'll never stop looking for it.

It is Doony's birthday and we gather with clumsy prettinesses around a dark, heavy table. Streamers and candles, our twelve-foot bright-yellow Burmese python, Sunshine, curled up on the buffet. Ry, to his brothers:

This isn't failing. It's just what fighting looks like.

Everybody knows glimpses of the infinite come easily and often, but don't stick around too long. And that's ok, cuz we all know infinity is there, expanding and contracting, breathing in and out, waiting for us to grasp it. Hearts are not placed on a linear timeline, but each moment is a sideways infinity. That's where we all figure we need to stay in order to stay here: in alignment with these shot-through notions of what is real. Body plus soul is moments.

In the candlelight, I tell the boys that they taught me this.

Sometimes? Thanks to you? I can see sideways.

* * * *

The circles continue.

They will be spirals, boys. We're getting somewhere, I promise.

* * * *

For my birthday, my drummer and bass player do the whole hyperactive triathlon with me. I worry that their hearts will give out or something, cuz they're not running on pain, but we make a sunshine morning of it and then they buy me breakfast. I thank every god I ever heard of for them, just like at band practice.

We just wanted to make sure you weren't having more fun than us.

Am I?

They glance at each other.

No.

* * * *

Wyatt's cartoons are about us, but only the brothers are shown. I am a dress hanging on the wall.

* * * *

My bass player's silhouette on the porch again, with another six-pack. We talk for hours, talk all night. He tells me that he's strange. He is not. Not unless normal is strange in a bonkers space-time. It's unusual, anyway.

Another unusual thing about this silhouette is that he fucks with time. A series of overlaid images, all of them with the same question/answer expression.

✳ ✳ ✳ ✳

Thanksgiving and we are raw and blank. We know we should do better, but we all forgot to get a turkey in our haste to make pies for each other. The car is busted, tilted in the driveway, waiting for money to happen.

I'll bike over to Stoner Shop.

Mom, you can't carry a frozen turkey on a bike.

I could . . . uh . . . stick it in a baby carrier, its little legs stickin' out.

That would be amazing.

I'll be right back.

Except this'll be the day you get hit by a bus.

Oh. With a turkey strapped to me. Almost worth it. Who gets a funny death?

Dead clowns aren't funny.

Probly wouldn't die anyway, just get sad.

We'd still eat your pies.

✳ ✳ ✳ ✳

We keep a drum kit in the basement and take turns shaking the kitchen floor with it. Whoever is cooking will count time signatures and memorize fills so that, when dinner's ready, music continues to fill the room with conversation. It's just nicer to focus on music than anything else.

I actually lost count when you started playing in . . . what was that, 14/16?

I dunno. I lost count then too.

Well the fifth or sixth time through, your fills got really solid. Lifting a pot lid.

Thank you. What did this used to be?

I, uh . . . lost track of dinner when I lost track of time signatures.

Adding amps and guitars means that townie musicians shyly join in sometimes, which makes us look up, pay a little more attention, listen to what they play. Like remembering that windows open.

♋ skeleton key

and don't forget to breathe

So Christmas must then be a swirl of ice-skating and Silly String and Nerf guns and more threats to bike frozen turkeys home and that Baby Bodhi—who's not a baby, he's just *the* baby, so he'll always be our baby—keeps us playing, playing, playing. In the basement, in the living room, in the studio, in the yard. Pogo sticks on the sidewalk and some inflatable bodysuits that turned my happy boys into giant multicolored balloons that helicoptered down the street.

Don't forget to have fun, Mom. That's all we've got left.

It's not all we've got. But ok.

Doony, hiding behind the couch with me while his brothers shoot us with their Christmas Nerf guns:

It's gonna be ok, Mom.

* * * *

My drummer:

When people find out that your songs are all literally true? That you aren't a poet at all. You're gonna be in so much god-damn trouble.

* * * *

Another record calls. And that's lightning: super quick jack-lighting, too much. Snow, guitars, horses, drums, buzzing amps, the Beautiful Cows, that shining, silver vintage mic in my face, blocking my view of dark wood in dim light, of my engineer's kind eyes over the console. Yelling for a living. Trying to hide in guitars, curl up in the warmth of amp tubes. *Will not puke when it gets so heavy*, perforating tissue. For months.

Cattle-fence jolts zap days outta my dumb head. Music is a hyperreality: crawl out a window in order to see the sky and you get what you asked for. Skies open.

* * * *

The cure for PTSD is strange. I sit in an office and track a mov-ing light across a bar with my eyes; in my hands are pulsing electrodes, keeping pace with the light. Crossing the picket lines of my psychology and physiology, I relive in vivid, cinematic fashion, the moments that fucked with time. A cop is standing on the front porch, the baby is gone, I drive in circles, his empty car seat behind me. A systemic response that engages every cell wants to fight and fly this chemo for the mind-self. Day after day, I collapse outside a building under a clock tower because the body can't face what the heart can't handle.

And the cure? Is to fuck with time. Now Doony was taken a long time ago, not always.

♋ bright

it won't last
keep your head down and follow the hood

My PTSD fading, triggers faltering in their failure to grip, I am fully present for the syringe of memory that is every song. When I step onstage, it is still to disappear the part of me with a name, but only cuz disappearing is right, is just, is smallness plus the muscles one needs in order to let a child or a song become. Background strength, hands without fingerprints, leaving the work, not leaving a trace. In no way did I create any babies or songs; they were born and they lived and I lived *with* them. If no one ever sees or hears these animals . . . I dunno, I think it might be better that way. Real life is pristine and secret.

And the stories? Everybody's life story, an earning of the telling. You can't really tell a story you didn't live. The songs gather mine and make them loud.

One gray morning, an electrician comes over to kill an alarm that won't stop yelling at us and gives us some quiet. Then, in the quiet, he tells us about a boot-camp trauma and the time sparkles for him because it was intense. Not great, just *real*, which is great. A cashier at the drugstore whispers a beautifully ludicrous fire story, full of birds in chimneys and a breathless rescue. A little kid feeding turtles at the reservoir down the street says that he remembers turtles from before he could speak, when there was no word for turtle. You can't really tell a story you didn't live. Life is the only art, the only entertainment. And we all like to compare notes.

How cool is that?

✳ ✳ ✳ ✳

Without PTSD, I cannot disappear. I have all my memories and no numb. My drummer has lived my disappearing act with me for so many years that he feels the loss too.

Your weapons were Band-Aids.
I needed them.
Now you're finally you.
Who's that?
You are the woman who wrote your songs.

✳ ✳ ✳ ✳

Spring and the liquor store between the silhouette's house and mine drench our present and clinch our future. He was always there, but on this corner, he steps out of the shadows; no longer a bass player, no longer a silhouette.

* * * *

INTERVIEW:

Q: What is meaning in a meaningless culture?

A: Real is everywhere and uncelebrated.

Q: Is that better?

A: It's good to look at the clowns as we inflate them to parade-float size. They're still just puffed up and lifeless. They aren't breathing; they're just full of hot air.

Q: But in the way. Taking up so much room.

A: Only if you equate attention with value do they obscure your view. If you know that fashion coming on to you is looking for money, you won't fall in love with it. You won't buy its books, its films, its records, its politics, its drugs, its anything. You won't buy into the insult. To do so—or to fight it—only imbues it with imaginary power.

Q: Did nature or nurture set us up for this?

A: Doesn't matter. This shit is *all* declawed by essence.

Q: So lonely, though. How many of us are left?

A: All of us. Some of us are just sleepwalking.

* * * *

In the summertime, I mow the lawn at midnight with a gently squeaking push mower, in my yellow nightgown, because it's cooler then. Bo leans out his bedroom window.

It's gonna be ok, Mom.

Looking up, I give him half a smile and he flashes me a full one.

＊ ＊ ＊ ＊

Our bright-yellow snake, Sunshine, is now fourteen feet long. She plays on the grass with us while the neighbors watch in fear. Ry cooks dinner on a tiny hardware store grill on the same lawn, which, according to our stoner neighbor, is not grass? But he's permanently baked, so we're not sure what to think about that. It *is* pretty pointy for a lawn. Our tiny piping plover, Clover, rides in Bodhi's pocket. Some sunshine.

Ryder, through our dinner's smoke:
   It takes years. But it's gonna be ok, Mom.

＊ ＊ ＊ ＊

By fall, my bass player and I no longer need the liquor store between our houses to drench our present. We sit in the yard in a cold breeze while summer-yellow Sunshine winds between us, stretching to the perimeter of the not-grass and then winding back again.
   We go back a long way. And we sorta just met.

＊ ＊ ＊ ＊

Bodhi and I must blast music in the car, so we prescribe winter cherries for each other. The only store open this late in the solid darkness is Stoner Shop. Which isn't really called that, it's just staffed by stoners, but . . . that's all we've ever called it. We play songs that scream into frigid air, too cold to snow, and we buy ourselves some goddamn winter cherries under fluorescent lights. A stoner chick works to focus her red eyes on the keys at her register, then gives up and charges us five bucks.

Pulling into the driveway, a quiet blacker than the winter darkness begins to eat at us again, so we keep the windows rolled up and play screaming peace at each other until we can camp out in the kitchen with our cherries. A brother wakes and joins us, then another, and the cherry pits pile up.

Tomorrow, we should go sledding.

Tomorrow we should definitely go sledding.

Tomorrow let's go sledding.

✳ ✳ ✳ ✳

It took years, but we built a menagerie; mostly rescues. We had three alligators, two dwarf swamp rabbits, and three orphaned mallard ducklings who all swam together peacefully. The ducks actually couldn't stand water, but they were good sports. They paddled around obligingly, then climbed out of the water and up *us*, balancing on top of our heads. Strange ducks, though I've never met a duck who wasn't quirky. The alligators and swamp rabbits circled each other gracefully without splashing. Clover the piping plover watched, interested, from our cupped hands.

We had two seagulls, four chameleons, a blue-tongued skink, a crow, two six-foot monitor lizards, an Asiatic leopard cat, a quince monitor, two tegus, a family of leopard geckos, and a hedgehog. Jars full of whatever eels and pipefish were caught in the salt marsh that morning, to be released in the evening, glowed green on the back porch. The indigo snake I spent my childhood looking for, shining dark blue, a dream come true, quite literally. Sparrows and chickadees flew in open doors and windows and then stuck around. Wild milk snakes and DeKay's brown snakes visited overnight and were then returned to their patches of tall grass.

We had a Great Dane who was severely upstaged by all of these creatures as well as the snakes we carried around on our shoulders. About eighty snakes in all.

The menagerie resonated. But no way were we not breaking a ton of zoning laws. Didn't look into it cuz I didn't wanna know. When pressed, I called it "homeschooling."

Or I just said: *Bodhi.*

✳ ✳ ✳ ✳

The UPS guy blinks when I answer the door in a bikini and motorcycle boots with a snake wrapped around each arm.

So. Y'all circus people?

✳ ✳ ✳ ✳

A Strange Angel listener-supporter reaches out in apology, tells me she can't help pay my studio costs until her business is off the ground. I ask her what that business is and she tells me it's community-supported agriculture, the model for my bumpy, organic, poison-free, un-shiny music business.

So the boys and I pool our money and support *her.* Every week, we get a basket of bumpy, organic, poison-free, un-shiny stone soup and we share it with the stoner dude next door, the townie musicians who helped me by drinking Captain Morgan on my floor so many years ago, and whoever on this island happens to need a potluck party and a basement full of noise. Eventually, our house fills with laughing people every weekend and we begin to know how it feels to shake off frostbite. Coming back to life outta numb *does* tingle, but the tingling is not intolerable. It's wonderful. It's really, really wonderful. Wyatt, with Roselius the crow on his shoulder:

Missing the world is missing the point.
Super fun here, huh?
Who knew?

✳ ✳ ✳ ✳

Love isn't blind. Love sees very clearly.

✳ ✳ ✳ ✳

A hurricane hits our island, boats floating up the street past our house. The National Guard parks a Death Star of a vessel in the water at the bottom of the street, which calms no one. Just makes a buncha people wearing raincoats and holding flashlights really nervous. Bodhi and I leave the house to buy supplies, but we don't know what that means really, so we go to the nature preserve instead, to see if the waves look cool. They do. Rearing up, chalk white and foaming black. We worry about the wild snakes.

Life hurts.
You just noticing this?

The grocery store is anticlimactic after the preserve and we still don't know what "supplies" means. So we cheat off other hurricaners' carts and buy what they're buying. Water and batteries, mostly. Long, scared lines of people.

They want more water?

I know, isn't water the problem?

Bodhi laughs and the cashier mumbles something incomprehensible. I squint at her.

I'm sorry?

She repeats whatever it was. I look at Bo.

What?

He shrugs. The man behind us asks me to hurry and a line of people behind him—stretching to the back of the store—peer over heads, looking agitated.

I didn't understand what she said.

She said you won a free turkey.

We did? Why?

I don't know. Could you please hurry?

The woman hands Bodhi a ticket and we wait in another line to collect our free turkey.

Life is funny.

You just noticing this?

Wish we had a baby carrier for it . . . its little legs sticking out.

When we get home with water, batteries, and a frozen turkey, the National Guard tells us to evacuate, then asks us to wait twenty minutes while a downed power line is removed. Twenty-five minutes later, they tell us the roads are impassable; to go home and wait out the storm, adding that we should be on the lookout for eleven-foot swells. I nod, pretending and imagining that I know what this means.

Later, around two a.m., wearing a raincoat and holding a flashlight in the dark swirl, alongside people doing the same, I stare at the broken ocean. It's aquamarine, video green. The water boils, dirty; the sky a clean, pinkish black. A neighbor dude catches my eye.

Where are we supposed to measure from?

I shake my head.

And if we count up to eleven . . . then whatta we do?

He laughs, watches a spacey, foaming water beast.

Sure is beautiful, though.

♋ pneuma

aquamarine and video green

Friends in the UK call, having seen news footage of people and houses being washed away.

It's looking bad. You have to get out of there.

Yeah? I don't have a TV. How bad?

You're in a red zone.

What's a red zone?

I don't know, but . . . well, it looks like you need to get to a blue zone.

We stick the turkey in the oven. The bamboo in our yard is blown sideways by screaming wind, and the water at the bottom of the street rears up, chalk white and foaming black, building the spacey, foaming water beast. Boat after boat sails up the street past our house. It's really beautiful. A blue zone.

* * * *

Apparently, caterpillars don't grow wings inside a cocoon. I had seen butterfly faces up close in Bodhi's butterfly room horror and had come up with a Frankenstein diagram of body parts for them that eventually worked to their advantage, but no. They break down entirely. Into a mush of DNA that reworks itself in order to grasp flight and color.

Are you saying we're DNA paste?

Yeah, but in a cool way. In black and white, waiting for a sequel.

What about the spiral thing?

. . . waiting for a prequel.

* * * *

INTERVIEW:

Q: Why this medium?

A: Aesthetics are aesthetics are aesthetics?

Q: Yeah, so . . . why music?

A: I didn't do this on purpose.

Q: I've heard that. How did it happen?

A: *How*, addressing the craft to serve a spark. *Why* is different in everybody's body, I think. I like that music tricks you with rhythm and melody.

Q: Tricks you into doing what?

A: Telling the truth. Which is embarrassing sometimes. But fully present, so you shake off shame. And the fact that people think rock music is stupid *and* pretentious helps me get away with substance.

Q: Sneak it under the radar?

A: Something like that.

Q: Set to music, speech seems *less* embarrassing.

A: Yeah! Words are given a new kind of verby personality then, that describes life living.

Q: And we're the protagonist?

A: We're . . . an eye-filter, a skin and heart awareness. The fail is thinking that's *you.*

Q: So shake off the *you* too?

A: Why on earth wouldn't you?

✳ ✳ ✳ ✳

Catbirds nest outside our back door, right off the kitchen. Four babies, barely hidden by wisteria. Fairly exposed.

Why? Why so close to us?

Maybe . . . birds unafraid of humans who don't mess with them are safer from predators who are afraid of humans and do mess with them?

Ok. So don't even look at 'em. Why do they make cat sounds?

Well, that I don't know.

My four babies, barely hidden, fairly exposed. My bass player gives us a picture of a catbird and we lean it against the wall on the radiator by the front door, where it stays for the duration. Not sure why, really, but it's a totem. I guess cuz we're not butterflies yet. Bodhi shrugs.

Butterflies're gross.

Wyatt:

The four of us are Mom, shattered.

He names a cartoon character "Catbird." It is all of us, integrated.

✳ ✳ ✳ ✳

My engineer, stirring his coffee with a toothbrush:

Kris. Don't cheat yourself of the finer things in life.

✳ ✳ ✳ ✳

Once, my bass player thinks he's getting hamburgers on the grill in our smoky yard and instead gets a me who can't breathe, so he waits. For an unshattering, I guess, and he's still so confusing and familiar. Strange and not strange, questioning and answering, too many overlaid memories to create a clear image . . . he's hard to type about.

Squinting out the window, he tells me that sometimes earthquakes happen before you're ready for them, so you store the event for future use. When it comes back, it's because it knows best. The crashing sweat spills in through cracks in your head as an external experience that happens inside you: a rememory. It builds itself in sound, color, texture, movement, weather, fight and flight.

Thinking I was cured, I found myself just . . . open. As open as all people are supposed to be. When my quake hits, it's because a system and a torquing have worked together to fuck with time. In a good way. DNA mush growing serious wings. The silhouette tells me not to go to the hospital.

They can't help you. No one can help you.

And this helps.

✷ ✷ ✷ ✷

Bodhi tells me he wants to start swearing.

How come, baby? Got some steam to let off?

Nah, just feel like I should probly grow up soon.

Hmmm . . . sorry.

He looks thoughtful.

I wanna start slow is all.

Okay. What do you wanna try first?

The C-word.

I look at him.

You wanna say the C-word?

Taking a deep breath, he whispers.

Crap.

✷ ✷ ✷ ✷

Ryder says our space-time orientation, still mired in touring, is responsible for both our confusion and our wherewithal.

I mean, "today is Chicago"? How is that not synesthesia?

Tuesday is blue Chicago.

And it smells like smoke and roses.

To me, Chicago sounds like a song I wrote about it. I apologize to the boys for teaching them what the world seemed like to *me*. I guess I was supposed to teach them what the world seemed like to norms, but I was never able to grasp that.

♋ soma gone slapstick

and we're back in chicago
when I jump out the window

The boys say the whole world turned out to be one of those hotel lobbies that looks disdainfully on their hopeful little animal-face paper plates waiting to be filled. Four little babies in pajamas, squeezing between loud businessmen and the polished creatures they call women. Hippie Mom built them to expect that in giving, one will meet like-minded folks and . . . well, not always.

Ryder looks dark, but Wyatt is inscrutable.

You know what, though? We were right.

✱ ✱ ✱ ✱

And the frantic is running out.

Wy skates past early spring flowers and a heron lifting its stick legs over sea grasses. Flips up his skateboard and peers soberly into the burning horizon. He lived. He kept breathing.

It's gonna be ok, Mom.
I'm starting to believe it.

✱ ✱ ✱ ✱

A jellyfish apocalypse:

Sunset. The frantic is running out and the tide is coming in. Racing toward the water, I make a plan to swim to the nearest buoy. I am not going to hear anything but water; everything will be removed from noise and the world will become wet music. I'm already hearing this washing clean when, through it, a man yells into the wind.

Girl! Hey, girl!

I am an adult, bikini and ponytails notwithstanding, so I stay focused on the ocean and dive in, let some actual girl answer that call, and swim toward the buoy. Immediately, I realize that something is not right. *Something* . . . is very, very wrong. But it's not a wrong I understand. Some things feel good and some things feel bad and sometimes you're hit with an interesting or a fucked-up, but rarely are we struck by anything brand fuckin' new and so weird we can't physically place it within our scope. All I can liken it to is an electrical storm focused entirely on what you thought was you, what you thought belonged to you.

I swim to the buoy cuz I'm no pussy, but I *am* now a dumbass rolling fish that doesn't know how to deal anymore, having been struck by lightning under the surface of the ocean. A body-wide cattle prod? Shark stick. Poseidon's joy-buzzer revenge. Somebody threw a car battery into the sea . . . uh . . . electric eels? I have no idea what is happening and I'm having trouble swimming straight. My heart isn't right, my breathing is bumpy, my skin is on a crawling fire. Kicking off the buoy, I hear that guy's voice again and briefly consider listening to what it's saying, but I want very much to get back to the sand and roll around *there* for a while, in earthbound agony instead of this weird, waterlogged prickling that has taken over my skin—the largest organ of my body—and some other ones too.

Lifting my head out of the water, I see a guy with a clipboard dancing on the shore; kind of hopping from foot to foot.

I tried to tell you!

Flopping through the water toward him, I carefully stand, ankle-deep in this new electrified wetness, and stare at him.

Tried to tell me what?

Gonionemus vertens!

I squint, dripping. He hops again.

We never get them here! What are your symptoms?

Looking down as if I might see my symptoms on me, I shrug. He checks his clipboard.

Burning skin? Difficulty breathing? Chest tightness? Muscle cramps? Pain?

Yes.

Like a thousand knives? Do you feel like you're gonna die?

Why? Am I gonna die?

You're supposed to feel a sense of impending doom.

I stare at him.

Jellyfish did this to me?

Clinging jellyfish. The Asian form. We never get them here.
They look like glass Christmas ornaments.

I didn't see anything down there.

Well, glass is clear. Can you tell me your symptoms?

I gotta go.

Oh. Should I just check off all of them?

Dragging my stinging legs through the sand.

Yeah. The doom one too.

Oh, cool.

Scribbling on his clipboard, he walks with me.

Really doom?

If you say so.

Palpable turmoil on his face. I nod.

Yeah. Doom.

He brightens.

Neuropsychiatric changes?

Yep.

Studying me hopefully.

Anaphylactic shock?

I don't . . . think I have that.

I was starting to get used to drowning on land. Tried to remember his clipboard's list of symptoms. Burning was not even close to what was wrong with my skin. More like a buncha syringes all at once. Chest tightness, what were the other ones? Anyway, probly.

Writing on the clipboard, then sudden concern.

Are you ok?

Well. I'm gonna be, right?

Yeah, but . . .
He shrugged sadly.
It takes years.

This turned out to be true.

✳ ✳ ✳ ✳

I fly away, play shows, come back to the boys, fly away again.
Rockets on my skates, but I've never known another life. Tuesday is blue Chicago and Friday is gray London and dreams
cloud up airplanes over the ocean. Always a guitar in the overhead compartment.

An English child on a flight to the Canary Islands slides across
many knees to sit on my lap and gaze out the window, humming. Suddenly, his little back stiffens and his eyes grow wide.

*Miss? When you die. Do you automatically move to a
haunted house?*

I think.

Um . . . let's try not to find out for a while.

He nods and turns back to the clouds outside, then grins.

I think it will be fun.

✳ ✳ ✳ ✳

In New Zealand, my Maori tour manager lets me climb a waterfall over black sand. This is the second waterfall I've climbed,
but the first illegal one.

Like, no white people're even allowed to look at it, Kris.
Hanging by my fingertips in the rushing water.
Geez, really? Should I go?
He squints enigmatically.
Kind of a wait-and-see thing.

✶ ✶ ✶ ✶

Home, and Bodhi finds himself in the ocean. I mean, as a *way*; something we all knew was coming. A surfer in need of a wave and this island's waves do not have the power to carry that passion for long.

Passions must be served, so, rockets on our skates, we run to California, looking for a wave.

♋ speedbath

I only wanted to swim out to sea

Diving into one of these waves, I find that the ocean has decided not to move toward the shore any longer. Physics is suspended and so is my breathing. Static fights with vision until gray wins and I go under. I breathe once, twice, then go under again and remember the skill I learned so many years ago: let saltwater have you. Holding your breath, you float, but letting go? You let go. It's all lit up and you're light and the water wins. I mean, of course.

A splashing next to me, and a man's hand shoots through the surface of the churning green salt.

I'm a lifeguard. Grab my hand. You're going to be okay, but we have to get you breathing again.

Hmmm.

Stay with me! What's your name?

He doesn't realize that the ocean is no longer moving toward the shore; that physics has been suspended. He still thinks saltwater doesn't take lifeguards. Holding me, he tries to swim but we go nowhere. He swims harder, keeps swimming. We don't move. The water is winning. I can see his eyes begin to gray out and he goes under. He breathes once, twice, and I lose my lifeguard to saltwater.

Over the surface of the ocean, I see Bodhi's face—a mirage, because he's at home, alone. Suddenly, my lifeguard pops up with a whistling breath, and we're sucked into a current that shoots both of us out of the riptide we were trapped in, tumbling us onto the sand. Eyes wide, he yells.

That was gnarly!!

And points at a still, dense, waveless patch of saltwater.

That's a dead zone.

We're still holding hands. Five lifeguards drive up in a beach pickup and tell us we're lucky we aren't dead. He looks up at them.

We know.

✳ ✳ ✳ ✳

A week later, the opposite of a dead zone, a rogue wave, broke my foot. People wailed and screamed in the aftermath of this crushing thing, pulling tumbled children out of the water. I limped to my truck, familiar with the feel of broken bones. Bodhi was charmed.

Mom . . . you'll be a crutches lady!

And I become a crutches lady. The homeless men and women who live in the park and call their plight *traveling light* begin refusing money and food for this reason, as if I'm Tiny Tim. So we sit and listen to their stories instead.

Those meth heads stole my pack. And they had a HOUSE. *Boy, did they teach me patience.*

More homeless in California than in any other state. They tell amazing stories of cold and heat and work and pain and true love and false hope and scars and wars . . . then thank us for sitting, for eye contact, for touching. Three incredibly free things to give.

* * * *

We play a show in a theater with an enormous plaster moon hanging from the ceiling, filling our view. Like . . . a moon-sized fake moon, it's nuts. I'm afraid this toy monster moon will fall on audience members and break them, but it just hangs over the crowd, glowing eerily. Closing the show with a song about the moon, the crowd sort of ducking under the song.

♋ you cage

I wish the moon wouldn't hang so low
hang over home

Then an actual moon the size of the goddamn moon lands outside my hotel room window. The one I was waiting for, the one I looked for above my wedding castle and didn't find. It found *me* when that silhouette stepped into the light, and now it shone on both of us. Takes years.

* * * *

Ryder watches the band sound check in a club in Pioneertown, California, the place where we fed coyotes cherry pie and heard god's harmonica whisper through pine needles when he was little. He's approached by a man who says nothing, just stares until he sees the eyes of a child across a checkerboard. Our desert dude who built our Moroccan lean-to, Wyatt's world of rain on sage, a game of checkers that never ended. I well up, step off the stage, and hug him.

How did you know it was Ryder? He's six foot five now.

And the desert dude smiles.

I'd know Ryder anywhere. Some checker games never end.

* * * *

Bodhi grabs his surfboard and runs back into the ocean, his wet suit shining. A bright-blue, roiling and wild ocean that is sometimes awfully cold, sometimes rippling with sharks. He's finally allowed to swim with sharks. But just yesterday, he watched a butterfly migration. Dragged two lawn chairs up to the garage roof and let clouds of monarchs fill the air and the trees in front of him; said it was maybe a little alarming at first but then he found it very beautiful. He may always prefer sharks to butterflies but . . . surfers are responsive. They know the wave is in charge. They know human nature and nature are one and the same. That a butterfly carries information you may not have yet.

Surfing is his music, surfboards his guitars. Corporate sponsorship his scary record company, indie heart his inspiration, hyper-life his drive. He develops his craft in solitude and shares it in public, but his skull didn't need to crack open in order to listen. *Bodhi* means awake. Born into laughter and living through loss built his muscle of presence; any pull away from this is immediately felt as an unbalancing and a surfer can't afford that. Sometimes a life-or-death thing.

This particular baby is all about balance. He inherited rockets on his skates, but only to balance my guitar on his skateboard in airport parking lots while we search for our rent-a-car, to balance his phone on the dashboard and navigate while we search for our hotel, to balance a sales sheet at the merch table in rock clubs, signing an occasional CD when listeners ask him to. To throw his board off a cliff in Santa Cruz and follow it with his body in a cold, drizzly surf competition.

He is taller than me. All the boys are. I held them until they held doors for me; until they held grocery bags and amps for me. They hold a strange dark hope in their eyes too. They are all smarter than I am. They're my heroes. Each boy gave maybe ten years of his life to the road, if you add up the hours, and they miss it.

Ferries?

Three ferries. Bitter cold, a ballroom, free caviar and coffee. I miss black tea and black bread. Oslo in the snow.

Yeah. But if you wanna do Oslo in the snow, I guess you gotta do Detroit in the sleet.
I'm game.

✸ ✸ ✸ ✸

My drummer, on tour in the UK last week:
I'll never forget your children's faces when their bus home was being towed away.

My bass player:
Homeless teaches you home.

We are each other's home.

♋ dog days

this is life and we didn't miss it

Fire finds you. California wildfires spark, build, come close, blow west, then south, and we are told to pack up and be ready to evacuate. While we wait for the call that the wind has shifted and it's time to leave, we wander down to the beach to watch a smoky sunset and see animals racing into the ocean. Ground squirrels, those little beach monkeys, and rabbits. Cops run into the water under a purple sky, helicoptering, urging the animals to turn around and swim back to shore; cop shoes and pant legs soaking wet. Orange sky.

When the evacuation call comes, we're driving home from the beach behind a giraffe in the back of a truck, for some reason. It gazes down at us through the windshield. I ask the woman on the phone where we should go, which way the wind has shifted.

Where are you now?

101, headed south. Behind a giraffe.

Follow the giraffe.

Bodhi loves this.

Could our lives be any more ludicrous?

Are you asking me? No.

So we follow the giraffe. What else're you gonna do?

❋ ❋ ❋ ❋

Sleepy in the sand, we watch Bo wax his surfboard, ready to dive headfirst into a freezing, roiling Malibu foam and paddle out to be a sea creature. The Pacific gets so cold. And the beach monkeys, just sitting there, watching, TV to them. Note to self: don't forget how *suddenly* an epiphany grabs your face and yells at it. Then kisses you on the cheek and wanders off. Love solves every equation, especially the one that keeps us here, manifested will, our atoms refusing to fly apart for another day. We're clear. And fucked up and making noise about it and being quiet about it. Maybe that's love too.

I mean, we think we're writing this story, cuz, yeah: your heart goes nutz. It's funny and funny is heartbreaking, but heartbreaking isn't funny. Still more of a wait-and-see swimmer, I can get edgy under my edges; these babies my expanding and contracting universes and me such a dumb little body, a swept-away sack of potatoes. Mothers? I dunno . . . truly, we were just present at goddings.

Find myself stare-hoping a prayer that stingrays and sharks leave the boy alone. Like that does any good. My jellyfish apocalypse still burns down my shoulders, so I use that scar to inform my mothering. Be patient with me. I watch babies very carefully.

Be careful, Bo.

I will. Careful doesn't do anything.

I know, I just have to say it.

I know. Goodbye, Mom. I love you.

This is always the last thing Bo says before he jumps into icy sharkness.

You know, it warms my heart that you say that? But it also chills me to the bone.

Yeah. Goodbye, Mom. I love you.

And the foam takes him again, but his muscles are severe with it before he chooses balance and response. The wave is in charge even if you don't allow for that, but he does. He's strong and quiet.

✳ ✳ ✳ ✳

Wyatt drew all of this a long time ago.

We paint our lives, Mom. We find the line and add the color. I only drew it because I could see it.

It's very beautiful.

It is.

Boys,

You came to me before you were born, always with a plan. Beauty beasts, like songs. In no way did I create you; you were born and you lived and I lived *with* you. Like songs. I guess if I'd known bear wranglers, zombie cows, and dead clowns were gonna play such a big role, I woulda tried to keep you a little safer. As it is, I didn't let go of your hands until recently, but, really, toward the end of your childhoods, I'm pretty sure you were guiding *me*. You know this already.

The youngest of us, the littlest boy, calls it The Parade when you aren't sure whether to laugh or cry. And he actually means *parade*: horns blaring and so in your face. The Mardi Gras we live, Jesus. Shakes your insides. Half the people here are thinking, *what the hell?* and the other half are divided. You know, sometimes simply about the spectacle: shiny objects, loud noises, *yay!* But also, *keep one foot in the street and one on the sidewalk in case we gotta make a break for it.* Fine line between party and conflict.

We were ready. To make a break for it, I mean, but also expectant, looking up at that cool sun. The universe is a *yes*, skin is happy, we're good animals, everybody, every body. Born that way, anyway. Muscles (your heart is a muscle), leading the way. The sun is shining.

Then we started fighting these wars, all different colors of wars, but the noise is always the same: violence and silence. The sound of feeling your shadow-way, fingertips first, future blues. It just got dark is all, highlights to follow years later when you begin to collect the pieces. But the Mardi Gras very sweetly wound its way through the wars, making heroes of you babies; it's shiny, it's noisy. So we *could* be about the spectacle. A bit. Warily. About the cool sun, anyway. The silence is as creepy as the violence if you aren't a monk; if you ask your human thumbprint to make an impression, leave its quirky dent. So, yeah, some raw trumpets, all whispery and dim.

Walking out onto the porch to watch a practice Mardi Gras stumble through the Bywater, all of us in a line, the dogs watching too. Angel's trumpet flowers on the dogs' heads cuz they were too distracted to shake them off. Angel's trumpet is poisonous but beautiful and nobody was eating the flowers, just wearing them. The music all husky, like a torn-up voice the morning after. The dancing was a line of movement crawling through bodies who weren't fighting possession. All a snapshot of what is and what's to come, because those are the same thing. Wear beautiful poison . . . we're bodies and shouldn't fight possession. You know this already.

Have seen more than our share of close-ups. You're not scared of anything if you've known worse and I'm so sorry you've known worse. We've done some fighting but never with each other. Some surviving, always *for* each other. Fighting is a hard thing to ask of a person, hard to call it a win. We're born so gentle. And, really, if you're strong and whole, you don't have to fight.

Is this fair? No. But only because there is no fair.

Is it okay? Maybe. And okay is all we ever asked for. Like all mothers, I'm happy I gave you life and I regret subjecting you to it. But? The universe is a *yes*, so in giving, you don't lose. I wanna repeat that so it sinks in, but y'all know everything already.

You do start to wonder how anybody, any *body*, could live through this. You wake up, hungover from another twisting fall, and know that this is life. This is what living is. You're a sweaty picture of life living itself. And look up: that cool sun.

Doony's childhood was a circular trauma, Ryder's an animal escape, Wyatt's a vivid cartoon, and Bodhi's a primal ocean. So *much* . . . when okay is all we ever asked for. The littlest boy, Bodhi, on the littlest bike, pedaling down Constance Street in New Orleans at sunset:

All scars are beautiful. Because you lived.

I stopped my bike then, with a squeak of brakes like an intake of breath. Stopped to take his picture saying that, so I'd never forget. The message or the delivery. Children scar better, the body finds it so necessary.

Laughed through all of it, shot each other with a lot of Nerf guns. I have to tell you to smile because I'm your mother, but I also have to *teach* you to smile. Because the pain had a life of its own. Like a man crawling through your window whose weapon is, he moves in.

But he also moves on. You know, you wake up walking. What else are you gonna do? Down some sidewalk and you're sure you just gave up but you're still walking. Giving up is something you're not really even *allowed* to do. I mean, what would it look like? It's not like they let you; you're on the hook for a buncha stuff. So that was hell just then, what the man who crawled through our window brought. Never forget that the devil is not a dude, just something lousy that happens to the weak. Heaven and hell are here, in the van, in the apartment, on the sidewalk, in the park watching birds with us. Obviously. Also: try for heaven. Obviously. Mostly cuz they are both contagious. Troubled people aren't always living their wars; they get dreamy. Believe the dreams too.

The devil carries pain in with him when he climbs in the window. Wears it, forces it on you like a housecooling gift. But he's not such a criminal as he is a guest. Because you are who you are. You study him, not wholly unwelcoming. A little welcoming, even, eyes still wide open to this future blue. Because the devil doesn't put his muddy feet up on your coffee table. He is strangely gentlemanly and strange. Not charming like they like to say, but he shines. Glistens, really, with the sweat of pain and nausea. Is a confusion, plays his cards wrong. You feel for him cuz he's an animal in the dark. And so are you; no shame in it. I mean, what else are you gonna be? Until the sun shines again. No hate in it either. If anything, you and the devil just shine a different light on love.

So you become a nomad, like him. He's gone now and you can't remember him leaving, but the residue will not leave your place. Stories and dreams become real when the devil catches your breath. Fairy tales and nightmares. You race outside: *maybe moonlight will wash me clean of another's sins*, but no. Not if you care. And you do. Like I say, you are gracious hosts. You are good people. I'm sorry. Because pain hurts you, all pain. Dicks only feel their *own* pain. Clarity comes as your hurt becomes mine and mine yours, and hell and heaven are still contagious, and ludicrous is funny. Always with the baffling and the beauty. *Then* moonlight washes you clean. When you're already clean.

And you are my sunshine. Suddenly and always. Open a window and happily-ever-after rushes in. A snapshot of what is and what's to come. Because those are the same thing.

So make your work exactly what it should be. Your Mardi Gras. You have this freedom because you're loved and you love your work. Open a window and it rushes in.

Fear? Maybe leave it as the question mark it will be when you step over it. Because life is good people, it feels our everything. You're life, sweating itself out of your pores. You know what, just open the window. Follow the hood. And almost grown up, you are all still my sunshine.

What else . . . music and sex are both sacred. But only if you know that.

Oh yeah, and if you're playing poker with a chimp? Let the chimp win.

That's all the maternal/material plane advice I have. All the other wisdoms I know came from y'all and therefore from heaven. Thank you. Still: repeated myself a lot . . . four boys and I was never sure who was listening, if anyone. I've been saying the same thing for decades. Same five things. I only really think, like, five things, as it turns out.

"Watch." The littlest one says this too. We're here to not miss anything. I really hope your eyes don't shut. They want to sometimes, I know. But every moment is a sideways eternity: points on the line of linear time that negate the concept of linear time.

And this is a dream. Dreams are still dreams, but this is one too. And all the more real for losing its hard edges.

And this is a song. Songs are still songs, but this is one too. Sometimes? Thanks to you . . . I can see it all sideways.

I love you

xo
Mom